READING ONORA O'NEILL

Onora O'Neill is one of the foremost moral philosophers writing today. Her work on ethics and bioethics, political philosophy and the philosophy of Kant is extremely influential. Her landmark Reith Lectures on trust did much to establish the subject not only on the philosophical and political agenda but in the world of media, business and law more widely.

Reading Onora O'Neill is the first book to examine and critically appraise the work of this important thinker. It includes specially commissioned chapters by leading international philosophers in ethics, Kantian philosophy and political philosophy. The following aspects of O'Neill's work are examined:

- global justice
- Kant
- the ethics of the family
- bioethics
- consent
- trust.

Featuring a substantial reply to her critics at the end of the book, *Reading Onora O'Neill* is essential reading for students and scholars of ethics and political philosophy.

Contributors: David Archard, Annette Baier, Marcia Baron, Melissa Barry, Simon Caney, Monique Deveaux, Katrin Flikschuh, Marilyn Friedman, Thomas E. Hill, Jr., Karen Jones, Neil Manson, Onora O'Neill, Suzanne Uniacke, and Daniel Weinstock.

Onora O'Neill, Baroness O'Neill of Bengarve, is Professor of Philosophy Emeritus at the University of Cambridge, UK. She is a former President of the British Academy, and former chair of the Nuffield Foundation, and now chairs the Equality and Human Rights Commission. In 2002 she delivered the BBC Reith Lectures, *A Question of Trust*. Her publications include *Towards Justice and Virtue*, *Bounds of Justice*, and *Autonomy and Trust in Bioethics*.

David Archard is Professor of Philosophy in the School of Politics, International Studies and Philosophy at Queen's University, Belfast, UK.

Monique Deveaux is Professor of Philosophy and Canada Research Chair of Ethics and Global Social Change at the University of Guelph, Canada.

Neil Manson is Senior Lecturer in Philosophy in the Department of Politics, Philosophy and Religion at Lancaster University, UK.

Daniel Weinstock is Professor in the Faculty of Law and member of the Research Group on Constitutional Studies at McGill University, Canada.

READING ONORA O'NEILL

*Edited by David Archard,
Monique Deveaux, Neil Manson,
and Daniel Weinstock*

Routledge
Taylor & Francis Group
LONDON AND NEW YORK

First published 2013
by Routledge
2 Park Square, Milton Park, Abingdon, Oxon OX14 4RN

Simultaneously published in the USA and Canada
by Routledge
711 Third Avenue, New York, NY 10017

Routledge is an imprint of the Taylor & Francis Group, an informa business

© 2013 David Archard, Monique Deveaux, Neil Manson, and Daniel Weinstock for selection and editorial matter; individual contributors for their contributions.

The right of David Archard, Monique Deveaux, Neil Manson, and Daniel Weinstock to be identified as the authors of the editorial material, and of the authors for their individual chapters, has been asserted in accordance with sections 77 and 78 of the Copyright, Designs and Patents Act 1988.

All rights reserved. No part of this book may be reprinted or reproduced or utilised in any form or by any electronic, mechanical, or other means, now known or hereafter invented, including photocopying and recording, or in any information storage or retrieval system, without permission in writing from the publishers.

Trademark notice: Product or corporate names may be trademarks or registered trademarks, and are used only for identification and explanation without intent to infringe.

British Library Cataloguing in Publication Data
A catalogue record for this book is available from the British Library

Library of Congress Cataloging in Publication Data
Reading Onora O'Neill/edited by David Archard, Monique Deveaux, Neil Manson, and Daniel Weinstock. – 1 [edition].
pages cm
Includes bibliographical references and index.
1. O'Neill, Onora, 1941- I. Archard, David, editor of compilation.
B1649.O554R43 2013
192–dc23
2012051110

ISBN 978-0-415-67590-1 (hbk)
ISBN 978-0-415-67598-7 (pbk)
ISBN 978-0-203-75879-3 (ebk)

Typeset in Goudy
by Taylor & Francis Books

Printed and bound by CPI Group (UK) Ltd, Croydon, CR0 4YY

CONTENTS

Contributors   vii
Acknowledgements   x

Introduction   1
DAVID ARCHARD, MONIQUE DEVEAUX, NEIL MANSON,
AND DANIEL WEINSTOCK

PART 1
Kant on action and reason   9

1 Moral worth and moral rightness, maxims and actions   11
   MARCIA BARON

2 Constructivist practical reasoning and objectivity   17
   MELISSA BARRY

3 Varieties of constructivism   37
   THOMAS E. HILL, JR.

4 Hope as prudence: practical faith in Kant's political thinking   55
   KATRIN FLIKSCHUH

PART 2
Agency, consent and autonomy   77

5 Informed consent and referential opacity   79
   NEIL MANSON

6 Respect for autonomy in medical ethics   94
   SUZANNE UNIACKE

CONTENTS

7 Independence, dependence, and the liberal subject   111
   MARILYN FRIEDMAN

PART 3
Some practical questions   **131**

8 Agents of global justice   133
   SIMON CANEY

9 Procreative rights and procreative duties   157
   DAVID ARCHARD

PART 4
Trustworthiness and trust   **173**

10 What is trust?   175
    ANNETTE BAIER

11 Distrusting the trustworthy   186
    KAREN JONES

12 Trust in institutions   199
    DANIEL WEINSTOCK

13 Responses   219
    ONORA O'NEILL

    Index   244

CONTRIBUTORS

David Archard is Professor of Philosophy at Queen's University, Belfast. He is the author of *Children: Rights and Childhood* (2004), *The Family: A Liberal Defence* (2010), as well as numerous articles and chapters in social, political, legal and applied moral philosophy, and co-editor of *The Moral and Political Status of Children* (2002), and *Procreation and Parenthood: The Ethics of Bearing and Rearing Children* (2010).

Annette Baier (1929–2012) was, for a large part of her professional life, Professor of Philosophy at Pittsburgh. She was President of the Eastern Division of the APA and elected to the American Academy of Arts and Sciences. She was the author of *Reflections on How we Live* (2009), *Moral Prejudices* (1995), *What Do Women Want in a Moral Theory?* (1983) and numerous publications in ethics, philosophy of mind, feminist philosophy and the history of philosophy.

Marcia Baron is Rudy Professor of Philosophy at Indiana University and Professor of Moral Philosophy at the University of St. Andrews. She has written extensively on Kant's ethics, including *Kantian Ethics Almost Without Apology* (Cornell 1995), as well as on an array of topics in moral philosophy and philosophy of law, including manipulativeness, rape, justifications and excuses, the imminence requirement for self-defense, and the standard of the reasonable person in criminal law.

Melissa Barry is Associate Professor of Philosophy at Williams College. Her recent work includes "Humean Theories of Motivation" in *Oxford Studies in Metaethics*, Volume 5, ed. R. Shafer-Landau (2010) and *The Normativity of Reasons* (OUP, forthcoming). She is currently writing on epistemic normativity.

Simon Caney is Professor of Political Theory at the University of Oxford, and a Fellow of Magdalen College, Oxford. He has worked extensively on topics in political philosophy, especially theories of distributive justice, equality, environmental justice, intergenerational justice and human rights. He is the author of *Justice Beyond Borders: A Global Political Theory* (2005) and co-editor of *Climate Ethics: Essential Readings* (2010).

Monique Deveaux is Professor of Philosophy at the University of Guelph, where she holds the Canada Research Chair in Ethics and Global Social Change. She is the author of the books *Gender and Justice in Multicultural Liberal States* (2006), *Cultural Pluralism in Liberal and Democratic Thought* (2000), and a co-editor of *Sexual Justice, Cultural Justice* (2007). Her journal articles and book chapters have addressed multiculturalism, human rights, and global poverty.

Katrin Flikschuh is Professor of Political Theory at the London School of Economics. She is the author of *Kant and Modern Political Philosophy* (2000) and has written widely on Kant, political philosophy, and the history of political philosophy.

Marilyn Friedman is Professor of Philosophy at Vanderbilt University. She has published widely in social and political philosophy, ethics, and feminist theory and is the author of *Autonomy, Gender, Politics* (2003), *What Are Friends For? Feminist Perspectives on Personal Relationships and Moral Theory* (1993) and the editor of *Women and Citizenship* (2005).

Thomas E. Hill, Jr. is Professor of Philosophy at the University of North Carolina, Chapel Hill. He has written widely on ethics, the history of ethics, and political philosophy. His books include *Virtue, Rules, and Justice: Kantian Aspirations* (2012), *A Blackwell Guide to Kant's Ethics*, editor (2009), *Human Welfare and Moral Worth: Kantian Perspectives* (2002), *Respect, Pluralism and Justice: Kantian Perspectives* (2000), *Dignity and Practical Reason in Kant's Moral Theory* (1992) and *Autonomy and Self-Respect* (1991).

Karen Jones is Senior Lecturer in Philosophy at the University of Melbourne. She has written extensively on trust, what it is and when it is justified. Her publications on this topic include 'Trust as an Affective Attitude,' *Ethics* (1996) and 'Trustworthiness,' *Ethics* (2012). She also works on emotion and rationality. Much of her work is from a feminist perspective.

Neil Manson is Senior Lecturer in Philosophy at Lancaster University. He is the co-author, with Onora O'Neill, of *Rethinking Informed Consent in Bioethics* (2007) and has published widely in applied philosophy, especially on issues to do with consent, informed consent, and the ethics of knowledge and communication.

Onora O'Neill, Baroness O'Neill of Bengarve, is Professor of Philosophy Emeritus at the University of Cambridge, UK. She is a former President of the British Academy, and former chair of the Nuffield Foundation, and now chairs the Equality and Human Rights Commission. In 2002 she delivered the BBC Reith Lectures, *A Question of Trust*. Her publications include *Towards Justice and Virtue*, *Bounds of Justice*, and *Autonomy and Trust in Bioethics*.

Suzanne Uniacke is Reader in Applied Ethics at the University of Hull. In July 2013 she will take up the Directorship of the Centre for Applied Philosophy and Public Ethics at Charles Sturt University, Canberra, Australia. She is the editor of the *Journal of Applied Philosophy* and has published widely in applied philosophy, ethics and philosophy of law.

Daniel Weinstock is a Professor of Law and Philosophy at McGill University. He has published over 100 scholarly articles across many fields of moral and political philosophy. His most recent work focuses on the political philosophy of cities, on the family as a political institution, and on equity and health. He is currently co-authoring a book on the ethical and political challenges of language teaching in multicultural societies, to be published by the University of Chicago Press.

ACKNOWLEDGEMENTS

Most of the essays in this volume were presented in September 2009 at a two-day event at the British Academy in London: 'Ethics and Politics Beyond Borders: The Work of Onora O'Neill'. The editors would like to thank the British Academy for their sponsorship of that event and for their organisational support. We would also like to thank de Gruyter press for permission to republish Katrin Flikschuh's contribution and Jake Bleiberg for his editorial assistance.

INTRODUCTION

David Archard, Monique Deveaux, Neil Manson, and Daniel Weinstock

Onora O'Neill – Baroness O'Neill of Bengarve – is one of the world's most prominent and distinguished philosophers. Her work has dealt with a very wide range of topics, ranging from the interpretation of the philosophy of Immanuel Kant, and the elaboration of a distinctly Kantian theory of moral agency, to moral and political philosophy and to the examination of some of the most important moral and political issues of the day. Though she has voiced scepticism toward attempts at applying philosophical theories to practical issues in too simplistic a manner, she has as a philosopher contributed to illuminating a great number of real-world ethical debates in philosophically sophisticated ways that betoken her keen awareness of the problems inherent in attempts at simply 'applying' philosophical theories to real-world controversies.[1] What is remarkable about O'Neill's work is that her writings in practical philosophy and even her non-academic interventions in the public sphere are deeply informed by her most general, abstract philosophical commitments. Rigorous philosophical theorizing about rationality and agency, drawing upon, and building upon a range of insights in Kant's philosophy, has been at the fore of her research and has shaped her approach to, and participation in, various applied philosophical topics and projects.

Strangely, perhaps, it is a matter of chance that O'Neill ended up being a philosopher at all. As an undergraduate she originally enrolled to study History with French and Latin at Somerville College, Oxford. The philosopher at her college – Elizabeth Anscombe – recognized O'Neill's aptitude for, and interest in, matters philosophical and, reportedly, passed on a one-line note to her college tutors – 'this girl is hungry for philosophy'.[2] In those days, student affairs were, it would seem, considerably less burdened by bureaucracy and her enrolment was changed to Philosophy, Psychology and Physiology. Having excelled at her undergraduate studies she gained a scholarship for postgraduate study at Harvard where she eventually ended up doing her doctoral dissertation under the supervision of John Rawls. But it was, arguably, Robert Nozick's graduate seminar that accentuated her interest in Kant. The seminar was focused on decision theory, but O'Neill found that account of rationality deployed to be overly thin. Kant – whose writings she had encountered as an undergraduate – seemed to offer something richer and more defensible, which led to her requesting Rawls as her doctoral supervisor. Her prize-winning doctoral dissertation was on universalizability, more specifically, on the problem of how to integrate the universality of certain kinds of rational norms – as found in Kant's categorical imperative – with the particularity of specific actions, without losing the normative dimension to either. A descendant of her doctoral dissertation was published as a monograph: *Acting on Principle* (Columbia University Press, 1975). After Harvard she took a post at Barnard College, Columbia University, where she remained until the late 1970s, when she returned to the UK, taking a post at the University of Essex.

During the 1970s O'Neill published on a wide range of research topics including rationality and agency, Kant's theory of objective space, global justice, rights theory, and the ethics of rearing and educating children. In the 1980s she continued to work on Kant, the ethics of child rearing and the family, and global ethics, the latter topic receiving a detailed treatment in her monograph *Faces of Hunger: An Essay on Poverty, Development and Justice* (George Allen and Unwin, 1986). Early in the decade she expanded her research interests into the area of medical ethics – though, as one might expect, O'Neill's medical ethics is one that is philosophically robust and focused upon ethically relevant aspects of agency. Abstract issues about agency continue as a research theme, with the ethics of consent emerging as a topic of interest, one to which she will repeatedly return over the next two decades. By the end of the decade the themes of Kant, agency, reason, normativity and ethics, all converge in the monograph outlining her distinctive development of Kantian constructivism *Constructions of Reason: Explorations of Kant's Practical Philosophy* (Cambridge University Press, 1989). O'Neill argues that a proper interpretation of Kant's constructivism about practical reasoning and its principles (or maxims) offers us a more defensible, adequate and robust framework for critically engaging with a wide range of ethical problems, including those that might seem to fall within the domain of *applied* ethics. But unlike some applied ethicists, who offer an 'off the peg' application of a sometimes thin understanding of Kant, or Mill, or Aristotle to give a deontological or consequentialist or virtue ethics 'solution' to an applied ethical conundrum, O'Neill as a Kant scholar herself, offers a clarified, revised version of Kantianism, at a very deep, sophisticated level.

In the 1990s O'Neill continued to develop, and elaborate upon, her research in these areas, in a wide range of articles and books. The start of the decade saw her leave Essex for Newnham College Cambridge, where she was elected Principal in 1992 – the head of the college – and remained so until her retirement in 2006. In terms of her philosophical work, her Kantian constructivism was further developed in *Towards Justice and Virtue*:

INTRODUCTION

A Constructive Account of Practical Reasoning (Cambridge University Press, 1996). Here O'Neill offers a thorough critical assessment of the relationship between rights-based theories of ethics and virtue ethics, with once again a focus on reason and agency. Her Kant-inflected critical philosophy is also developed in *Bounds of Justice* (Cambridge University Press, 2000), and Kant (on Religion and Reason) provides the focus of her 1996 Tanner Lectures at Harvard.

The end of the 1990s found O'Neill entering a new area of research – *bioethics* – that might seem to be at some distance from Kant and abstract thinking about reason and agency. Bioethics is a discipline that studies ethical problems that arise from biotechnological developments. Not all bioethics is philosophical, and not all philosophical bioethics exhibits the rigour and analytic subtlety of O'Neill's work. Her new research interest in bioethical issues coincided with her playing an increasing role in public and policy affairs, some of which are directly concerned with bioethical matters. In the 1990s O'Neill was a member, then chair, of the UK's Nuffield Council on Bioethics. Later in the decade she was a member (and acting chair) of the UK Human Genetics Advisory Commission. Her contribution to public life in the UK was recognized in the honours system with the award of a CBE – (*Commander of the Most Excellent Order of the British Empire*). In 1999, she was appointed a life peer in the UK House of Lords, taking the title Baroness O'Neill of Bengarve.

The new millennium saw her continue her research on many of the topics highlighted above, but with a widening of her communication to audiences beyond philosophy and even beyond the academy. In *Autonomy and Trust in Bioethics* (Cambridge University Press, 2002), based upon her 2001 Gifford lectures, she offers a critical perspective on the way that notions of autonomy (including Kant's notion of autonomy) are misunderstood and misused in bioethics, together with a neglect of the importance of trust. Philosophical and ethical issues to do with trust and placing trust are at the core of her 2002 Reith Lectures – a prestigious public broadcast lecture series in the UK. These lectures were published as *Question of Trust* (Cambridge University Press, 2002). Applied philosophical themes, including the critical evaluation of bioethics and a stress on the ethical importance of trust, emerge once more in *Rethinking Informed Consent* (Cambridge University Press, 2007) (co-authored with Neil C. Manson).

Communication and the ethics of communication are central topics in *Rethinking Informed Consent*. But the ethics of communication has also been an important, if implicit, aspect of many different areas of O'Neill's work: her constructivism lays great stress on the importance that norms be *communicable* to others; her work on consent, and on trust, similarly involves a critical focus on normative aspects of, and the normative role of, communication in securing consent or in signalling trustworthiness. In recent years this interest in the ethics of communication has become more explicit with

O'Neill's work on freedom of the press and freedom of speech, data protection regulation, transparency, accountability, and communicative norms more generally.

With over 130 articles, and nine books, on a wide range of philosophical topics, any volume on Onora O'Neill's work, especially one entitled *Reading Onora O'Neill*, poses its editors with a problem of selection. We could not hope to offer a fully comprehensive critical commentary upon all of O'Neill's work whilst at the same time doing justice to the rigour and subtlety of her work. We have therefore decided to restrict our focus to some key areas. A recent volume focuses specifically on O'Neill's Kantian philosophy from the perspective of Kant studies and Kant scholarship, and the present volume does not duplicate that focus. Whilst Kant does feature heavily in many of the critical commentaries below, the collection opens with critical discussion of a topic that has been central to a great deal of O'Neill's philosophy, sometimes explicitly, sometimes less explicitly, and sometimes indirectly: the nature of reason and agency. As noted above, O'Neill takes Kant's insights about reason and agency very seriously. But O'Neill has not simply taken Kantian views of reason and agency and applied them to philosophical and ethical problems; she has sought to get to the very heart of the issues about reasoning and agency that were Kant's concern, and to improve upon Kant's way of engaging with and resolving those issues.

In 'Moral Worth and Moral Rightness, Maxims and Actions' Marcia Baron focuses upon a key challenge for O'Neill's constructivism (and also for Kant), one that is directed at its fundamentals. On O'Neill's constructivist theory, maxims are of central moral worth. But this poses the challenge of what we say about the moral worth of particular *actions*. Kant seems to suggest that the connection is found in whether or not the action is done *out of* duty. But, Baron argues, an action might 'fit' with a maxim that passes the test of the categorical imperative but not be done *out of duty*: does such an action inherit the moral worth of the maxim or not? If it does, *how* is this so? Baron argues that neither Kant nor O'Neill has offered us an adequate answer here.

O'Neill's distinctive take on Kantian constructivism is also subjected to critical evaluation in Melissa Barry's 'Constructivist Practical Reasoning and Objectivity', which seeks to clarify the scope and ambitions of O'Neill's constructivism. O'Neill's work, especially in *Towards Justice and Virtue*, seems to suggest that she aspires to offer a constructivist account of *reasoning* and the authority of reasons. Barry argues that this is much more problematic than the more modest project of seeking to offer a constructivist account of ethical norms that rests upon an unanalysed notion of rational authority as its foundation.

Thomas Hill's 'Varieties of Constructivism', as the title suggests, also focuses on O'Neill's constructivism but here seeks to clarify the scope and

INTRODUCTION

limits of O'Neill's constructivism by comparing it with other forms of constructivism, including Kant's own, and the political constructivism of John Rawls. Like Barry, Hill also seeks to press O'Neill on the question of what, if anything, provides the foundation for the constructivist process.

Still with Kant, but with a different focus, Katrin Flikschuh's 'Hope as Prudence: Practical Faith in Kant's Political Thinking' engages with the topic of O'Neill's 1996 Tanner Lectures: Kant's philosophical theology and its implications for the notion of religious *hope*. Flikschuh argues against what she sees as O'Neill's overly secular interpretation of Kant.

O'Neill's work on reason and agency ranges way beyond a focus on Kant. She has applied her rigorous thinking about reasoning and agency in a normative context to other phenomena, such as that of *consent*. A certain kind of consent has received a great deal of attention in political philosophy: consent as agreement to be bound by norms. The kind of consent that O'Neill has focused upon is *permissive* consent, where an act of consent by one party renders permissible an action that would otherwise remain impermissible. In his 'Informed Consent and Referential Opacity' Neil Manson considers the importance of the problem of referential opacity to O'Neill's understanding of consent. This problem is one familiar from discussions in philosophy of language whereby the truth-value of propositional statements is not preserved with the substitution of distinct, co-referring words or phrases. Manson argues that O'Neill has a broader understanding of referential opacity than that employed in philosophy of language. For her what matters is that we consent to things described and conceived in different possible ways. Manson shows how an impoverished understanding of information gets in the way of being clear about how and why we should secure informed consent. He suggests that the problem of referential opacity goes to the very heart of what consent requires and offers two possible solutions that O'Neill makes use of. One downgrades the importance of consent and shifts the focus from the provision of information to norms of good communication. The second sees the problem of different subjective understandings of what we are agreeing to (or proposing) within the context of her own interpretation of Kantian ethics and the Categorical Imperative.

In her 'Respect for Autonomy in Medical Ethics' Suzanne Uniacke challenges O'Neill's characterization of what might be required of doctors in the name of respecting patient autonomy. O'Neill draws a contrast between a rich, robust and full sense of autonomy as personal independence, self-direction and self-expression and a 'minimalist' sense of autonomy as 'mere, sheer choice'. O'Neill believes that in contemporary medical practice it is the 'minimalist' understanding of a respect for patient autonomy that is in play and that in effect this amounts to little more than a right to refuse treatment. Uniacke suggests that in fact more is in play. She does so by analysing the reasoning in the important English legal case of *Burke* [2004] and [2005] and by offering distinct senses in which a doctor might respect a competent patient's expressed wishes. In particular, she distinguishes between 'compliance' respect that treats the other's wishes as determinative and 'consideration' respect that requires the doctor only to take some account of the other's wishes. Moreover, a key sense of consideration respect is of a respect for the patient's wishes *as* the patient's wishes. Attending to this sense of what it is to respect the patient's wishes suggests that O'Neill is mistaken to conclude that only the 'minimalist' sense of autonomy is respected in medicine.

In her 'Independence, Dependence, and the Liberal Subject' Marilyn Friedman makes use of the work of O'Neill to explore how we should understand the notions of independence and dependence. Friedman reviews various critical claims made about the value of independence and endorses O'Neill's view that independence is best construed as relative to different areas of human life and as admitting of degrees. So construed it is neither mythical nor impossible to attain. Friedman also endorses O'Neill's view that independence can be for good or ill, as can dependency. However, O'Neill is, Friedman thinks, right to emphasize the particular importance and value independence can have for women by drawing attention to the particular harms to which a woman's dependency can expose her. Friedman also argues that the independent, or autonomous, liberal citizen should remain a key element of the standard for establishing the legitimacy of political principles such as those of justice. However, she also believes that O'Neill's account fails to accommodate those citizens, such as the severely cognitively impaired, who cannot engage in critical political reflection. Friedman offers a modified liberal theory of legitimacy that can accommodate such persons.

Much of O'Neill's work has sought to *apply* sophisticated Kantian ideas about reason and agency to practical ethical issues. In addition to bioethics and medical ethics, O'Neill has made major contributions to debates about the scope of procreative rights and global justice.

In 'Agents of Global Justice' Simon Caney develops and deepens O'Neill's argument that theories of global justice must not only articulate the principles that ought to govern the relations among states, and among people, they must also take on the task of defining who the agents of these principles might be. This question becomes interesting and complex once it is observed that a natural answer that we might provide to this question, namely, that states ought to be the primary agents of global justice, will not do, given the fact that many of the states in the world today are weak or virtually non-existent. Caney broadens O'Neill's account, which articulated the roles that transnational companies and non-governmental organizations might take on in the non-ideal context of weak and of failed states, and deepens it by couching the account of agents of justice in a more encompassing theory of legitimacy and international law.

David Archard in 'Procreative Rights and Procreative Duties' rehearses some of the themes that O'Neill has developed in her writings on procreation and child-rearing. O'Neill, in keeping with her emphasis on grounding our views of our ethical responsibilities on the basis of an account of our duties rather than of our rights, argued for limits on procreative rights that take into account the duty to provide children with a minimally decent life. Archard shows just how difficult it is to define the limit clearly, given, among other things, the importance of child-rearing even to those individuals who are through no fault of their own incapable of ensuring a minimally decent life for their children, and given also the difficulties inherent in identifying a threshold of well-being that might warrant the claim that a person's existence is preferable to her non-existence.

The final group of essays picks up on a theme that has featured heavily in O'Neill's research in the twenty-first century: the ethics of trust, trustworthiness and the institutions and procedures that secure or hinder the intelligent placing of trust.

Annette Baier, whose philosophical views on trust differ considerably from O'Neill's, takes the opportunity in 'What is Trust?' to lay out some of these differences. Arguing that she confuses the ethically richer notion of *trust* with a less rich notion of *reliance*, Baier warns that the monitoring and supervision that O'Neill proposes as instruments to bolster trust will have the opposite effect. Trust necessarily entails vulnerability – 'willingness to be vulnerable to the trusted' – and there is simply no getting around this. Trust also requires trustworthiness, but the reverse is also true: one cannot establish one's trustworthiness, according to Baier, if another does not risk trusting them. She argues that repairing the broken trust of institutions (such as that of medicine) would best be done through self-monitoring rather than constant external monitoring, which can damage the web-like climate of trust.

Karen Jones, like Baier, has developed her own distinctive philosophical account of trust. In 'Distrusting the Trustworthy', she too focuses on trustworthiness and placing trust, arguing that O'Neill's view of trust is overly rationalistic and downplays the essential affective aspects of trust and placing trust. These affective dimensions affect our judgment of whom and when to trust, with far reaching consequences. Distinguishing between 'basic trustworthiness' and what she calls 'rich trustworthiness' Jones argues that the latter highlights the issue of reliable signaling in matters of trust. Jones furthermore draws our attention to the ways in which affective judgment can cause us to fail to trust the trustworthy by disrupting signals and their reception. Such failures can in turn carry serious social consequences, including generating 'pathologies of distrust', such as those fuelled by racial or cultural prejudice and bias.

In the final critical paper of the volume, Daniel Weinstock's 'Trust in Institutions', Weinstock builds on some of O'Neill's most recent, path-breaking work on trust, more specifically on her diagnoses of a contemporary 'crisis of trust'. O'Neill has noted that there is something of a contradiction between, on the one hand, the avowals people tend to make to the effect that they do not view the holders of important social responsibilities as trust-worthy, and on the other, the behaviour people display in continuing to actively place trust in those people they claim to distrust. Weinstock shows that there is an intuitively plausible explanation, which has to do with the fact that in certain contexts it may actually be prudentially rational to act as if one trusted people that one does not consider trustworthy, all things considered. Weinstock goes on to argue that the kind of trust that matters in modern, complex societies is trust in institutions – specifically in the rules and oversight mechanisms that govern them rather than the individuals that happen to hold offices within them, and that the sources of information through which citizens are provided with relevant information with which to determine whether or not to place their trust in institutions, should focus on these rules and mechanisms.

This volume has its roots in a two-day conference 'Ethics and Politics Beyond Borders: The Work of Onora O'Neill' held at the British Academy in September 2009, convened by David Archard, Monique Deveaux, and Daniel Weinstock. Versions of many of the papers in this collection were presented at that conference (the papers by Barry, Hill, Flikschuh, Manson, Uniacke, Caney, Archard, Weinstock). The remaining contributions, as with the conference presentations, were sought from those whom the editors believed would be able to offer a useful critical perspective on various aspects of O'Neill's work.

The editors are extremely pleased that Onora O'Neill agreed to produce an extended essay to conclude this volume. Her essay not only responds to the various critical appraisals of her work in this volume, but takes the opportunity to provide a critical overview and self-assessment of her own work. We hope that the essays in this volume will provide a useful and engaging resource both for those who are interested in the work of one of the world's leading philosophers, but also for those who share O'Neill's interests in a wide range of philosophical topics, including rationality, agency, global justice, the ethics of children and the family, consent, informed consent, trust and trustworthiness, and, in the background to all of this, the ever-present framework of Kantian philosophy.

Notes

1 O'Neill's views on the connection between philosophy and issues of public policy are best expressed in her paper 'Applied Ethics: Naturalism, Normativity, and Public Policy', in *Journal of Applied Philosophy*, vol. 26, no. 3, 2009, pp. 219–229.
2 'This Girl is Hungry for Philosophy': an interview with Onora O'Neill, by Kimberley Hutchings. *Women's Philosophy Review*, no. 28, 2001–2, 7–21, p. 7.

Part 1

KANT ON ACTION AND REASON

1

MORAL WORTH AND MORAL RIGHTNESS, MAXIMS AND ACTIONS

Marcia Baron

My essay has a narrow focus: it explores a question – and likely disagreement – I have concerning one aspect of Onora O'Neill's very rich, very influential 'Consistency in Action'.[1] There is much that I agree with in that essay, and I have learned a great deal from it, as I have from O'Neill's other work. My disagreement is small in relation to the scope of her essay, but it is not a mere quibble. I hope to elicit from Prof. O'Neill some remarks on maxims and the relation between a maxim's passing muster – the maxim's passing the test of the Categorical Imperative (CI) – and the moral worth of an action that has that maxim. I can best introduce my question by quoting a passage from 'Consistency in Action'.

> [R]ightness and wrongness and the other 'categories of right' standardly used in appraisal of outward features of action are *not* the fundamental forms of moral acceptability and unacceptability that he [Kant] takes the Categorical Imperative to be able to discriminate. Since the locus of application of Kant's universality test is agents' fundamental principles or intentions, the moral distinction that it can draw is in the first place an intentional moral distinction, namely that between acts that have and those that lack moral worth. In an application of the Categorical Imperative to an agent's maxim we ask whether the underlying intention with which the agent acts or proposes to act—the intention that guides and controls other more specific intentions—is consistently universalizable; if it is, according to Kant, we at least know that the action will not be morally unworthy, and will not be a violation of duty.[2]

I completely agree with O'Neill that the fundamental form of moral acceptability that the CI is supposed to be able to discriminate is not the rightness of actions. Insofar as it is a test,[3] the CI tests the agent's maxim. So far we are in agreement. (My use of 'maxim' does not reflect any disagreement; see note 2.) What I want to question is O'Neill's claim that the CI distinguishes between acts that have and those that lack moral worth.

My question thus concerns the relation between an action's moral worth and a maxim's passing the CI test. Does the fact that a maxim is universalizable entail, on Kant's view, that the action that has that maxim is morally worthy?[4] (The question can be asked with respect to any formulation of the CI; since I am discussing O'Neill's paper, I frame the question in terms of universalizability when I do not present it simply in terms of passing the CI test.)

Here is an initial answer, to be examined and expanded on in the course of this short essay: No, it does not entail it, and we can see that by recalling that on Kant's view, an action has moral worth only if it is done from duty. An action whose maxim is universalizable need not be done from duty. Therefore, an action whose maxim is universalizable may, but need not, have moral worth. Recall Kant's shopkeeper who refrains from cheating in order to maintain his good reputation (G 397). His maxim – 'In order not to harm my reputation, I will treat all my customers honestly rather than cheat those I think I can get away with cheating' – is universalizable, but he does not act from duty, and his action lacks moral worth.

The negative answer – the position that the fact that a maxim is universalizable does not entail, on Kant's view, that the action that has that maxim is morally worthy – is only tentative, because we need to examine just what is meant by 'done from duty'. 'Done from duty' may mean that it is done for the reason that it is morally required. This is the narrow, and more standard, notion of 'done from duty' (or of 'acting from duty'). Acting from duty thus understood is what is sometimes referred to as acting from duty 'as a primary motive'. But there is also a broader notion, which encompasses both acting from duty as a primary motive and acting from duty in the following sense: I act primarily for some other reason, but I am guided in so acting by my sense that what I do is morally recommended, or at least morally permissible. My commitment to morality thus plays a motivational role, but only a secondary one. This is sometimes referred to as acting from duty 'as a secondary motive'.[5]

There are different views of just what acting from duty as a primary motive involves. On my view, acting from duty as a primary motive (more precisely, doing x from duty at t_1) is not compatible with *acting from* an inclination (more precisely, doing x from an inclination at t_1) but is compatible with *having* one or more inclinations (inclinations that may, but need not, conflict with duty). I have written extensively on this elsewhere[6] and will not repeat it here; I want only to acknowledge that Kant scholars differ on this.[7] There is also room to question whether it makes sense to speak of conduct that is guided by a commitment to morality – a commitment to putting moral considerations before other considerations in the event of a conflict – as acting from duty as a secondary motive, the worry being that this does not count as acting *from duty*.[8] I have no investment in calling it 'acting from duty', and agree that there is clumsiness in the term. The point in drawing the distinction is to highlight the role played by a commitment to morality in actions other than those done from duty as a primary motive, and to suggest that the value in acting from duty lies mainly in that commitment.

When Kant says (in *Groundwork* I) that an action has moral worth only if it is done from duty, he is using 'done from duty' in the narrower sense. He is not saying that what is crucial for an action to have moral worth is that it be done in such a way that the agent's commitment to morality plays a role in guiding and constraining the agent's choice. I wish he were. It is hard to see why acting from duty as a primary motive should have special value. Acting from duty is certainly of value; it reflects a commitment to putting morality before competing considerations. Yet it is hard to understand why actions done from duty as a primary motive should count as more worthy – or, more precisely, worthy in a way that actions guided by duty but not from duty as a primary motive are not.

It is important not to overstate the emphasis Kant places on acting from duty as a primary motive – and thus on the moral worth of actions. As I and others have noted, *Groundwork* 397–401 should not be read as if the aim were simply to provide an account of the moral worth of actions; it is crucial to understand *Groundwork* 397–401 as part of Kant's development of the idea of a supreme moral principle, a principle that guides without borrowing anything from inclination.[9] Appreciation of the role of Kant's discussion of actions done from duty in elucidating the concept of good will and thereby developing the principle that guides it, mitigates somewhat the force of the claim that only *these* actions have moral worth. Nonetheless, the claim stands.

In most of his ethical writings, Kant's emphasis is indeed on what I am calling acting from duty as a secondary motive. What matters is that the agent subordinates inclination to duty, i.e., that the agent is committed to putting morality before competing considerations. What matters is not best understood by speaking of isolated actions and asking of each action what motivated it, but rather by considering the agent's conduct over time. But in *Groundwork* I, virtually the only work where he speaks of the moral worth of individual actions,[10] and the only work where he does so in a way that suggests he might be offering an account of the moral worth of actions, he clearly ties the moral worth of actions to acting from duty as a primary motive.

Qualifications and clarifications duly taken into account, it is clear that insofar as Kant concerns himself with the moral worth of individual actions, his position is that an action's moral worth hinges on whether the action was done from duty as a primary motive. That being the case, I don't see how the universalizability of a maxim can entail that an action with that maxim is morally worthy – unless my claim that an action whose maxim is universalizable need not be done from duty is false.

Is it false? Am I wrong in thinking that an action whose maxim is universalizable – or, put in more general terms, an action whose maxim passes the CI test – need not be done from duty? Kant does, after all, say that an 'action from duty has its moral worth ... in the maxim in accordance with which it is decided upon' (G 399).[11] Might it be, then, that to act on a maxim that passes muster *is* to act from duty? I don't think so. This much is clear: that the action's moral worth resides in its maxim does not entail that any action whose maxim passes the CI test is morally worthy. It can still be the case – and I believe it is the case – that only some maxims that pass the CI test have moral worth.

If we were to accept the position that any action whose maxim is universalizable is morally worthy, and thus that any action whose maxim is universalizable has to have been done from duty, we would be forced to hold that in each of the examples Kant gives in *Groundwork* I of actions that lack moral worth, the maxim is not universalizable. Thus, we would have to hold that the maxim of refraining from overcharging inexperienced customers because it is good business policy to do so – or put differently, of treating one's customers fairly with the aim of thereby having a more successful business (and more to the point, of thereby increasing one's wealth) – is not universalizable. Perhaps this position can be defended, but I don't see how. I see no reason why that maxim would not be universalizable.

Am I wrong in thinking that Kant holds that an action has moral worth only if done from duty as a primary motive? I wish I were. I tried hard, in my earlier work, to avoid saddling Kant with that view, but could not find a way to avoid it. But perhaps someone will argue that we should jettison the distinction between primary and secondary motives and propose a new way of understanding 'done from duty' according to which it makes sense both to ascribe to Kant the view that an action has moral worth only if done from duty and to hold that every action whose maxim is universalizable was done from duty. I don't see how this could go, but I mention it as a way one might support O'Neill's claim that the CI distinguishes between acts that have moral worth and those that lack it.

I have focused in this short essay on one area of disagreement I have with Prof. O'Neill: I do not believe that the CI distinguishes between actions that have and actions that lack moral worth. I fully agree that the locus of application of the CI is an agent's maxim, but I am not convinced – and I doubt – that a maxim's passing the CI test entails that actions with that maxim have moral worth.

My discussion has been limited to the *Groundwork*, because that is the only work with anything remotely like an account of the moral worth of actions. That Kant says so little elsewhere about the moral worth of actions is, in fact, an added reason for doubting that the moral worth of actions has the significance that O'Neill suggests it has. I am curious to hear why, insofar as the CI tells us anything about the moral status of actions we are contemplating undertaking, she holds that it is the action's moral worth, not the action's moral rightness (or permissibility) that the CI can disclose. I understand that it cannot tell us about the action's rightness if this is understood as referring only to its 'external' features; to borrow from an example J.S. Mill discusses in a footnote to the second edition of *Utilitarianism*, it matters what the agent's aim is in saving someone from drowning, not merely that he is saving someone from drowning.[12] But once it is clear that the rightness in question is not mere 'external' rightness and must reflect the agent's aim, why suppose that the CI is more able to discern, or more fundamentally applies to, the moral worth of an action than to its permissibility?

In closing, I want to reiterate that I agree with O'Neill that it is maxims, not actions, that are the locus of application of the CI. In addition (though a closely related point), isolated actions are of far less importance in Kant's ethics than conduct; what matters most is how the agent conducts himself or herself. But the moral worth of actions seems to me of minor significance.

Notes

1 'Consistency in Action', in her *Constructions of Reason: Explorations of Kant's Practical Philosophy* (Cambridge University Press, 1989), p. 86. First published in *Universality and Morality: Essays on Ethical Universalizability*, ed. N. Potter and M. Timmons (Reidel, 1985): 159–86.
2 'Consistency in Action', p. 86. In a footnote added in *Constructions of Reason* (n. 3, p. 84), O'Neill indicates that she would not now use the term 'intention' as she did throughout this essay. In keeping with that footnote, I'll use 'maxim' or 'practical principle' rather than 'intention' in presenting her view.
3 I shall not take up the question here of to what extent the Categorical Imperative is a test. For discussion, see Barbara Herman, *The Practice of Moral Judgment* (Harvard University Press, 1993), esp. Ch. 7.
4 I am not certain that O'Neill thinks that it does; perhaps she is saying only that we can tell that it is at least not morally unworthy. That is indeed suggested by the last sentence of the quotation above. But the previous sentence seems to suggest more than that, namely, that the Categorical Imperative can distinguish between acts that have and acts that lack moral worth.
5 This terminology was first used in print by Barbara Herman in her 'On the Value of Acting from the Motive of Duty', *Philosophical Review* 90 (1981): 359–82, later published as a chapter of her *The Practice of Moral Judgment*. I developed the distinction a bit differently in my 'The Alleged Moral Repugnance of Acting from Duty', *Journal of Philosophy* 81 (1984): 197–220, and in *Kantian Ethics Almost without Apology* (Cornell, 1995). Herman gives the secondary (or as she

also calls it, 'limiting') motive a smaller role: it filters out impermissible actions. I envision it as playing a larger regulative role.

6 See my *Kantian Ethics Almost without Apology*; 'Acting from Duty,' in *Groundwork for the Metaphysics of Morals*, ed. and trans. by Allen Wood (Yale University Press, 2002), pp. 92–110 (published in German as 'Handeln aus Pflicht in *Kants Ethik*', edited by Karl Ameriks and Dieter Sturma (Mentis Verlag, Paderborn, 2004), pp. 80–97; and 'Acting from Duty (GMS I, 397–401)', in *Kant's* Groundwork for the Metaphysics of Morals. *New Interpretations*, edited by Christoph Horn and Dieter Schönecker (Walter de Gruyter Verlag, 2006), pp. 72–92.

7 Allen Wood, for instance, holds that an action not only cannot be done from duty and at the same time *aus Neigung* (and on this I am in agreement with him) but that it also cannot be done from duty *mit Neigung*. See Allen W. Wood, *Kantian Ethics* (Cambridge University Press, 2008), p. 26.

8 See my *Kantian Ethics Almost without Apology*, pp. 129, 134–35, and 190–91.

9 This is particularly well explained in Christine M. Korsgaard, 'Kant's Analysis of Obligation: The Argument of *Foundations I*', *Monist* 72 (July 1989), reprinted in her *Creating the Kingdom of Ends* (Cambridge University Press, 1996).

10 He also speaks of the moral worth of individual actions in the *Critique of Practical Reason*. See my *Kantian Ethics Almost without Apology*, pp. 184–86.

11 For those suspicious that crucial words were omitted, here it is without the ellipsis: 'action from duty has its moral worth *not in the purpose* to be attained by it but in the maxim in accordance with which it is decided upon' (G 399; his italics). I omitted that bit to highlight the part that lends some support to the view that any action whose maxim passes the CI test is morally worthy.

12 The example, from the Rev. J. Llewellyn Davies, is discussed in n. 3 to Ch. 2 in the second (1864) ed. of *Utilitarianism*, but was dropped from later editions.

2

CONSTRUCTIVIST PRACTICAL REASONING AND OBJECTIVITY

Melissa Barry

I have learned a great deal from Onora O'Neill's work in many areas of philosophy. In this paper, I shall focus on her work on the foundations of moral philosophy, and in particular on her constructivist account of practical reasoning, which aims to vindicate the principles of reason from the ground up without appealing to idealized foundational elements. I shall suggest reasons for thinking that, contrary to O'Neill's intention, this account is in the end best characterized as a form of limited constructivism, for it, like the views she tends to be critical of, seems to rely on idealized conceptions that are not fully vindicated by constructivist reasoning. I think the same can be said about Korsgaard's constructivist account, which has similar ambitions. The similarity is instructive, as it suggests that the problem lies not with the details of the accounts but with the project of trying to give a constructivist vindication of practical reasoning itself. Since I think it is unavoidable that we start with foundational normative notions, and indeed that we conceive of these realistically if objectivity is to be preserved, I do not take this to be an objection, except insofar as constructivists like O'Neill and Korsgaard claim to achieve something more radical. If I am correct, however, they should characterize their aims differently.

Given space limits, I shall focus mainly on O'Neill's constructivism here, and in particular on the account she develops in *Towards Justice and Virtue* and 'Constructivism in Rawls and Kant'.[1] Near the end of the paper, I'll briefly discuss Korsgaard's constructivist account in relation to O'Neill's. I'll begin with a discussion of the contrasts between (1) realism and constructivism, and (2) limited and complete constructivism, before turning to O'Neill's account. While I cannot do justice to her view here, I hope to make plausible the claim that it implicitly relies upon foundational ideals that are not constructively vindicated.

Realism and constructivism

A realist about principles of reasoning, substantive or formal, regards these as true independent of our beliefs or practices of reasoning, and as the foundation for all justification. He denies that they can be constructed from anything else for the simple reason that the anything else would, in order to construct in a way that is justified, need to rely upon a claim about which starting points and procedures of construction are appropriate, and the only notion of 'appropriate' suited to the task is that the principles are *reasonable* or *reason-giving*. A realist in this sense may think that constructivist reasoning can be useful for some restricted domain, such as political morality or even the morality of right and wrong.[2] But he will insist that the basic building materials for this construction, whether substantive or formal principles, must be conceived of realistically.[3] This is a form of *limited* constructivism.

As this possibility makes clear, constructivist views differ in how ambitious they take the constructivist project to be. *Limited* constructivism does not attempt to provide a constructivist account of all of its materials. While it proposes procedures that agents can use to establish principles for guiding action in a given domain, it does not attempt to justify either the starting points or the procedures themselves in a constructivist manner. It takes these to be justified in some nonconstructivist fashion and uses them to reason constructively to justified conclusions. In particular, limited constructivism does not regard practical reasoning itself as vindicated by a constructivist procedure.[4] *Complete* constructivism, in contrast, aims to constructively vindicate all of the principles of practical reasoning.

As O'Neill notes, Rawls has defended different varieties of limited constructivism over the years. In A *Theory of Justice*, he justifies the assumptions behind the Original Position, from which principles of justice are to be constructed, by arguing that they are in reflective equilibrium with our considered moral judgments. He thereby uses a nonconstructivist, coherentist method of reasoning to establish what look like robustly metaphysical starting points and procedures for constructivist reasoning.[5] In later work, in contrast, he argues that the ideals from which constructivist reasoning must begin are justified by virtue of the fact that they are embedded in liberal democratic societies, to which he restricts the application of his argument. In both cases, the starting points of constructivist reasoning – the conception of persons involved, and the limitations on information and reasoning – are not themselves vindicated by constructivist reasoning. As O'Neill notes, in the first case, Rawls seems to rely ultimately upon a realist foundation; in the second, he falls back on a form of relativism or communitarianism with liberal content. Neither type of foundation is able to provide real vindication, she argues, since each relies on ideas that agents need have no reason to accept, either because they rely on metaphysically and epistemologically problematic notions or because they appeal to particularities of a community to which the agent addressed does not belong.[6]

In contrast to these forms of limited constructivism, O'Neill aims, and takes Kant to aim, at the more ambitious task of giving a constructivist vindication of practical reasoning itself. While many philosophers have interpreted Kant as some form of rational intuitionist, either about formal or substantive principles, O'Neill denies that Kant thinks there is an independent order of reason that determines the correct principles of practical reasoning. Any such principles must be constructed by agents who find themselves in circumstances that pose problems requiring reasonable solutions.[7] As O'Neill puts the idea, Kant tries to 'show how a conception of reasonableness can be constructed out of the capacities and materials which human agents actually have at their disposal.'[8] This is meant to be a form of *complete* constructivism, in that it attempts to provide a constructivist vindication of practical reasoning itself. Through this vindication, O'Neill hopes to show that while realism must be rejected, objective reasoning about conduct is possible. I turn now to the details of her account.

O'Neill's constructivist account of practical reasoning

As I have noted, O'Neill denies that there are independent facts that determine which principles of practical reasoning are correct. Instead, she claims,

> ... 'reason' is just the name we give to whatever may be most authoritative for orienting thought and action. If no metaphysical system or empirical discovery provides foundations for reasoning, reason will be no more than the term we use for the necessary conditions for any coordination, however minimal, by those among whom the reasoning is to count.[9]

If reason designates the necessary conditions for any coordination, we must look at the coordination problem itself for guidance. She notes that for Kant, ' ... the very predicament of a plurality of uncoordinated agents is all we can presuppose in trying to identify the principles of practical reason ... '[10] What guidance does the predicament itself provide? If agents are to coordinate, O'Neill claims, they must find a way to organize their thinking and acting together. For this they need to find a way to agree upon some common authority. If they do not share their starting points, however, they cannot rely upon any particular beliefs or norms: 'In a world of differing beings, reasoning is not complete, or we may say (and Kant said) not completely public when it rests on appeals to properties and beliefs, attitudes and desires, norms and commitments which are simply arbitrary from some point of view. ... '[11]

The only reasonable strategy, O'Neill suggests, is negative rather than positive: it is for the parties to reject all arbitrary assumptions. 'All they can do is to refuse to treat any of the various faiths and beliefs, traditions and norms, claims and propositions they variously adhere to as having an unrestricted authority for organizing thinking and doing.'[12] This suggests that the most fundamental principle of practical reasoning is 'to reject principles and strategies that are not followable by all.'[13] If a principle is not followable by all, she claims, then it will not be a possible way of coordinating with others. She characterizes this as a doubly modal claim: 'reasons for action *must* be held *capable* of being followed or adopted by others.'[14] Two elements of this formulation require further interpretation: (1) in what sense must a principle be 'followable', and (2) by which others? I'll consider these in turn.

According to O'Neill, to be reasonable a principle must be followable in both thought and action by ordinary agents. Judgments about followability must not rely on idealizing assumptions about the capacities, capabilities, or vulnerabilities of the agents to whom principles are to apply. Instead, they should be based upon empirically accurate generalizations about agents and the conditions of action.[15] Followability in thought requires that a principle be intelligible and that it not strike those to whom it is offered as arbitrary (i.e. unconvincing) given their starting points.[16] Followability in action requires, first, that a principle not demand action of an agent that she cannot perform, and second, that it be such that all agents can coherently adopt it together.[17] These considerations provide constraints on any principles of reason. When they are ignored, O'Neill claims, 'coordination and communication fail.'[18] Taken together, they show why the categorical imperative is the supreme principle of reason,[19] for it expressly aims to avoid arbitrary starting points and principles that cannot be coherently adopted by all agents together.[20]

Here, then, we have O'Neill's constructivist line of reasoning, which moves from an identification of the initial target (a plurality of uncoordinated agents), to a specification of a necessary condition on any principle that can serve to coordinate (i.e. the requirement that any principle be *followable* in thought and action), to the conclusion that the categorical imperative is the supreme principle of practical reason (and so the principle to use in constructing additional principles of practical reasoning). In Chapters 6 and 7 of *Towards Justice and Virtue*, O'Neill illustrates how this principle can be used to arrive at an account of both justice and required virtue. For the domain of justice, it reveals why any principle of injury must be rejected. Since the ordinary and predictable result of a commitment to injuring would injure some and thereby incapacitate them for action, the principle itself is non-universalizable.[21] For the domain of required virtue, universalizability rules out inclusive principles of indifference to and neglect of others since no vulnerable agent can coherently accept that these be universalized.[22]

The second element in need of interpretation in O'Neill's account concerns which agents should be included in the domain of ethical concern. Instead of trying to identify a theoretical criterion for determining which agents have ethical standing, O'Neill regards questions of ethical standing as primarily practical, arising for particular agents in particular circumstances. The starting points for such judgments are the interlocking assumptions about others on which agents base their activities. These presuppositions are disciplined by the demands of acting and responding effectively in the world. They include both that there are others whom one's activity will affect, and that those others have certain capacities, capabilities, and vulnerabilities.[23] Such assumptions cannot coherently or honestly be rejected when one turns to the question of who has ethical standing, she argues: 'What is assumed for purposes of activity must also be assumed in fixing the scope of ethical consideration.'[24] These assumptions, when accurate, provide the basis for an account of the scope of ethical consideration agents have reason to accord. People cannot reasonably exclude from the domain of ethical consideration others with whom they take themselves to interact. Since in the contemporary world most agents are linked to some distant and future others, this approach yields a cosmopolitan view of the proper scope of ethical consideration.[25]

Substantive normative commitments in O'Neill's constructivist account

As this brief summary makes clear, O'Neill's constructivist account of practical reasoning starts from the predicament of a plurality of uncoordinated agents and asks which principles of reason such a plurality could appeal to. If the constraint of followability is not respected, she claims, coordination and communication will fail.[26] This language can make it sound as if she intends the justification for the constraint of followability to be instrumental in nature. Further examination suggests that this is not what she has in mind, however. As background, it will be helpful to look more carefully at how such an instrumental argument might go. I'll take as my example Gauthier's argument in 'Why Contractarianism?' where he offers an instrumental justification for the claim that any principles agreed to by agents seeking coordination should ideally avoid arbitrariness and so prescribe equal advantage for all agents.

In Gauthier's account, agents seek to coordinate their reasoning and action in order to maximize their individual preference satisfaction. Rational agents so conceived will see that they will do better if they adopt a system of mutually advantageous constraints on their action.[27] This reasoning is enough to enable them to escape the initial predicament of a plurality of uncoordinated agents, Gauthier argues, but it leaves open the question of what the content of the agreed upon constraints should be. Gauthier's argument in favor of a principle of equal advantage is that any principle that stops short of this will strike some of the agents involved as arbitrary in the sense that they will view their unequal position as due to conditions that need not be the way that they are (as judged against a hypothetical pre-social condition). Their sense that unequal principles are arbitrary will lead them to regard such principles of cooperation as coercive, in place only because the other party is stronger, and so to pressure the more advantaged party to agree to a principle of equal advantage. This in turn will predictably lead to instability. These considerations, Gauthier argues, suggest that the principle of equal advantage is uniquely suited as a means to ensure a stable form of coordination among self-interested rational utility maximizers.[28]

One problem with this argument is that it seems clear that sufficiently large disparities in strength and resources among agents may make it rational for the more advantaged agents to reject a principle of equal advantage, even in the long term. How much instability will severely disadvantaged agents be in a position to cause, after all? Deprived of resources such as education, political and social influence, and economic power, they may well find that they need to acquiesce in a very unequal arrangement in order to obtain the basic means of survival and functioning. If so, then an instrumental justification for accepting principles that all agents will regard as non-arbitrary is unlikely to succeed. For my purposes here, however, the success of this argument is less important than its form. It claims that the principle of equal advantage is justified as a principle of coordination because it is a uniquely effective means to stable cooperation for a plurality of uncoordinated agents when nothing about the content of preferences is assumed. In this account, the nonarbitrary treatment of other agents with whom one is trying to coordinate is of interest only because, and insofar as, it is a necessary means to stable cooperation.

O'Neill's claim that coordination and communication will fail if the constraint of followability is not respected is not meant in this strictly instrumental sense, I think. The problem with a principle that agents regard as arbitrary is not, or not primarily, that it leads to instability. It is, more fundamentally, that only a non-arbitrary principle constitutes a *reasonable* solution, in a noninstrumental sense of reasonable, for a plurality of uncoordinated agents with different starting points. Such a principle is reasonable in the sense of providing the only plan that is *not unreasoned* due to being arbitrary. Likewise, it is the only principle that can be openly communicated (i.e. fully public) since all can accept its justification, and the only principle that allows free, as opposed to coerced, interaction. In contrast to metaphysical truths, which may strike some as arbitrary, O'Neill claims, a non-arbitrary principle such as the categorical imperative is uniquely suited to solve the coordination problem in a reasonable way.

As she says, 'The touchstones of abstraction and universalizability ... will be available for all ... '[29]

My concern with this account is that the initial doubly modal claim that any principle of coordination must be *followable* may not be as minimal in its commitments as O'Neill suggests. In her view, the followability of a principle in thought involves (1) being intelligible, and (2) not striking any agents as arbitrary (i.e. unconvincing) given their starting points. The followability of a principle in action involves (1) being such that each agent can act on it given his capacities, capabilities, and vulnerabilities, and (2) being such that all agents can coherently adopt it together. The first clauses here do indeed look uncontroversial as necessary conditions for any reasonable principle, for they seem simply to express the idea that if an agent *ought* to adopt a principle then she *can*, in the sense that she has the capacity to cognitively grasp its meaning and act on it. While some philosophers have rejected even this minimal requirement because they worry that it may hold normative standards hostage to the contingencies of individual psychologies, I am inclined to grant it.[30] Any principle that fails to respect *ought implies can* should not qualify as reasonable.

The second clauses, however, seem to embody, in subtle form, the Kantian ideal of respect for rational agency without constructively justifying it. We can perhaps begin to see this if we remind ourselves what is on the table at this juncture. We have an abstract but nonideal characterization of the agents' capabilities, capacities, and vulnerabilities based on empirical premises that do not carry normative significance in their own right. We also have the fact of the predicament of a plurality of uncoordinated agents and the intuitively plausible requirement that any principles offered as a solution be *followable* in the sense of being cognitively graspable and not beyond an individual agent's capacity to act. What justifies the additional requirements that any candidate principles must strike each agent as non-arbitrary given his starting points and be such that everyone could coherently adopt them together?

The predicament alone dictates only that the agents find some way or other to coordinate or order their interactions. It seems that a solution here needn't even involve *reasoning* together, since order might be established by the imposition of force. Even if the agents opt to reason together, however, the reasoning might take the form of a mutual exchange of threats (e.g., as in the Cold War), or, more positively, of an agreement on mutually advantageous constraints, as Gauthier suggests. That these seem to be possible solutions suggests that nothing about the predicament itself dictates that the Kantian solution uniquely embodies 'the necessary conditions for any coordination.'[31]

Something more must be built into the initial conception of the predicament, then. O'Neill claims that the predicament shows that agents need to find some way to agree upon a common authority, and that any authority that appeals to arbitrary commitments will be unacceptable. She presents the requirement that principles not seem arbitrary or unjustified to agents to whom they are to apply as a minimal, intuitive requirement on any reasonable principle. Further, she suggests that the requirement that everyone be able to coherently adopt a principle together simply embodies a requirement of consistency. Are these minimal, formal requirements? I'll suggest a few reasons for thinking that despite their minimal appearance they may already embody a commitment to the substantive Kantian ideal of interaction between free and equal rational agents.

Consider first the requirement that principles not seem arbitrary (i.e. unconvincing) to the agents in the plurality. In what sense is this an intuitive, minimal requirement on any reasonable principle? A version of the principle that does seem uncontroversial is one that says that it is a requirement on any reasonable principle that it not strike *reasonable* agents as arbitrary or unconvincing. That seems clearly correct but also trivial, for all the work will be done by one's account of which agents qualify as reasonable and why. There may well be good grounds for regarding some agents as not fully reasonable, and so to deny that their dissent should count against a principle's reasonableness.

If, unlike O'Neill, we are not skeptics about reason's capacity to identify at least some independent normative truths, and we also believe that we have succeeded in identifying some well-grounded principles, we will likely not think it is reasonable to agree that the mere fact that other agents in the plurality remain unconvinced should disqualify these principles as reasonable. There is nothing arbitrary about a well-grounded principle; indeed, being well grounded seems a paradigm case of the non-arbitrary and may even constitute the primary meaning of this notion. We do not regard the denial that the Earth is flat as arbitrary, despite the dissent of flat Earthers, because we think that the claim is well founded and that flat-Earthers are unreasonable. Reasonable agents, we think, would not find this claim arbitrary.

It may seem that even an apparently well-grounded principle must be acknowledged to be arbitrary for purposes of coordinating with agents who disagree, and so unreasonable on *this* basis at least. However, I think the sense in which it must appear unreasonable for purposes of coordination is merely an instrumental sense, in that it would lead to a failure of coordination with agents who refuse to accept it. It need not seem unreasonable in the further, noninstrumental sense that O'Neill seems to have in mind, i.e. of being an arbitrary and so unreasoned principle for coordination. To regard it as unreasonable in this sense, we would need to have some reason to think that the judgments of other agents, and indeed those agents themselves, deserve equal respect so that their disagreement counts as sufficient reason to remove from consideration a principle we regard as well founded. But we need not think *this* in order to coordinate with people. We can think, instead, that the others are unreasonable to reject the principle and continue to regard it as the most reasonable choice despite their dissent, while also admitting that some other principle of coordination is instrumentally justified because these people are too unreasonable to appreciate the well-grounded principle.

To illustrate, if we are deciding between options A and B and we think there are strong reasons to choose A, it seems unreasonable to flip a coin in order to decide which to choose. The weight of reasons, after all, favors A. Upon adding another agent who disagrees and judges that B is better, and with whom we need to coordinate our decision, does it make sense to flip a coin? It may. But the sense in which it does will depend on how we regard the other agent. If we regard him as unreasonable but still a person with whom we must coordinate, we may agree to the fair coin flip as a way to coordinate, but we need not regard the coin flip as representing the only reasonable solution in any but an instrumental sense. If, however, we think the other person is equally reasonable and so deserves to have his judgment given equal weight and respect – despite our disagreement over substance – then we will regard the coin flip as reasonable in the further noninstrumental sense that it is the only *not unreasoned* strategy given that all parties are equally reasonable and deserve to have the decision procedure reflect this fact by not privileging anyone's judgment over anyone else's. If we do not already have a reason to respect the other person and his judgment, however, this will seem like the wrong way to understand why the coin flip makes sense. Indeed, we may even regard the fact that we have to bracket our substantive commitments in order to coordinate with this unreasonable agent as intellectually or morally objectionable, particularly if the domain in question is all of morality and not merely the political domain.

Even if we agree with the Kantian constructivist that there are no good grounds for accepting any metaphysically robust conception of agents or norms, and so agree that any principles based upon these are epistemically unjustified, we may still have other reasons to think that the agents who disagree with us do not deserve to have their views count as possible disqualifiers of principles we find appealing. We may view them as selfish, silly, or unintelligent, and so deny that their viewpoints deserve equal standing with ours. Here too, we may grudgingly admit that adopting a principle that treats their judgment as having equal standing is the only instrumentally rational way to coordinate with them given that they insist on being given an equal voice, but we need not regard this principle as reasonable in the further noninstrumental sense of being the only reasonable (i.e. not unreasoned) strategy given the fact that other agents find our preferred principles arbitrary or unconvincing. That fact would only matter if we thought *they* mattered.

What one needs to accept to think that O'Neill's use of the principle that proposals not strike agents as arbitrary is justified, then, seems to be the distinctly Kantian idea that the judgment of every agent in the plurality should be respected in the sense that every agent should be given a justification that she can accept as at least not unreasoned given her own starting points. And this just seems to be a way of claiming that each agent's rational autonomy should be respected. The reason the Kantian thinks the plurality must adopt nonarbitrary principles is that adopting any other principles would express a lack of respect for the agents who find them arbitrary, i.e., it would disrespect their capacity to think for themselves and to interact with others only on terms they can accept. If so, then what is presented as a minimal and formal principle carries substantive moral content.

The related requirement that a reasonable principle must be such that all agents can coherently adopt it together seems to be based upon similar Kantian commitments. That the same principle should apply to all, so that all can act together on the same reason, will only seem plausible if we think all agents are of equal worth. However if, like Nietzsche, we believe that there are distinctions of merit between people that imply they deserve different treatment, then we will deny that reasonable principles must meet this requirement and indeed believe that there is good reason why they should not. And of course one needn't be a Nietzschean to claim this. Milder versions of the same idea are found in other hierarchical normative systems. My aim is not to defend any such system but to note that the principle that everyone be able to coherently adopt a principle together rules out these positions from the start without clear justification for doing so. Coordination needn't fail in such systems, I would argue, only coordination that respects all agents equally.

It might seem that O'Neill's argument regarding the scope of ethical concern can do some work here, for it might seem that the presuppositions of these agents' activities show that even *they* regard those with whom they interact as equally rational agents in the relevant sense. I doubt that this argument can do the necessary work, however. First, it is not obvious how we should go about determining what the presuppositions of a given activity are. If I set out to cheat someone with a bogus investment scheme, for example, it can look as if what I presuppose is that he is rational enough to be able to follow the reasoning I offer in support of the scheme but ignorant or gullible enough to miss the crucial features that would reveal that it is a fraud. Why not think that this more fine-grained characterization of the presuppositions of my activity is the empirically accurate one? (Indeed, a more generic presupposition that the agent has a general capacity for rationality would seem to make my confidence in my scheme unfounded, for then I would have little reason to expect him to be deceived.) If this more fine-grained characterization of my presuppositions seems more accurate, then it will not be the case that the presuppositions of my activity reveal that I already take those with whom I interact and must coordinate to be rational agents in a sense needed to block the objections raised above.

Second, even if it can be shown that an agent's activity does presuppose that the agents with whom she interacts are rational in the broad sense of possessing a general capacity for rationality, it is not clear how this fact alone, or this fact together with an appeal to consistency, could show that she is already committed to treating those who have this capacity with respect. Why would presupposing, for strategic purposes, that others are rational commit one to thinking that their rationality has any normative standing? At most, this presupposition seems to involve the belief that as a descriptive matter these agents *have* a certain capacity, but this alone does not imply that one must treat this capacity in any particular way. An appeal to consistency would only work, it seems, if one's activity presupposed that this capacity had value, but no reason has been given why strategic interaction must presuppose this (and indeed, many forms of strategic interaction seem expressly to deny it, as they intentionally mistreat the rational agency of others).

What is needed to determine the normative significance of any capacities, capabilities, and vulnerabilities presupposed by agents in their activities, I think, is a substantive normative view about which of those features have value and why. Capacities and vulnerabilities can be an invitation to abuse or protect, and which way they point can only be determined by a view about what value they have. For the case at hand, what is needed is a general theoretical defense of the claim that rational agency as such is valuable (and so should be protected and enabled). Leaving this as a practical question to be addressed by particular agents in particular circumstances of interaction, as O'Neill counsels, will not guarantee rational agency appropriate moral standing.[32]

In summary, the claim that 'reason will be no more than the term we use for the necessary conditions for any coordination'[33] makes it sound as if O'Neill is constructing the principles of reasoning from the ground up, but in the end it looks as if the initial requirement of *followability* has respect for autonomy built into it. If we start only with an abstract and banal characterization of the capacities of agents and the conditions of action, with no specific assumptions about the value of these capacities and the proper norms for interaction, it seems that we may only have reason to endorse the range of options considered by Gauthier. We have an additional, noninstrumental, reason to make sure that the principles appealed to are nonarbitrary and coherently adoptable by all only if we have some further reason to respect the rational autonomy of the other agents in the plurality. And for this we seem to need a non-constructed substantive ideal of agency and interaction. *Ideal* coordination may fail if Kantian restrictions are not respected, but coordination as such doesn't seem to.

A brief comparison with Korsgaard's constructivism

A comparison with Korsgaard's constructivist account of practical reasoning may be instructive.[34] Korsgaard claims that a formal principle, the categorical imperative, serves as the procedure of construction for substantive principles or reasons. Like O'Neill, she regards this procedure as largely negative or constraining in nature, telling agents which actions cannot be rationally willed. Also like O'Neill, she regards formal principles of this kind as easier to justify than substantive principles, and thinks they are best defended by showing that they provide the unique solution to a predicament the agent is in. Thus, the structure of justification in Korsgaard's constructivist account is similar to O'Neill's. Instead of focusing on the predicament of a plurality of agents who need to coordinate, however, Korsgaard begins with the predicament of the agent who needs to unify his will, and indeed himself, in order to act.

The basic problem faced by the human agent, she claims, is created by the structure of its mind. Because the mind is self-conscious, i.e., conscious not only of things in the world but also of its own beliefs and desires, the agent has the capacity to distance himself from his beliefs and desires and call them into question. This, in turn, generates a problem: once he has stepped back, on what basis should he go forward? This problem can be characterized in two ways, which Korsgaard thinks amount to the same thing. First, once the agent has stepped back from his desires he needs some way to determine which of these potential grounds for action he should count as *good* grounds, i.e., which desires he should treat as reason-giving.[35] Alternatively, once the agent has stepped back and recognized all of the desires acting on him, he needs some way to distinguish his will from these desires in order to constitute himself as a unified and autonomous source of action.[36] As we'll see below, it is the latter idea that is central: the need for reasons is understood in terms of the agent's need to regard his will as unified and autonomous.

To solve this basic problem, the agent must select a principle with which to identify his will, that is, he must will in a lawlike way: ' ... we impose the form of universal volitional principle on our decisions in our attempts to unify ourselves into agents or characters who persist through time ... The function of the normative principles of the will ... is to bring integrity and therefore unity – and therefore, really, existence – to the acting self.'[37] Willing according to the categorical imperative is required to have a will that is distinguishable from the forces working on it, then. It is what makes having an active and autonomous will possible.[38] This principle provides a solution to the agent's need to constitute his will as an autonomous source of action not by offering an external standard that might be rejected, but by providing an internal or constitutive standard of willing without which he could not will at all. As Korsgaard says, ' ... the laws of practical reason govern our action because if we don't follow them we just aren't acting, and acting is something that we must do. A constitutive principle for an inescapable activity is unconditionally binding.'[39] Since the categorical imperative provides the unique solution to the agent's problem of how to constitute his will, its normative authority is beyond question.[40]

It is by willing in accordance with this constitutive principle that the agent is able to construct substantive principles or reasons for action. Since in Korsgaard's account the categorical imperative leaves the domain of the law open, it is up to the agent to choose the content of the laws that constitute his will. Some will be proposed by desires, others by contingent features of his situation, such as his social role or ethnicity, which provide 'practical identities' under which he values himself. Finding himself drawn to various activities and practical identities, he recognizes that he needs to endorse some of these in a lawlike way to have a unified and autonomous will. As a result of endorsing considerations in this procedurally appropriate way, he creates reasons for action where before there were only inclinations to engage in certain activities. This form of self-legislation frees him from determination by his desires; it also makes his will, not external normative facts, the source of reasons.[41]

Following Kant, Korsgaard argues that there is one limitation on the identities that the agent can choose. Since it is his humanity, or self-conscious mind, that creates his need for a unified will or identity, if he endorses any desires or identities at all, he must endorse his human identity as valuable (and so the humanity of others).[42] He may fail to realize this, but carrying out reflection properly would reveal that these commitments rationally follow from endorsing anything.[43] This last point appeals to a constitutive standard of reflection: ' ... the activity of reflection has rules of its own, rules, which ... are constitutive of it. And one of them, perhaps the most essential, is the rule that we should never stop reflecting until we have reached an answer that admits of no further questioning. It is the rule, in Kant's language, that we should seek the unconditioned.'[44] A solution that endorses particular practical identities but not the value of humanity fails because it stops before reaching an unconditional answer.

The constructivist strategy of justification here is similar to O'Neill's: it starts with a specification of an agent's capacities and predicament, and through an analysis of these it arrives at a normatively binding principle that is to serve as the procedure of construction for additional principles of action. I argued above that in O'Neill's account, the standard for successful coordination was a distinctly Kantian ideal of interaction among autonomous rational agents, not a necessary condition for coordination as such. While I do not have space to argue fully for this point here, I want at least to suggest that the standard for successful willing that emerges from Korsgaard's analysis is likewise a distinctly Kantian ideal of agency, not a necessary condition for willing as such. Here, as in the case of O'Neill's argument, there are alternative conceptions on offer that seem to provide potential solutions that do not require embracing the Kantian ideal of the activity in question.

A well-known alternative is a Humean account of the sort Frankfurt develops, according to which the will is unified and autonomous by virtue of a certain kind of coherence between first- and second-order desires.[45] An agent whose second-order desires are firm and not subject to doubt, and whose first-order desires conform to these has, on the Humean view, a stable and individually distinctive foundation for willing that is largely immune to passing changes in his first-order desires. Here stable second-order desires are the reference point for determining what the agent really wants (or wants to want). This allows us to distinguish between action rooted in the agent's identity-constituting, second-order commitments, which the agent regards as expressive of his unified self, and action that is the product of a motivationally efficacious first-order desire at odds with his identity-constituting commitments, which the agent may experience as a form of compulsion. It is the former that represents the agent's autonomous and unified will. In this manner, the account provides a way for the agent to regard his will as distinct from the desires acting on him. Autonomy here is achieved through the reordering of desires, not through stepping back from the whole set of desires and willing according to a principle of reason. On initial appearance, at least, these stable, psychologically deep, coherently ordered motivations seem potentially to provide the resources for a solution to an agent's need to constitute his will as a unified and autonomous source of action. Moreover, they seem to do so without requiring that the agent endorse his own or others' rational agency.

We might understand the Idealized Mafioso that Korsgaard discusses in these Humean terms.[46] This character knows what his goals are, is stably committed to them, and pursues them effectively. In the stability, deep-rootedness and coherence of his commitments, he appears to have found what he regards as a satisfactory solution to his need for a unified and autonomous will, without stepping back from all of his desires, and without endorsing the value of his own or others' rational agency. Of course, he does not engage in genuinely autonomous willing in the Kantian sense, but he has arguably found a solution to his need for unified and autonomous agency. Pressed to characterize his activity, he might agree that he is not willing in a full-blown Kantian sense, but that is unlikely to concern him.[47]

To insist that this is not really *willing* seems to rely on the intuition that willing cannot be genuinely unified and autonomous unless it has a foundation other than desire (regardless of how coherent or expressive of the agent's unique personality his desires are). This depends upon an intuitive contrast between the passivity of desire and the active nature of reason. While appealing, this contrast does not, I think, establish that willing in a principled or lawlike way is necessary for the possibility of having a unified and autonomous will, for the ideal Humean agent certainly seems to have a unified will and autonomous will distinct from his first-order desires. Ideal Kantian willing may fail if the categorical imperative is not followed, but willing as such doesn't seem to. In Korsgaard's constructivist argument too, then, it appears that the formal principle that constitutes the procedure of construction is rooted in a non-constructed substantive normative ideal of agency. Her analysis of willing is essentially normative in nature: the internal standard of willing describes the activity ideally performed, ruling out other forms as incorrect or defective because they do not manifest the same independence from passively given desires.

A similar point, I think, can be made regarding the claim that it is a constitutive standard of reflection that it seek the unconditioned (through tracing the rational preconditions of its activity until it finds an answer that it would be incoherent to deny). When describing what is wrong with the Idealized Mafioso, Korsgaard claims that since he is a human being who chooses based on reflection, he is subject to this constitutive rule of reflection: ' ... following that rule would have led the Mafioso to morality, and, since he was reflecting, he ought to have followed it, and therefore he ought to have arrived there.'[48] It seems clear that Korsgaard regards the requirement to seek the unconditioned as a non-constructed norm for reason's activity that applies simply in virtue of its correctness. Here too, the materials of construction are treated as normative apart from a constructivist justification for them.

While Korsgaard attempts to defend principles of reasoning by articulating the conditions of the possibility of willing and reflecting, what she identifies are the conditions of the possibility of an ideal Kantian form of activity. At the bottom of this constructivist account is a substantive normative ideal of agency and reflection.

The need for realist foundations

We have seen that both O'Neill and Korsgaard attempt to justify the categorical imperative as the procedure of construction by arguing, in different ways, that it constitutes the unique solution to a predicament that agents face. O'Neill focuses on its role in solving the coordination problem, Korsgaard on its role in rendering the will unified and autonomous. I have argued that while each shows that the categorical imperative provides an attractive ideal solution to the predicaments considered, it does not provide a uniquely reasonable solution. Instead, each relies on a substantive normative ideal of the activity in question, an ideal that is not constructively justified. This suggests that these forms of *unlimited* or *complete* constructivism are more accurately characterized as forms of *limited* constructivism after all.

This discussion points to two lessons, both of which count against the aim of providing a constructivist justification for practical reasoning as such. First, the distinction between formal and substantive principles in Kantian constructivism is misleading insofar as it suggests that formal principles can be defended without appeal to substantive normative ideals. Both Korsgaard and O'Neill regard formal principles as less arbitrary and question-begging in that the constraints they impose are largely negative in nature. In each case, however, it seems that the formal principle appealed to rests upon a prior ideal conception (of coordination or agency).

This discussion also suggests that, regardless of whether the foundational elements in constructivism are viewed as formal or substantive in nature, whatever serves as the foundation cannot itself be constructed, as it constitutes the basis on which all constructivist reasoning must be conducted. While some restricted stretch of the reasoning for a given set of norms may indeed be constructivist, in the sense of providing an articulation and defense of a specific normative ideal, the basic judgments and principles of practical reason cannot be constructed, on pain of regress. If we cannot avoid direct appeal to non-constructed principles at the foundation of reasoning, what we need is an epistemology that helps to identify ideal epistemic conditions and general methodological principles regarding how to assess rival judgments about principles. At some point we require criteria for assessing the central normative claims that serve as the starting points of arguments, not further arguments.

Scanlon's constructivist account of the morality of right and wrong provides an interesting contrast to these *unlimited* forms of constructivism. It explicitly appeals to just the sort of substantive value that seems to be at work in O'Neill's and Korsgaard's accounts, i.e. the value of rational agency. At the core of his account is the Kantian ideal of justifiability to others, which requires living with others on terms that they could not reasonably reject. This value, Scanlon claims, is an expression of respect for rational agency.[49] Scanlon justifies the value of rational agency, in turn, by appealing to realistically conceived substantive reasons.[50] Likewise, he justifies particular claims regarding which principles can be reasonably rejected by appealing to substantive judgments about reasons.[51] Both the foundational value of rational agency, then, and subsequent judgments regarding which moral principles are a concern for justifiability supports are defended through direct appeals to substantive normative judgments. The practical reasoning rooted in these notions is constructivist, however, in that it is framed by the organizing idea that potential principles must be assessed according to whether they could be reasonably rejected by agents on whom they'll have an impact. Thus, while Scanlon is a constructivist about the domain of morality that concerns right and wrong, he is not a constructivist about the value of rational agency and the related ideal of justifiability, nor about the substantive judgments that go into the process of reasoning one's way to ethical principles. The result is a *limited* form of constructivism in which the value of rational agency and the related ideal of justifiability to others, along with substantive judgments about reasons, provide significant positive guidance in assessing proposed principles of interaction without determining the result. If my arguments above are plausible, this is a more defensible form for constructivism to take, for it acknowledges the need for foundational principles that cannot be constructively justified.[52]

I have argued that O'Neill's defense of the principle that any reasonable principle must be *followable* subtly relies upon a similar appeal to the substantive value of rational agency. Likewise, I've suggested that Korsgaard's constructivism relies upon a Kantian ideal of agency and reflection. If so, then their constructivism, too, is really limited in nature. I do not view this as a flaw since I do not think we can avoid starting with at least some normative propositions that we regard as justified. However, it means that they may need to give up the ambition of providing a constructivist vindication of practical reasoning itself.

While I have argued against the possibility of complete constructivism, I think limited constructivism potentially has an important role to play in justifying principles. By leading us to focus on differences in the distinctive *targets* of evaluation (i.e., principles of interaction for a plurality of uncoordinated agents, as in O'Neill's account, or principles of willing for an agent who faces the task of unification, as in Korsgaard's constructivist account), this approach provides a fruitful epistemological device for extending our normative thinking in a disciplined way. In particular, it may help us to unpack the content and implications of what are in many ways very appealing ideal conceptions of agency and interaction. Since we cannot assess an ideal without understanding its commitments and implications, constructive reasoning will constitute at least a part of the defense of such ideals. Their ultimate vindication, however, will need to come from elsewhere.

Notes

1 O'Neill (1996) and (2002).
2 Scanlon, for instance, seems best characterized as a substantive realist about reasons but a constructivist about the domain of morality concerning right and wrong. See Scanlon (1998).
3 Of course, he will agree that he owes an epistemological account of how we can access these basic starting points.
4 O'Neill (2002), 356.

5 Rawls (1971), Chapters 1–3.
6 O'Neill (1996), 44–48.
7 O'Neill (2002), 354–61. Korsgaard agrees with this way of conceiving of the task. See, for instance, Korsgaard (1996), Lectures 3 and 9.
8 O'Neill (2002), 357.
9 O'Neill (1996), 60.
10 O'Neill (2002), 358.
11 O'Neill (2002), 359.
12 O'Neill (2002), 358.
13 O'Neill (1996), 60.
14 O'Neill (1996), 57.
15 O'Neill (1996), 40–44, 48, 62.
16 O'Neill (1996), 57 and (2002), 358.
17 O'Neill (1996), 57–60.
18 O'Neill (1996), 63.
19 O'Neill (2002), 359.
20 O'Neill (1996), 58–59.
21 O'Neill (1996), 163–64.
22 O'Neill (1996), 194.
23 O'Neill (1996), 93–106.
24 O'Neill (1996), 106.
25 O'Neill (1996), 121.
26 O'Neill (1996), 63.
27 Gauthier (1995), 707–9.
28 Gauthier (1995), 709–13.
29 O'Neill (1996), 212.
30 It seems to me, however, that even taking this principle to be intuitively justified as a starting constraint involves taking some principle of reason to be normatively basic, in which case not every principle will be constructively justified.
31 O'Neill (1996), 60.
32 O'Neill (1996), 93.
33 O'Neill (1996), 60.
34 See Korsgaard (1996), (1997), and (2009) for the development of this view.
35 Korsgaard (1996), 92–94.
36 Korsgaard (1996), 227–28.
37 Korsgaard (1996), 228. Korsgaard distinguishes between the categorical imperative, which requires lawlike willing while leaving the domain open, and the moral law, the domain of which includes all rational agents. It is the former that's a constitutive standard of willing. The latter is justified by an additional argument.
38 Korsgaard argues that the agent must will according to the hypothetical imperative as well, for if an agent always fails to take the means to his ends he will never really *will* an end but merely follow his strongest desires (1996, 230). In (2009) Korsgaard suggests that the hypothetical imperative can be regarded as an extension of the categorical imperative and not a separate principle. I shall focus here on the categorical imperative's role in unifying the will.
39 Korsgaard (2009), 32.
40 Korsgaard (1996), 235–36.
41 Korsgaard (1996), 104.
42 See Korsgaard (1996, Lecture 4) and (2009, Chapter 9) for somewhat different ways of developing this argument.
43 Korsgaard (1996), 121–23.

44 Korsgaard (1996), 257–58.
45 See Frankfurt (1969), (1988), and (2002). Frankfurt distinguishes between desires, which are dispositions to action, and volitions, which are desires that actually determine one's action. A second-order volition is a second-order desire that some first-order desire determine one's action (or constitute one's will). In Frankfurt's view, it is second-order volitions that are essential to an agent's identity as a person (1969, 8–14). For simplicity, I'll ignore this distinction here and speak in terms of second-order desires.
46 See Korsgaard (1996), Lecture 9.
47 Enoch (2006) points this out as well.
48 Korsgaard (1996), 257–58.
49 Scanlon (1998), 106, 168–71.
50 Scanlon (1998), 1–13 and 162, 178. This is a shift from the claim, in his original formulation of the view, that the value of justifiability to others is rooted in a contingent desire. See Scanlon (1982, 111). It's worth noting that on his view realism commits one to mind-independent truths but not to Platonism.
51 Scanlon (1998), 194, 204–6, 213–18, 241–47. See also Scanlon (1998), Chapter 1.
52 Some critics have claimed that Scanlon's reliance on substantive normative judgments when assessing principles of interaction renders the constructivist structure for the morality of right and wrong otiose. I do not have space to discuss that objection here. If correct, it provides more evidence for the idea that a commitment to substantive realism is unavoidable for nonskeptics.

Bibliography

Enoch, D. 'Agency, Shmagency: Why Normativity Won't Come from What is Constitutive of Action,' *Philosophical Review* (2006), Vol. 115, No. 2, 169–98.

Frankfurt, H. 'Freedom of the Will and the Concept of a Person,' *Journal of Philosophy*, LXVI, no. 23 (December, 1969), 5–20.

———'Identification and Wholeheartedness,' reprinted in *The Importance of What We Care About* (Cambridge: Cambridge University Press, 1988), pp. 159–76.

———'Reply to Michael E. Bratman,' in S. Buss and L. Overton (eds.), *The Contours of Agency: Essays on Themes from Harry Frankfurt* (Cambridge, MA: Bradford MIT Press, 2002), 86–90.

Gauthier, D. 'Why Contractarianism?' Reprinted in S. Cahn and J. Haber (eds.), *Twentieth Century Ethical Theory* (Englewood Cliffs, NJ: Prentice Hall, 1995), 701–13.

Korsgaard, C. *The Sources of Normativity* (Cambridge: Cambridge University Press, 1996).

———'The Normativity of Instrumental Reason,' in G. Cullity and B. Gaut (eds.), *Ethics and Practical Reason* (Oxford: Clarendon Press, 1997), 215–54.

———*Self-Constitution: Agency, Identity and Integrity* (Oxford: Oxford University Press, 2009).

O'Neill, O. *Constructions of Reason: Explorations of Kant's Practical Philosophy* (Cambridge: Cambridge University Press, 1990).

———'Vindicating Reason,' in P. Guyer (ed.), *Cambridge Companion to Kant* (Cambridge: Cambridge University Press, 1992).

———*Towards Justice and Virtue: A Constructive Account of Practical Reasoning* (Cambridge: Cambridge University Press, 1996).

———*Bounds of Justice* (Cambridge: Cambridge University Press, 2000).

——'Constructivism in Rawls and Kant,' in S. Freeman (ed.), *Cambridge Companion to Rawls* (Cambridge: Cambridge University Press, 2002), 347–67.
——'Constructivism Vs. Contractualism,' in Philip Stratton-Lake (ed.), *On What We Owe to Each Other* (Oxford: Wiley-Blackwell, 2004), 19–31.
Rawls, J. *A Theory of Justice* (Cambridge, MA: Harvard University Press, 1971).
Scanlon, T. 'Contractualism and Utilitarianism,' in A. Sen and B. Williams (eds), *Utilitarianism and Beyond* (Cambridge: Cambridge University Press, 1982), 103–28.
——*What We Owe to Each Other* (Cambridge, MA: Harvard University Press, 1998).

3
VARIETIES OF CONSTRUCTIVISM

Thomas E. Hill, Jr.

Introduction

In recent years there has been remarkable expansion and development in Kantian ethics. This includes the serious study and interpretation of Kant's texts and the philosophical reconstruction, critique, defense, and extension of its major themes. In the English-speaking world John Rawls has been a major inspiration for this development, through his lectures at Harvard perhaps even more than his writings. There have been many prominent contributors to the continuing discussions of Kant's ethical writings and Kantian themes in ethics, but arguably none has been more insightful, philosophically astute, or faithful to Kant's deepest thought than Onora O'Neill. As one who has had the privilege of learning from her work in this area from its earliest stages, I am pleased to review here some of its highlights and then, more specifically, to comment on how it differs from Rawls' theories that are also, in a broad sense, 'Kantian' and 'constructivist.'

O'Neill's basic ethical constructivism, drawn from Kant, is most explicitly presented in her book *Constructions of Reason*, though it builds on her earlier book *Acting on Principle* and its practical implications are developed in the more recent books *Towards Justice and Virtue* and *The Bounds of Justice*, and other essays.[1] Her constructivism differs from both 'Kantian constructivism' and 'political constructivism' as proposed by John Rawls, which are the main contrasting ideas to be considered here. There are, of course, other so-called 'constructivist' positions in ethics, especially in 'meta-ethics', as these terms have come to be defined by advocates and critics. Prominently Christine Korsgaard has presented ideas that are broadly Kantian and constructivist,[2] and from time to time I have proposed a modest kind of Kantian constructivist thinking in normative ethical theory.[3]

In several papers O'Neill makes a point of distinguishing Rawls' constructivism from her own.[4] She calls attention to important ways in which Rawls deviates from Kant, and she raises serious philosophical objections to Rawls' theory of justice. My plan here is to review some of these contrasts and objections with the aim of anticipating some possible misunderstandings, identifying the deepest disagreements, and exploring whether her constructivism at the fundamental level might be compatible with certain aspects of Rawls' constructivist thinking.[5]

Reviewing O'Neill and Rawls together is appropriate because they both have contributed importantly and influentially to the understanding of Kant's ethics, to the further development of broadly 'Kantian' political philosophy, and to the renewal of philosophical attention to practical concerns. My specific interest in O'Neill's objections to Rawls stems also from my hope that the alternative 'Kantian' constructivist framework that I have sometimes proposed for *normative* ethics, despite appearances to the contrary, need not necessarily compete with O'Neill's deepest aspirations for the constructive powers of reason. The appearance of incompatibility may be due largely to differences in our aims and in our confidence that philosophy can fully vindicate its own starting-points. We also evidently disagree about the value of asking what ideal Kantian agents *would* agree to, which plays a central role in my view, as opposed to asking what real human agents can agree to, which is O'Neill's preferred way of thinking.[6] My main aim here, however, is to explore the contrasts, real and apparent, between the constructivisms of O'Neill and Rawls, not my own attempts to develop an alternative.

O'Neill's Kantian projects: aims, limits, and development

Kant had extraordinary ambitions for moral philosophy but also a strong sense of its limitations. O'Neill defends and follows Kant in both his fundamental ambitions and insistence on not over-reaching the limits of our capacities as philosophers. Many commentators, friends and critics alike, exaggerate Kant's ambitions – Kant's friends to derive more from Kantian theory than O'Neill thinks possible and Kant's critics to blame Kantian ethics for attempting the impossible. Drawing more from Kant's First *Critique* than most commentators do, O'Neill emphasizes that at the core of Kant's critical method was the rejection of arbitrary authority. Too long, Kant argued, metaphysicians had pronounced their Ideas to be necessary truths discovered by reason but had rested their arguments on unsupported premises simply declared to be self-evident. A critical use of reason was supposed to restrict the scope of legitimate metaphysics, just as at the same time it restricted the scope of claims based on empirical science.

Even the use of reason in these critical projects, O'Neill argues, must be 'vindicated' through the ongoing public use of reason. The problem with 'realism', 'foundationalism', and traditional 'rationalism' in ethics is that they cannot survive reason's critique of their authority to assert their starting points. The same critique of arbitrary claims to authority explains why O'Neill's constructivist moral philosophy must work from a fundamental principle that many have regarded as too formal, insubstantial, even 'empty', to guide moral deliberation and judgment. This fundamental principle is the famous universal law formula of the Categorical Imperative – to act only on maxims through which one can at the same time will that they be universal laws. O'Neill argues that this is a fundamental principle of thought as well as action. Reason can vindicate restriction of its use to thinking and acting in ways that are compatible with its supreme principle along with Kant's three great maxims – 1) to think for oneself, 2) to think from the standpoint of everyone, and 3) always to think consistently.[7]

From these seemingly sparse starting points, O'Neill argues, further principles can be derived or constructed, for example, prohibitions of coercive force, polemical debate, deception, disrespect, and indifference to the welfare of others. These are restrictions imposed by the fundamental principle because the maxims of the prohibited actions cannot be shared by everyone. These maxims cannot be *consistently shared, publicized* and *communicated* to everyone in a reason-governed way. The derivative principles are very general negative principles that establish strong presumptions, but not absolute prohibitions, against certain types of acts (coercion, deception, etc.). More specific requirements of virtue and justice need to be worked out by appropriate thinking and judgment that is sensitive to differences in context. Fundamental principles can guide and must constrain applications to practical problems but do not by themselves provide determinate answers to all our moral questions. These are basic themes that O'Neill has developed and defended throughout her philosophical career. They are the background for her later work on famine relief, toleration, trust, and justice across state boundaries.

More specifically, in her first book, *Acting on Principle* (Nell 1975), O'Neill offered a subtle and thorough defense of this ambitious Kantian thesis that the Categorical Imperative (in particular, the universal law formula) can ' ... guide action, and does so with considerable precision' (p. viii). In addition, she argues that so long as it is applied as a guide to decision making (as opposed to judgments about others or acts in one's past), its results are not seriously counterintuitive (p. 129). In order to make the case O'Neill chose to interpret maxims as the specific intentions of a particular person at a particular place and time. She addressed the problem of multiple act-descriptions by assigning a maxim to each of the component acts in a composite act if an act is intended under several descriptions as, for example, when someone raised his gun, fired it, and killed his enemy (p. 41). We can then assess all aspects of what was done by testing their maxims using the Categorical Imperative. O'Neill added a further stipulation to Kant's test to avoid certain kinds of troublesome maxim, such as 'I will buy clockwork trains but not sell them.' Maxims, such as this one, were not to be rejected simply because neither the maxim nor its contrary could be willed consistently as universal law.

A more important, but controversial, supplement was that 'We must intend some set of conditions sufficient for the successful carrying out of our intentions and the normal and predictable results of successful execution' (p. 73). Thus, to use O'Neill's example, a person who intends to rob a bank for profit must consistently intend not only 1) his maxim, 2) that everyone adopt and act on his maxim, but also 3) the normal and predictable results of his successfully acting on his maxim (e.g. his enjoying the stolen money), and 4) the normal and predictable results of everyone's adopting and acting on that maxim (e.g. banks closing or vastly increasing their security measures).

In *Constructions of Reason* (1989) O'Neill modified her presentation of the Categorical Imperative and made explicit her understanding of Kantian constructivism. Maxims are still the principles of action of particular agents at particular times, but the same maxim can be retained over time and can be adopted by many people. Maxims may or may not be explicitly, consciously, or completely formulated. Significantly, the maxim 'must incorporate just those descriptions of the agent, the act, and the situation upon which the doing of the acts depends' (p. 84). Now, the intentions to perform the specific acts by which we carry out our primary aims are no longer considered maxims. Rather, 'Maxims are those *underlying principles* and intentions by which we guide and control our more specific intentions' (p. 84).[8] It is these more general, life-governing fundamental maxims that are to be tested by the Categorical Imperative.

The earlier supplementary stipulation that we intend the normal and foreseeable results of our intentions is replaced by five proposed principles of rational willing regarding the means and ways to implement one's primary intentions (p. 91). These are: 1) we must intend *some sufficient* means to whatever is fundamentally intended; 2) we must seek to make some sufficient means available if they are not; 3) we must intend *all* necessary and *some* sufficient components of our fundamental intention; 4) the specific intentions we act on must be consistent; and 5) foreseeable results of our specific intentions must be consistent with our fundamental intention. In short, if rational, we will implement our fundamental maxim in ways consistent with that maxim, subsidiary intentions, and foreseeable results.

The Categorical Imperative test, on her view, remains limited in various ways. For example, because our maxims can be based on mistaken beliefs and self-deception, and we can sometimes fail to act on our maxims, the test does not show whether our act is in itself ('objectively') right or wrong but only whether acting on the maxim has or lacks moral worth.[9] As she says, 'It tells us what we are *to avoid* if we are not to act in ways that we can know are in principle not possible for others' (p. 103). It tests the mutual consistency of sets of relevant intentions and principles and thereby rules out certain ways of acting, but '[I]t does not thereby generally single out action on any one set of specific intentions as morally required' (p. 103). Despite the limited negative function of the Categorical Imperative test, O'Neill says, 'Rather than presenting a dismal choice between triviality and implausible rigorism, a universalizability test can provide a rational foundation for ethics and maintain a serious respect for the diversity of content of distinct ethical practices and traditions' (p. 102).

Similar themes may be found in the work of others who interpret and extend Kant's practical philosophy, but O'Neill's contribution has been special, if not unique, in several ways. Among these, I think, are the following.

First, she takes Kant's *Critique of Pure Reason* seriously as laying out a method of critical thinking applicable to both theoretical and practical matters. This is where she finds Kantian resources for resisting the idea that we can base ethical and political judgments on 'foundations' of rational intuition, theology, or moral sentiments. Accordingly, she rejects the idea that that morality is based on consciousness of a metaphysically real, intrinsic 'value' that exists independently of rational thought.

Second, she argues forcefully that the single most fundamental and comprehensive principle of *both theoretical and practical reasoning* is expressed by Kant's universal law formulation of the Categorical Imperative – to act only on maxims through which one can at the same time will that they be universal laws. In the most general terms, reason is a capacity that can be used theoretically (as in mathematics and science) and practically (as in morals and politics), and its core requirement for reason-governed thinking and choosing is to seek and follow the conclusions of theoretical and practical inquiry that one can, when thinking critically and consistently, regard as (in some sense) understandable and acceptable from everyone's point of view.

Third, O'Neill argues that Kant's other formulations of the Categorical Imperative must be interpreted as expressing essentially the same requirement as the universal law formulation, and more specific principles of virtue and justice must be derivative from this same principle. Her view, then, is opposed to interpretations of Kant's ethics that treat as distinct and foundational Kant's humanity formula – to treat humanity in each person, never simply as a means, but always as an end in itself.[10]

Fourth, O'Neill takes seriously the limitation that the universal law formulation only rules out bad maxims and so requires us to use our judgment to find mutually acceptable positive policies in the light of empirical facts, context, and appropriate consultation with others. The power of reason in ethics is also limited, on her view, because ethical questions cannot be settled by science, theology, or intuition. The derivative negative moral prohibitions, moreover, are only presumptive, not absolute. And, because our particular maxims may reflect our mistaken or self-deceptive understanding of our circumstances and reasons for acting, testing them by the Categorical Imperative can only guide us to conscientious or 'morally worthy' choices, not necessarily to acts that are morally permissible in light of the actual facts.

Fifth, O'Neill consistently and austerely insists on not importing idealizations into her interpretation of Kant's procedure for testing maxims by the Categorical Imperative. For example, we are not to reflect on whether we can will our maxims as universal laws from behind a 'veil of ignorance'.[11] All the more, we are supposed to think of our maxims as possible universal laws for our imperfect world, not for an ideal world of fully rational, informed, equal, conscientious, and mutually respecting persons.[12]

What I have summarized here I take to be the core of O'Neill's Kantian constructivism, but in subsequent essays she develops and illustrates how the core ideas might lead us to general maxims of virtue and justice, and guide our deliberation about specific practical problems. This development of her broadly Kantian perspective can be seen in her later books, *Towards Virtue and Justice* (1996) and *Bounds of Justice* (2000). Importantly she also contrasts her Kantian constructivism with the constructivism (or rather several versions of constructivism) developed and described by John Rawls. The Rawlsian versions, she argues, are more remote from Kant's texts, narrower in scope, and subject to several serious objections. My aim here is not to resolve this controversy in favor of one idea of constructivism or another. Instead I will simply highlight some points of contrast, separate some issues, and raise questions from a would-be mediator's perspective.

Points of agreement and general objections to Rawls' constructivisms

In his Dewey Lectures, 'Kantian Constructivism in Moral Theory' Rawls describes Kantian constructivism as a moral theory that stands in contrast to utilitarianism and intuitionism as described by Henry Sidgwick in his *Methods of Ethics*.[13] These lectures were transitional between Rawls' *A Theory of Justice* and *Political Liberalism*. In *A Theory of Justice* Rawls draws from some aspects of Kant's ethics and uses a kind of reasoning that has come to be called constructivist, but in *Political Liberalism* he is more explicit about the materials, process, purpose, and limits of construction. In the latter work, Rawls distinguishes his own political constructivism from his reconstruction of Kant's ethical constructivism. Rawls' last work, *The Law of Peoples*, describes two further perspectives for constructing liberal principles regarding international relations.[14] The details of these various forms of constructivism are complex and reflect subtle changes in Rawls' thinking. The main features of the Rawlsian constructivist approach, however, are well known. Here I will first note a few similarities between O'Neill and Rawls regarding constructivism, and then summarize briefly a few differences, focusing primarily on features of Rawls' theory that O'Neill finds objectionable.

On at least the following points I think O'Neill and Rawls are in agreement. *First*, both follow Kant in granting that, at least for purposes of determining just principles of social organization, claims to authority must be justified from a perspective that does not include the prior assumption that we know and comprehend divine or noumenal wills. Deep aspects of religious life are not denied, but construction of principles of justice cannot presuppose theological beliefs. (Kant's attribution of principles to rational noumenal wills is a conclusion, not a premise, of his ethical thought.) *Second*, no one can be assumed to have direct intuitive or perceptual access to correct principles of justice and moral truths – these are not entities that can be simply 'seen' even by 'the light of reason'. *Third*, the existence of historical traditions and actual agreements, though relevant to particular decisions, cannot be foundational. The more basic standard is what people *can* share, not what they actually consent to. *Fourth*, principles of justice and morality are somehow constructs of the thinking and willing of persons who are, in some appropriate sense, free, rational, and equal. What this assumption amounts to and how it plays out in theory and practice is a matter of disagreement, but the assumption is explicit in Rawls' work (especially in the early stages) and seems at least implicit in O'Neill's Kantian constructivism.[15] *Fifth*, we live in a very diverse and imperfect world, and our theories and their use must ultimately reflect respect for each person and concern for their welfare. The philosophical disagreement is about how to interpret, defend, and apply such values to our circumstances in this diverse and imperfect world and what kind of success we can reasonably hope for.[16] *Sixth*, justification of moral and political principles is an ongoing, perhaps never-ending, task in which proposals must be presented and tested in public discourse in which no voice is supremely authoritative and all conclusions are subject to critique and possible revision. This, of course, applies to philosophers' theories as well as particular moral and political claims. Unless I am mistaken, these points are commonalities and should not be lost when we concentrate on some significant disagreements.

O'Neill's main objections to Rawls' versions of constructivism, I think, fall under three main headings: (A) Rawlsian constructivisms are not Kant's and so are only misleadingly called 'Kantian constructivism'. O'Neill does not deny that Rawls was aware of important ways in which his versions deviated from Kant's, but she highlights these differences to show the advantages of Kant's position, not just to reclaim the label 'Kantian' for Kant. (B) Rawls' constructivist procedures are always concerned with what agents of an ideal kind *would* endorse, but the more widely defensible constructivist procedure (Kant's Categorical Imperative) is concerned only with what real human agents *can* endorse (or at least 'share,' 'communicate,' and find 'intelligible'). (C) Rawls' constructivist procedures, and therefore their results, presuppose ideas that are arbitrary, which apparently means 'not vindicated' (or perhaps 'not evidently possible to vindicate') by reason. The objection is that Rawls builds his theory from various starting points that are arbitrarily assumed to have authority for us, and in the process of construction he makes use of ideas of 'the rational' and 'the reasonable' that are not themselves vindicated. The result is a theory that is too narrowly restricted in that it arbitrarily excludes those who do not fit its assumptions, for example, 'outsiders', non-democrats, and 'marginalized' people.[17]

Under each of these headings are more specific points that need to be addressed in a thorough treatment of these contrasts, but for now I will focus on the last objection in order to question whether the contrasting views are as deeply incompatible as they initially appear. My interest is less in the details of Rawls' various constructivist procedures than with whether his sort of approach to problems is clearly objectionable for the reasons O'Neill articulates. I set aside the first controversy about which view best reflects Kant's own thinking, for several reasons. One reason is that, as O'Neill and others have rightly noted, Rawls' theories in A Theory of Justice and Political Liberalism obviously deviate substantially from Kant's ethics and even more from Kant's account of justice in Part I of The Metaphysics of Morals. For Kant scholarship the appropriate comparison would be with O'Neill's interpretation of Kant's ethics (as in her Constructions of Reason) and Rawls' reconstruction of Kant's ethics as explicitly presented in the Dewey Lectures, the essay 'Themes in Kant's Moral Philosophy', a brief section of Political Liberalism,[18] and Rawls' published lectures on Kant.[19] In these works Rawls did ascribe certain views to Kant, primarily to contrast Kant's view with other views (such as rational intuitionism and his own 'political conception' of justice). With characteristic modesty, Rawls was reluctant to publish the lectures on the history of moral and political philosophy and expressed doubts that he understood Kant sufficiently.[20] Discussing the relative merits of O'Neill's and Rawls' proposed readings of Kant's texts would be a worthwhile project, but more than I can undertake here.

The second line of objection (about what agents *can* versus *would* will) is important for contemporary constructivist thinking as well as for interpreting of Kant's moral philosophy, but it raises large questions and I have briefly commented on it elsewhere.[21]

I turn then to the third category of objections.

Arbitrary authority and restricted domains: a problem for Rawls?

This line of objection is perhaps the most important one: that is, Rawls' constructivist procedures, and therefore their results, presuppose ideas not vindicated (or, perhaps, not possible to vindicate) by reason. To be vindicated by reason presumably is to be justified, or shown true or supported, by good reasons without reliance on premises and procedures that are not, cannot be, or are evidently unlikely to be so supported.[22] In other words, the grounds for accepting the premises and procedures of thought cannot be arbitrarily assumed to be authoritative for us. Obviously straight-line deductive reasoning cannot provide the deepest vindication because it relies on premises and inference rules that cannot all be supported in the same way without circularity. This, I take it, is partly why O'Neill thinks the 'vindication of reason' itself must be recursive, public, and an ongoing task that can never be fully completed. She follows Kant's refusal to accept arbitrary authorities in religion, metaphysics, politics, and ethics. A crucial background for her critique of Rawls and others is that, from her own studies and Kant's, she is convinced that reason can vindicate as necessarily rational for every agent's choices only the universal law formula of the Categorical Imperative along with the general principles of means-ends coordination.[23] Other very general practical principles, she argues, can be derived by applying these most fundamental principles to recurring kinds of human interactions, but she believes that the derivative principles are mostly general prohibitions or presumptions against such things as deception, coercion, manipulation, disrespect, and indifference to others' welfare. From these we can publicly deliberate about and institute more specific policies and organizations as justifiable for various identified contexts.

As I understand her position, then, O'Neill has no general objection to proposing and arguing for principles that, like Rawls', are designed for specific contexts. The crucial question for her, presumably, is whether or not such principles can be justified for that context by rational arguments that *can* survive critical scrutiny of the deepest kind, which includes scrutiny of all their assumptions and modes of reasoning needed to support them. Because she believes that only Kant's universal law formula can be vindicated in this way, she must think that Rawls' starting points are arbitrary unless they can be derived from that formula. Neither she nor Rawls apparently think that such a derivation is possible. From her point of view, then, his starting points are arbitrary. Rawls, however, evidently does not share her belief that Kant's universal law formula, as she interprets it, is the one and only supreme principle of choice and thought that can be fully vindicated. He does not claim ultimate vindication for his initial normative assumptions but rejects her idea that only the universal law formula and what can be derived from it is non-arbitrary. This remains a deep disagreement, not easily resolved.

Rawls and O'Neill agree, however, on the obvious point that our thinking about theoretical and practical matters must start somewhere and that we should not assume that our starting points are fixed and uncontestable. Rather, we should take them as provisional and subject to revision under further critique. Whether they can be justified must emerge over time in 'public' accessible discourse. In Rawls' view, to make progress we need to make proposals, drawing provisionally from ideas that open discussions to date give us some good reason to rely on. Some may hope that the proposals can ultimately be vindicated in O'Neill's Kantian sense, but even those skeptical of success in that project must stand somewhere and need to work out the implications of their stance. The Rawlsian metaphor appropriate for moral and political theories, I think, is not a ship permanently 'anchored' or fixed in place by its working assumptions,[24] but rather a ship we choose to anchor for now with provisional assumptions in order to review the theoretical ship's problems and potential, propose repairs and improvements, so that it may better serve its purpose and everyone affected. Investigation may convince us that the ship needs to be scrapped and replaced, maybe even that we can live better without ships, but all that depends on the specifics of the case.

In sum, the key question is *not* whether Rawls' theories apply to specific contexts, make use of conditional arguments,[25] or contain ideas that have not yet been sufficiently scrutinized and vindicated. The question is whether, after all is considered, it is evident that the practical use of Rawls' theories in the limited ways and context he proposes essentially rests on assumptions that cannot possibly survive critical scrutiny. If, as I believe (despite the efforts of Kant and O'Neill), no theories so far have been vindicated completely, perhaps the better question is whether provisional use of a proposed theory is more likely to survive critical scrutiny (or at least deserve further attention) than use of other available theories or none. Judgment is required here; and if different theorists initially estimate that different types of theory are more promising to develop, the discipline stands to learn from their efforts and public discussion of the competing alternatives. Assuming that the question for now is which among the several imperfect moral and political theories developed so far are still worth pursuing, we need to examine specific objections to their assumptions, development, and claims to authority.

Further objections: are specific features of Rawls' theories arbitrary?

Turning to more particular aspects of Rawls' work, here are a few thoughts about the issues regarding arbitrary assumptions.

Reliance on instrumental reason, desires, and idealizations

O'Neill points to a number of features of Rawls' theories that are potentially objectionable. For example, she calls attention to his extensive reliance on purely instrumental reasoning within the theory. In A *Theory of Justice* this is the standard for the initial reasoning of parties to the original position and Rawls' later argument that a just life and a good life for a person generally converge in a closed society well-ordered by his two principles of justice. Also, at least in the earlier versions, Rawls justifies the 'primary goods' by reference to the *desires* that everyone is supposed to have, whereas in Kant's theory (and O'Neill's) unexamined desires as such have no weight in rational deliberation. Again, Rawls admitted he had to make rather arbitrary stipulations to ensure that his principles would cover duties regarding future generations.

The reliance on desires is less prominent in Rawls' later statements of justice as fairness, where 'the two moral powers' to some extent replace actual desires in constructivist thinking.[26] Rawls' later work, however, prompts other concerns from O'Neill's perspective. The particular points mentioned so far are aspects of a more general disagreement about whether the elements of a theory need to be justified independently. In the case of complex theories or models that make use of idealizations and simplifications, Rawls believed that what matters is not whether each theory-defined feature of the model can be justified independently but whether the use of a construction, as a whole, serves a legitimate purpose better, all considered, than alternatives (including having no theory). This is apparently a major point of disagreement because Rawls repeatedly uses theoretical terms, acknowledged simplifications, thought-experiments, and artificial devices of representation in complex overlapping arguments for his practical conclusions. Rawls contends that all these elements are helpful, maybe even necessary initially, for addressing the problems he raises, and he held that the pieces need not be justified *independently* as corresponding exactly to actual 'real-world' conditions. Instead, the value of his use of his various simplifying, idealizing, and contextualizing devices was to be found in how well the whole package served as a step towards resolving the problems he initially identifies.

Wary of all this, O'Neill evidently suspects that any conclusions will be tainted by this process of using assumptions that are not strictly true, models that do not fit our imperfect conditions, and simplifications that simply bypass issues that need to be addressed. Her objection is not the classic complaint 'garbage in, garbage out' but rather that in large part Rawls' theory is problematic because it is front-loaded with well-intended idealizations that blind us to real and important human vulnerabilities and weaknesses. Perhaps a better metaphor for her view of Rawls' idealizations is 'fiction in, fiction out'.

As a general matter of philosophical method, I think both O'Neill and Rawls have a point here. Artificial elements serve well enough in theories of other kinds, and holistic thinking is not in principle objectionable; but also simplifications and idealizations can lead to conclusions that, if unrestricted, are useless or dangerous. As thousands of pages of Rawls' commentaries demonstrate, these dangers are not easily averted by a theorist's occasional mention that he is doing 'ideal theory' that may not apply directly to actual conditions. Nevertheless, these liabilities are not necessarily decisive against cautious use of Rawlsian strategies. It depends on whether they serve a good purpose and whether the use of the output unjustifiably ignores the fictions of the input.

Reliance on ideas drawn from our culture

Another common objection is the charge that Rawls, especially in his later work, relies unduly on ideas familiar in Western democratic societies. O'Neill's objection is not that these ideas were born and raised locally, but that they are not universally shared, are assumed without justification, and liable to be used in a way that arbitrarily 'excludes' outsiders and marginalized people.[27] Whether or not it is objectionable to draw on and make use of ideas from within one's culture depends on how and why one uses them. We can, for example, use ideas and concepts in both conditional and dogmatic arguments, use them for both proposing and for imposing, and use them in theories of both restricted and unlimited scope. What seems clear in principle is that we should not use them in dogmatic arguments to impose our ideas universally. In principle Rawls, Kant, and O'Neill seem to agree on this.

What O'Neill adds, and Rawls resists, is that in using culture-specific assumptions, even if they are provisional, tentative, and restricted in scope, a philosopher should aspire that they be accessible and publicly defensible to everyone regardless of culture. Rawls apparently came to believe that 'reasonable' people, using non-coercive public reason alone, will inevitably disagree about *moral* principles and their sources, and so he tried to work out an internally consistent and appealing version of *political* principles that could win an overlapping consensus of those committed to broadly Western democratic values.[28] This seems to reflect a striking difference in optimism about what 'public reason' can accomplish, but the appearance may be partly due to other factors. Rawls has no objection to arguing about the superiority of justice as fairness, utilitarianism, or classic natural law theory in classrooms and philosophy conferences that engage in 'public' discourse in Kant's sense. And his political theory is at least consistent with optimism that the best reasoning in such arenas will tend to vindicate justice as fairness over time. What he came to doubt is whether his comprehensive moral theory, or anyone's, could fairly win the allegiance over time of enough citizens who are free to think for themselves so that a just, liberal society based on his comprehensive theory could be stable for the right reasons. Given that, he also doubted that he, and others, could legitimately use in *political* arguments (on 'constitutional essentials') the comprehensive *moral* commitments that they believe to be best supported by reason.

Reliance on stipulated criteria of 'reasonable'

Does Rawls' reliance in *Political Liberalism* on his stipulated definition of 'reasonable' arbitrarily exclude 'outsiders' and 'marginalized people'?[29] This question raises legitimate worries, but fewer, I think, than some readers have suspected. For example, some may worry that by stipulating a particular definition of a common normatively charged word, such as 'reasonable', Rawls is merely adopting a 'persuasive definition' designed to change attitudes without offering any convincing reasons.[30] But definitions can be stipulated for a useful purpose, placed in a theory for good reasons, and explained clearly enough to avoid misleading the readers. The definitions need not correspond exactly to familiar usage, whether in law or everyday life. Besides, Rawls probably did not gain much support by borrowing the unearned emotive force of the term 'reasonable' because it seems to have raised at least as many doubts and objections as pledges of allegiance. In any case, I doubt that this is the source of O'Neill's objection.

Another common objection to Rawls' use of 'reasonable' rests on the mistaken thought that Rawls uses the term to identify who has rights and whose interests matter in a just state. This is just a misunderstanding, and it is not the basis of O'Neill's legitimate concern. Rawls uses his criteria of reasonableness not as a condition of having rights or value but rather to explain the limited scope of the arguments that he thinks he can and needs to offer to satisfy his 'liberal principle of legitimacy' regarding the government use of coercive force.[31] His arguments and assumed standard may be misguided, but the point was surely not to deny adherents of 'unreasonable' comprehensive doctrines (or unreasonable doctrineless people) civil rights and good standing under his political principles. Rawls' principles extend protections of free speech and practice of religion, for example, to all sorts of unthinking, superstitious, dogmatic, reciprocity-denying people, so long as they, like everyone else, limit their overt behavior to familiar (liberal) restrictions on harming, threatening, and imposing on others. He argues for voluntary restraint in public discourse, limiting oneself to arguments that do not presuppose one's own particular religious and philosophical commitments. There may be good reasons to oppose the proposal, but not to confuse it with an enforceable restriction of civil rights.

A more serious concern that O'Neill may share is that, by limiting liberal justification to the 'reasonable,' Rawls encourages applications of his theory that ignore the interests of people with disabilities, special vulnerabilities, limited education, and so on (see the essay by Baier in this volume). This may be so, and if so, it would be troublesome. But it is not obvious yet that this is a necessary consequence or that it was unwarranted to stipulate criteria for reasonableness for the intended purpose. As I understand his view, Rawls restricts efforts to justify political principles to people whose comprehensive moral and religious doctrines are reasonable because he believes that philosophical arguments do not fail just because they are now rejected by people who have no commitment to time-tested epistemological standards or to finding common principles. Details matter, but the general idea seems plausible enough. In philosophy, as in any discipline, there are limits on what kind of objections we must regard as carrying weight. The question is not whether unreasonable individuals are to be denied moral standing in general or shut out of public debates but what kind of speakers he must be able to convince before he should count a political principle warranted for the purpose and context he proposed. This stipulation and other features of his theory may be misused and abused in application, but this sort of liability is common to most theories and may not cut deep.

Reliance on 'an overlapping consensus'

A more serious challenge to Rawls' *Political Liberalism* would be whether its appeal to the idea of an overlapping consensus[32] gives undue weight to arbitrary authorities in satisfying the liberal principle of legitimacy. That standard regards political principles for coercive use of power as not fully justified unless an overlapping consensus of diverse reasonable comprehensive religious and moral doctrines could develop in its favor. An overlapping consensus is not a mere *modus vivendi* but a stabilizing agreement on the common use of political principles that is grounded in part by the convergence of arguments from different perspectives about fundamental questions. Setting aside the doubts about Rawls' restriction to 'reasonable' doctrines, one might worry that he tries to get justification out of an anticipated (or hoped for) actual agreement among groups of people who are arbitrarily committed to different authorities. Even if all comprehensive doctrines that are 'reasonable' (by Rawls' standards) come to endorse a common set of political principles, the emergence of this overlapping consensus may seem of little value because the starting points of each may be arbitrary (by O'Neill's standards).

This is a large issue, but one suggestion for now is this. The kind of possibility of consensus that Rawls was most concerned about, as he later explained, was not whether or not actual agreement would in fact emerge some day.[33] The crucial point for Rawls was whether or not overlapping consensus is *possible*, that is, whether or not adherents of the diverse comprehensive doctrines have good and sufficient reasons to join a consensus for political purposes. They need not accept as true Rawls' initial theory of justice, or any competing comprehensive moral or religious theory other than their own, but they need to have reasons from within and without their own doctrine sufficient to accept the political principles for their world which is characterized by 'the fact of reasonable pluralism'. Only then, Rawls argues, can we have a just political order that is stable for the right reasons.[34]

If this is right, Rawls does not infer political legitimacy from actual agreement, even among adherents of 'reasonable' comprehensive doctrines. From O'Neill's perspective, this should count as a good thing because by Rawls' account those 'reasonable' people can all be basing their agreement on arbitrary presuppositions in their various doctrines. The larger issue in the end is about whether there are available to each person sufficient good reasons to join a consensus, not whether or not they all actually come to see this. Even so, Rawls' best possible scenario is a convergence of reasons that are relative to diverse and incompatible commitments and so arbitrary by O'Neill's standard. Although each party to the consensus would be *thinking for himself* in a sense, their private reasons would be impossible to vindicate *from the point of view of everyone* because (by hypothesis) the diverse reasonable doctrines are *inconsistent*.

Concluding note about remaining questions

Here we seem to have hit upon a bedrock disagreement, and so it may be well to turn attention to underlying sources of disagreement and broader questions. For example, is it possible to vindicate any choice-guiding principles without starting from some points that we take (without vindication) to be fixed?[35] Can we rest with Kant's grounds for thinking the universal law formula of the Categorical Imperative is such a principle? Are there no arbitrary commitments in the Kantian conception of a person, or in the understanding of what can be shared, communicated, and followed by everyone? Can we even understand what ultimate vindication would amount to? And, however we answer those questions, can cautiously constrained constructivist thinking that shares some structural features with Rawls' constructivism be a legitimate way of working towards solutions to practical problems?

Notes

1 Onora O'Neill, 1989, 1996, 2000, 2003a, 2003b, and Onora [O'Neill] Nell, 1975.
2 Korsgaard, 1996, 2008, 2009.
3 My proposed normative constructivism arguably is closer to Kant's texts than Rawls' version is, though the proposal is less ambitious than O'Neill's constructivism about the ultimate vindication of its basic principles. The main idea, admittedly an extension and modification of Kant's explicit views, is described briefly in Hill, 1992, chs. 2, 4, and 11, developed further in Hill, 2000, chs. 2, 4, and 8, Hill, 2002, ch. 3, 2003, and 2008.
4 See especially O'Neill, 1989, ch. 11, 206–18; 1996, ch. 2, 38–48; 2000, ch. 4, 65–80; 2003a and 2003b.
5 Rawls' work on justice evolved through two editions of *A Theory of Justice*, many essays, *Political Liberalism*, *Justice as Fairness: A Restatement*, and *The Law of Peoples*. See Rawls, 1971/99, 1993/6, 1999a, 1999b, 2001. Somewhat different versions of constructivism, then, emerge with different claims about its aim,

intended audience, justification, and context for application. O'Neill's constructivism too developed and she has commented on Rawls' versions in several essays over time. In a brief discussion, then, it is best to focus on some larger issues and keep our suggestions somewhat tentative.

6 See Hill, 2002, ch. 3, 61–95, and 2011.
7 *Constructions of Reason*, 26–27, 45–47; Kant, *Critique of Judgment*, 135–37 [5: 294–95].
8 A note indicates that on reflection she would drop the first use of 'intentions' in this sentence.
9 See the essay by Baron, this volume, Chapter 1.
10 For example, Donagan, 1977.
11 Compare Rawls, 1999a, 502.
12 Compare Hill, 2000, 46–55.
13 Rawls, 1999a, 303–58.
14 Rawls, 1999b, 30–35, 68–70. This work presents an elaborate sketch of how Rawls thought his main lines of his theory of justice might extend to international justice. The uses of 'original position' thinking are for (a) determining domestic principles for liberal democratic societies, (b) determining foreign policy principles for liberal democratic societies, and (c) for determining principles that should be acceptable for international relations (strictly relations among 'peoples') not only to liberal democratic societies but to 'decent hierarchical societies'.
15 O'Neill apparently does not object to 'abstracting' features of real moral agents, such as minimal rationality, freedom, and equality under the moral law, for use in constructivist arguments. Her objection, rather, is to 'idealizing' them in the ways that she believes Rawls and others do.
16 Rawls shows optimism about the *possibility* of a 'realistic utopia' but apparently not about the possibility of vindicating his starting points in the way that would satisfy O'Neill's Kantian aspirations. For the idea of a realistic utopia, see Rawls, 1996, 4–7 and 11–23.
17 O'Neill, 2003a, 353 and 359.
18 Rawls, 1999a, 303–58 and 497–528; 1993/1996, 90–102.
19 Rawls, 2000, 143–322.
20 The point, I take it, was that he had not yet been able to understand by his high standards of seeing the deepest ideas all connected and structured into a whole coherent system, at least not as well as he thought he understood Hobbes and Rousseau. See Rawls, 2000, editor's foreword, xviii, and Rawls, 2007, editor's preface, xiv-xv.
21 Hill, 2002, ch. 3, and 2011.
22 A further qualification that O'Neill's constructivism requires is that the 'good reasons' be of a kind that ultimately every (rational) person *could* find 'intelligible' and share, but her negative test for maxims implies that even this possibility is not sufficient for a consideration to be a good positive reason for endorsing the procedures and results. For sufficiency, as I understand the position, there must be no alternative to the proposed 'good reasons' that can be found intelligible and shared by everyone. If so, then the test is *formally* similar to T.M. Scanlon's – basic principles of action must be ones that no person who is minimally rational (O'Neill) or appropriately responsive to the relevant reasons (Scanlon) can reject. Scanlon, 1998.
23 O'Neill, 1989, 91–92.
24 The 'anchoring' metaphor is taken from O'Neill, 2003a, 359.
25 For example, Rawlsian conditional arguments of the form, 'If certain specified basic ideas common in Western democratic societies are valid within a domain,

then, given certain facts, certain specified practical principles are valid within that domain.'
26 Rawls, 1993/1996, 81; 1999a, 312, 367, 386, 397–98.
27 For example, see again O'Neill, 2003a, 359.
28 Burton Dreben, Rawls' good friend and sometimes interpreter, emphasizes this. See his 'On Rawls and Political Liberalism,' in Freeman, 2003, 316–46, especially 319 and 326. Dreben expresses his own view more bluntly than Rawls would have, for example: 'Rawls is a good enough thinker not to argue against those who do not believe in liberal constitutional democracy' (319) and ' ... What do you say to an Adolf Hitler? The answer is [nothing]. You shoot him. You do not try to reason with him. Reason has no bearing on that issue' (326).
29 Rawls, 1993/1996, 48–65.
30 The term was Charles Stevenson's in an essay of that name (Stevenson, 1938).
31 The principle is: 'our exercise of political power is fully proper only when it is exercised in accordance with a constitution the essentials of which all citizens as free and equal may reasonably be expected to endorse in the light of principles and ideals acceptable to their common human reason' (Rawls, 1993/1996, 137).
32 Rawls, 1993/1996, 133–54.
33 Rawls, 1993/1996, paperback (1996) edition, 'Reply to Habermas,' 390.
34 This was a main point I argued in 'The Problem of Stability in Political Liberalism,' Hill, 2000, 333–52.
35 See the essay by Barry, this volume, Chapter 2.

Bibliography

Donagan, A., 1977: *The Theory of Morality* (Chicago: Chicago University Press).

Freeman, S., 2003: *The Cambridge Companion to Rawls*, S. Freeman ed. (Cambridge: Cambridge University Press).

Hill, T. E., Jr., 1992: *Dignity and Practical Reason in Kant's Moral Theory* (Ithaca: Cornell University Press).

——, 2000: *Respect, Pluralism and Justice: Kantian Perspectives* (Oxford: Oxford University Press).

——, 2002: *Human Welfare and Moral Worth: Kantian Perspectives* (Oxford: Oxford University Press).

——, 2003: 'Treating Criminals as Ends in Themselves' in *Annual Review of Law and Ethics*, Band 11, 17–36.

——, 2008: 'Moral Construction as a Task: Sources and Limits,' *Social Philosophy and Policy*, 214–36.

——, 2011: 'Kantian Constructivism as Normative Ethics' in M. Timmons ed., *Oxford Studies in Normative Ethics* (Oxford: Oxford University Press).

Kant, I., 1996: *The Metaphysics of Morals*, ed. M. Gregor (Cambridge: Cambridge University Press), here abbreviated as MM. Citations for Kant's works are to volume and page in the standard Academy edition.

——, 2002: *Groundwork for the Metaphysics of Morals*, ed. T. E. Hill, Jr. and A. Zweig (Oxford: Oxford University Press), here abbreviated as '*Groundwork*' or 'G'.

——, 1951, *Critique of Judgment*, tr. J. Bernard (New York, Hafner Publishing Co).

Korsgaard, C., 1996: *Sources of Normativity* (Cambridge: Cambridge University Press).

——, 2008: *The Constitution of Agency* (Oxford and New York: Oxford University Press).

——, 2009: *Self-constitution: Agency, Identity, and Integrity* (Oxford: Oxford University Press).
Nell [O'Neill], O., 1975: *Acting on Principle* (New York: Columbia University Press).
O'Neill, O., 1989: *Constructions of Reason: Exploring Kant's Practical Philosophy* (Cambridge: Cambridge University Press).
——, 1996: *Towards Virtue and Justice: A Constructive Account of Practical Reason* (Cambridge: Cambridge University Press).
——, 2000: *Bounds of Justice* (Cambridge: Cambridge University Press).
——, 2003a: 'Constructivism in Rawls and Kant,' in Freeman, 2003, 347–67.
——, 2003b: 'Constructivism vs. Contractualism,' *Ratio* XVI 4, 319–31.
Rawls, J., 1971/1999: *A Theory of Justice* (Cambridge, MA: Harvard University Press).
——, 1993/1996: *Political Liberalism* (New York: Columbia University Press).
——, 1999a: *Collected Papers*. S. Freeman, ed. (Cambridge, MA: Harvard University Press).
——, 1999b: *The Law of Peoples* (Cambridge, MA: Harvard University Press).
——, 2001: *Justice as Fairness: A Restatement*. E. Kelly, ed. (Cambridge, MA: Harvard University Press).
——, 2007: *Lectures on the History of Political Philosophy*. S. Freeman, ed. (Cambridge, MA: Harvard University Press).
Rawls, J. and Herman, B., 2000: *Lectures on the History of Moral Philosophy* (Cambridge, MA: Harvard University Press).
Scanlon, T.M., 1998: *What We Owe To Each Other* (Cambridge, MA: Harvard University Press).
Sidgwick, Henry, 1962: *Methods of Ethics*, 7th edition (Chicago: Chicago University Press).
Stevenson, C.L., 1938: 'Persuasive Definitions,' *Mind* 47(187), 331-50.

4

HOPE AS PRUDENCE
Practical faith in Kant's political thinking

Katrin Flikschuh

The exalted epithets often bestowed upon a ruler ('the divinely anointed', 'the administrator of the divine will on earth and its representatives') have frequently been censured as gross and dizzying flattery, but, it seems to me, without grounds. Far from making the ruler of a country arrogant, they should rather humble him in his soul, if he is intelligent (as must be assumed) and considers that he has taken on an office far too demanding for any human being – namely, the most sacred office that God has on earth, that of trustee of the Right of mankind – such that he must always remain concerned about having in some ways offended against this 'apple of God's eye'[1]

Introduction

In *The Moral Gap* John Hare concludes that Kant fails in his attempt to translate revealed Christian religion into terms that fall within the limits of reason alone – terms that would allow Kant to close the gap between moral perfection and human finitude without necessary appeal to the living Christian God (Hare, 2002, pp. 38–68). Faith in the direct presence of God and his sustaining grace are practically necessary to enable us to strive for moral perfection in the face of our acknowledged moral limitations. Hare's primary Kantian text is *Religion Within the Limits of Reason Alone*; he begins from the problem of evil and suggests that, given its declared rootedness in the human heart, the individual agent could not without divine assistance perform the envisaged moral revolution towards the good.

In her Tanner Lectures on *Faith and Reason* Onora O'Neill takes a very different view when she concludes that 'although the surface of *Religion* presents a view of reasoned religion that seemingly takes Christian faith and scriptures seriously, Kant's philosophical theology does not endorse religion in any straightforward way. Slightly below the surface of the work is a view of reason and of reasoned interpretation that assigns no unique status to religious hopes' (O'Neill, 1996, p. 308). Moral hope, not religious faith, is the relevant catchword: without hope, practically free yet rationally finite beings could not act with the intention to effect change in the causally ordered world. If, for Hare, the gap bridged by religious faith consists in the distance between moral perfection and moral fallibility, for O'Neill practical hope overcomes what would otherwise constitute the 'great gulf' (O'Neill, 1996, p. 271) between freedom and nature in Kant's philosophy.

Hare and O'Neill represent opposite extremes of possible readings of *Religion* between which a number of intermediate positions might locate themselves: while Hare may seem to many to insist upon an all too determinate interpretation of the idea of God within the framework of Kant's moral philosophy, O'Neill's approach will strike others as altogether too humanistic, depriving Kantian practical faith of all transcendent connotations. There is a further point of contrast between Hare and O'Neill. As noted, Hare starts from the idea of moral perfection, arriving at necessary belief in a living God via the problem of human evil. Strikingly, O'Neill bypasses the question of evil entirely, concentrating instead on the relation between *Religion* and Kant's historical and political writings. Hare's focus is ethical, O'Neill's political. This may help account for the interpretative distance between them. While one may resist Hare's close alignment of Kant's ethics with specific doctrinal commitments, there is a sense in which ethics, conceived as the morality of good willing, defines a realm of agent-interiority in relation to which (a sufficiently Protestant reading of) the idea of a Christian God seems at least not implausible. By contrast, Right is about external moral relations between agents. Right abstracts from intrapersonal good willing – and we should surely in any case leave God out of an enlightened political morality. Given Kant's distinction between virtue and Right there is *prima facie* plausibility in conceding that practical faith in the ethical realm may have the inward orientation traditionally associated with Christian religion whilst simultaneously insisting upon the radically secular character of practical hope in relation to political agency.

Should Kant then be read as offering two parallel conceptions of practical faith – one ethical and one political – where the first is infused with remnants of religious thought while the second repudiates all reference even to the *idea* of God? This, too, seems unsatisfactory. Despite his insistence upon the distinctness of Right from virtue Kant holds that they jointly comprise the domain of morality. It is then not unreasonable to expect there to be some point of contact between faith in ethics and faith in politics. Yet identification of such a connection may prove elusive. Acknowledgement of the non-determinability of final sources is itself a central tenet of Kant's philosophy. This is Karl Ameriks' diagnosis in his study of the contrast between Kant and his early critics: the latter's quest for philosophical certainty culminated in the revised Kantianism of German Idealism which saw itself as improving on what Ameriks calls the modesty of Kant's approach by tying up (what seemed to Reinhold, Fichte, and Hegel) Kant's numerous philosophically loose ends (Ameriks, 2000). An especially relevant aspect of Ameriks' analysis concerns the tendency he detects among Kant's early critics to mend shortfalls in human theoretical knowledge by appeals to the powers of practical reason. Questions in relation to which Kant concluded no theoretical answer is available to us – God, the soul, freedom – Reinhold and Fichte put to rest by means of the thesis of the primacy of practical reason. In consequence the metaphysical space left open by Kant's acknowledgement of theoretical limitation came to be closed off: in the face of the powers of practical reason affirmed by Reinhold and Fichte the limits of theoretical reason became irrelevant. Ameriks notes a similar tendency among current Kantians: the thesis of the primacy of practical reason when advanced as a bulwark against metaphysical impulses is a thesis which has its roots in early German idealism, though it is now routinely attributed to Kant.[2]

Ameriks' modest yet metaphysically sympathetic reading of Kant allows for philosophical loose ends within Kant's system: it allows for ultimate theoretical answers to practically significant questions to 'lose themselves in intelligible grounds' (*DoR*, AA VI: 246). Arguably, it is only against a background of acknowledged theoretical limitation that the question of practical faith is significant. The doctrine of the postulates in the second *Critique* is often said to have a faith-enabling function. Yet the postulates do not assert the *primacy* of practical reason. Nor do they declare the limits of theoretical knowledge irrelevant from a practical point of view. A postulate of practical reason is 'a theoretical proposition which is not as such demonstrable, but which is an inseparable corollary of an a priori unconditionally valid practical law' (*CPR*, AA V: 123). Warranted subjective endorsement on practical grounds presupposes acknowledged theoretical indemonstrability. The importance of the doctrine of the postulates to Kant's ethics is contested, with some declaring superfluous what others deem indispensable.[3] In his political philosophy, too, Kant invokes postulates: the postulate of practical reason in regard to Right is as central to his property argument as the postulate of public Right is to the transition from private to public Right. There has been far less discussion of these and other instances of acknowledged theoretical indemonstrability in relation to his political philosophy.[4] My principal aim in this article is to articulate a plausible notion of practical faith in relation to Kant's political morality which, though non-religious, preserves some of the transcendent connotations that Ameriks suggests are lost in all too eager resorts to the thesis of the primacy of practical reason. I begin by saying a little more about Hare's and O'Neill's respective accounts of practical faith and noting my disagreements with them. I then propose a reading of practical faith that divides it into hope in relation to ethics and prudence in relation to political morality. While hope has more obviously transcendent connotations than prudence,

I suggest that certain aspects of Kant's political philosophy are indicative of acknowledged theoretical unknowability, lending Kantian prudence transcendent overtones. I briefly return to the question of a possible connection between hope and prudence in my concluding comments.

Practical faith: religious and secular

Hare and O'Neill agree that *Religion* seeks to translate theological doctrines into moral terms. While O'Neill endorses Kant's project, Hare declares it a failure. A plausible preliminary characterization of Kant's dilemma according to Hare is that although Kant characterizes the problem of evil in Christian terms his attempted solution relies on the 'stoic maxim', according to which 'a person herself must make or have made herself into whatever, in a moral sense, whether good or evil, she is to become' (Hare, 2002, p. 60). The Christian conception of evil locates its source not in the flesh but in the will. Kant similarly exonerates human beings' sensible nature when he declares 'the human being is evil means: he is conscious of the moral law and has nonetheless admitted its (occasional) violation into his maxim' (R, AA VI: 32).[5] The propensity to evil is a feature of a person's power of choice (*Willkür*). It consists in a deliberate prioritizing of sensible incentives over moral ones. Evil is innate in the individual person considered as a member of the species; no human being lacks the propensity to evil. The propensity is radical in the sense that a person's evil disposition 'spoils the basis of all [his] maxims' (R, AA VI: 37). The individual person does not originally adopt an evil disposition. There is no morally neutral disposition: a person is either fundamentally good or radically evil. Although the human being naturally has both a propensity for evil and a predisposition towards the good, given that he can only be *either* radically evil *or* fundamentally good, we must think him innately evil. Yet the propensity towards evil, though innate, is also self-incurred. This may sound paradoxical; however, theological doctrine affirms something similar. The story of the Fall portrays evil as self-incurred; the related doctrine of original sin claims it to be innate. Each new member of the species inherits from Adam and Eve the evil they deliberately brought upon themselves and all their progeny. Evil thus originates in the human species in a deliberate act of moral transgression by the human will. Had Adam and Eve not knowingly transgressed against God, the idea of human moral autonomy could not have taken root. This is not to deny that the idea of the moral law itself is prior to the possibility of doing evil. It is, however, possible to do evil non-autonomously: *Willkür*, not *Wille* adopts the evil maxim – indeed Kant thinks human beings incapable of autonomously willed, 'devilish', evil (R, AA VI: 37). Still, the original deliberate commission of evil as the first step towards moral autonomy marks mankind's exodus from God's moral tutelage.

This is not Hare's assessment. For Hare, Kant's revolution in disposition from evil to good is impossible for the individual human person to achieve absent God's active assistance. Hare's analysis is guided by his account of the moral gap. 'Morality has a structure with three parts to it: the moral demand, our defective natural capacities, and the possible being (the authoritative source of the demand)' (Hare, 2002, p. 23). This three-part structure entails that 'without the doctrines [of traditional Christianity], or some functional equivalent, we are left in the moral gap, with the attendant sense of failure and the conceptual difficulty that we seem to be under a demand that is far beyond our capacities' (Hare, 2002, p. 25). The problem of evil epitomizes human moral frailty more generally and God's assistance is needed not just in relation to overcoming evil but for leading a morally good life more generally. Hare adopts a notably individualist line of analysis: whereas Kant reads the proposition 'man is by nature evil' to assert that the problem of evil is a problem for the human species, for Hare we are all sinners and each in need of God's forgiveness: 'how [else] can a person become a new man?' (Hare, 2002, p. 53). If a person starts from a fundamentally evil disposition how can he morally transform himself without external assistance? Other human beings are of no help here. Hare attributes to Kant a view according to which the mutually corrupting effects of our co-existence with others constitute part of the problem. Besides, a being whose moral capacity is equal to mine cannot, presumably, achieve for me what I cannot achieve for myself. How can my moral equal bring about a moral revolution in me that I cannot bring about in myself? My moral equal, too, confronts the moral gap. Only a being higher in moral status than me can come to my assistance in my struggle to overcome my evil disposition.

It is not entirely clear what precise form divine assistance must take for Hare. Is God's assistance needed because a corrupt heart cannot see its own corruptness, hence cannot even fathom the idea of the good? This cannot be Kant's view, given his claim that capacity for evil presupposes consciousness of the moral law. Is God's assistance then required for him to be able to will the revolution in disposition? This too seems problematic, for if the evil person cannot think himself capable of willing his moral revolution, his evil disposition cannot be self-incurred. Is it simply that given his opacity to himself the moral revolutionary needs assurance from God that the intended revolution has succeeded? But then God's assistance arrives at the point at which the crucial work has been accomplished already. Hare would retort that these ambivalences regarding the extent of God's assistance are Kant's, not his. Hare conceives of Kant as caught on the two horns of a dilemma. On the one hand, Kant subscribes to the Stoic maxim, on the other hand, he holds that God's assistance is needed: 'either Kant means to reject the notion of extra-human assistance, or he means to retain it' (Hare, 2002, p. 62). Moreover, Kant's attempt to avoid the dilemma by reconciling Christian doctrine with the Stoic maxim fails. The attempted translation of theological doctrine into secular morality renders 'scrutable the inscrutable doctrines of Christian faith' (Hare, 2002, p. 51). Kant has us 'think of God the Son as humanity in its moral perfection, God the Holy Spirit as the good disposition which is our comforter, and God the Father as the Idea of holiness within us' (Hare, 2002, p. 54). Thus translated we can view the evil person as rescuing himself from eternal damnation. Yet if it is the idea of our own holiness that we must call upon for inner moral strength in accomplishing our revolution, we are literally, if rather elaborately, pulling ourselves up by our own bootstraps: 'Kant has subtracted from the traditional understanding of God's work in salvation any mediating role for anything that is not already human', leaving him with 'an incoherence in the pure religion of reason' (Hare, 2002, p. 65).

In *Religion* Kant is not concerned with evil as raising the spectre of eternal damnation. Although the analysis of evil is in part guided by the story of the Fall, Kant's morally evil person transgresses not against God's will but against the moral law within herself. If the evil person transgressed against God's will, it would be up to God to forgive her. Yet in relation to the moral law God is one rational being among many – the evil person's transgression is against herself, humanity, and all rational beings, including God. God is not uniquely placed to forgive her. Indeed, arguably, the one uniquely placed to do so is the evil person herself. This has to do less with any Stoic maxims than with Kant's location of evil in a person's basic moral disposition. Evil is radical in that it spoils the basis of all maxims. A person's disposition is the basis of all her maxims. So it is not the relation between herself and God that is spoilt by evil, but the relation between a person and herself, more precisely, between a person and her capacity for goodwill. The principal victim of her evil disposition is the perpetrator herself – in a metaphorical sense it is she, not God, who needs to forgive herself. If, therefore, on Hare's theological account God forgives by rescuing the repentant person from her evil disposition, then on Kant's account, the evil person forgives herself by resolving to make moral revolution within herself. While God's *assistance* may yet be needed, God in effect lacks the power to forgive the evil-doer her moral transgressions against herself.[6]

One notable feature of Hare's diagnosis of Kant's secular 'translation' is his tendency to evaluate Kant's moral account by the standards of a theological conception of the problem of evil. A second feature is the individualistic orientation of his analysis. Yet, while Hare interprets evil as a problem of each individual person in her relation to God, Kant is emphatic in his characterization of evil as a problem for the human species. Evil is innate and self-incurred in relation to each *as member of the species*. In one sense, this ups the stakes of moral responsibility. In aiming at moral revolution within himself the innately evil person contributes to the moral progress of humankind as a whole: each individual person's decision to remain evil thus has moral repercussions for humankind as a whole. In another sense, however, the view of evil as a shared human problem lightens the burden of each. The resolve to moral revolution does not in itself ensure immediate success. Many failed attempts in good faith are to be expected; the route of moral progress is potentially endless. The task is a collective one, and the idea and establishment of an ethical commonwealth indispensable. Although Kant does speak of the 'reciprocal spoilage of the moral disposition' between persons, this is a function of individuals remaining in an ethical state of nature with one another. Only as members of an ethical society tasked with the maintenance of morality can individuals together withstand the temptations of evil. 'So far as we are able to tell, the government of the good principle is attainable only through establishment and extension of a society based on principles of virtue' (R, AA VI: 94): this is the visible church whose establishment is conceived by analogy with the exit from the political state of nature and into the civil condition.

O'Neill's account of practical faith emphasizes its social dimension. O'Neill begins her interpretation of *Religion* not from theological doctrines but from Kant's doctrine of method as set out towards the end of the *Critique of Pure Reason*. Kantian reasoning imposes a self-discipline that reflects acknowledgment of insurmountable human limitations: 'we *accept* that our grandest cognitive ambitions must be set aside and we *adopt* a form of cognitive discipline to protect ourselves from error' (O'Neill, 1996, p. 274). The discipline of reason is threefold. First, reason is 'negative' or formal in character: we cannot legitimately postulate, let alone prove, the existence of a supersensible world by mere appeal to the authority of reason. Second, reason is non-derivative in that it 'does not derive from more fundamental standards' (O'Neill, 1996, p. 274). We cannot assert that the authority of reason emanates from God's will, or that it is a function of our biological make-up. Third, reason is lawlike, meaning that its directives must be intelligible to all its addressees, i.e., to all reasoning beings. Reason thus conceived is an indispensable tool of thought and action for finite rational beings but delivers them no reassuring higher-order certainties. A version of the primacy of practical reason thesis drives O'Neill's approach: 'This meagre conception of reason is unlikely to yield proofs of human freedom or immortality or of God's existence. However, Kant notes that our reasons for being interested in the soul and in God are primarily practical and raises the question whether "reason may not be able to supply us from the standpoint of its practical interest what it altogether refuses to supply in respect of its speculative interest" (CPR, A805 / B833)' (O'Neill, 1996, p. 277). Seemingly metaphysical questions are in fact symptomatic of practical problems we face – most acutely, the problem of agency itself: how can we be confident that our agency effects change in the causally governed order of the world? One might think this itself a metaphysical question; however, for O'Neill the discipline of reason demands that we set aside our metaphysical impulses: insofar as the question of practical efficacy arises in the practical context it can only meaningfully be answered from within that context.

O'Neill's outline of the discipline of reason informs her approach to the idea of moral hope which she gleans from *Religion*. To say that the grounds of religious faith must lie within the limits of reason alone is to disallow any 'leap of faith' (O'Neill, 1996, p. 279) by means of which we transport ourselves from the sensible into a supersensible world. Such leaps are literally fanciful – they imagine content and meaning where the discipline of reason offers only method. If, therefore, we are to understand religious commitments within the limits of reason, their substantive grounds cannot lie in reason itself but must lie in the practical problems to which such commitments, suitably translated, supply a response. 'The reasons that Kant offers interpret religious trust or commitment fundamentally as a mode of hope: religious faith cannot be a matter of knowledge and must be a matter of taking a hopeful view of human destiny' (O'Neill, 1996, pp. 280–1). Religious faith as a mode of hope relating to human destiny is a response to the practical question: what ought I do? – meaning, here, 'will what I do make any difference at all?' Doubts about the efficacy of my agency arise from consciousness of the 'great gulf' between nature and freedom. The latter represent two mutually irreducible standpoints defining the nature of human existence: on the one hand, we cannot but experience the world as causally ordered, on the other hand, we cannot but think ourselves practically free.[7] Given our irreducible commitment to both these standpoints, 'we must assume that there is some sort of degree of coordination of nature and freedom' (O'Neill, 1996, p. 282). More traditional articulations of hope in the coordinate relation between nature and freedom might have taken a theological form; in the first *Critique* Kant himself retains a strong allegiance to traditional approaches when he conceives the idea of God as originating within the domain of theoretical reason. Yet with the thesis of the primacy of practical reason, the basic impetus is seen as emanating from the other side of the great gulf; the idea of God becomes a postulate of practical reason and one the agent entertains as a mode of hope that arises not prior to action but from action itself. The agent hopes that his agency will not prove futile; although he cannot be certain, he hopes that God will ensure happiness in proportion to virtue.

But if theoretically grounded belief in God is at bottom incoherent such that religious faith, to be meaningful, must be seen as practically grounded, *must* we think of practically grounded faith in religious terms at all? Under O'Neill's treatment, religious faith undergoes a series of subtle translations which begin in the negative discipline of reason and end in an increasingly secularized articulation of hope. Practically grounded religious faith is one possible form of practical hope among several. 'Might we not construe the task of moral progress as a this-worldly, shared and historical, perhaps incompletable task rather than one that will provide each of us an occupation for an eternal afterlife?' (O'Neill, 1996, p. 286). O'Neill discovers a this-worldly view of reasoned hope in Kant's historical and political writings, in which the role of God as guarantor of the link between nature and freedom is increasingly noticeable for its absence. In many respects, *Religion*, too, takes a more noticeably secular approach to the idea of God than the second *Critique*. *Religion* articulates the idea of an ethical commonwealth by analogy with a juridical commonwealth; the suggestion is that underlying this visible church with its particular theological doctrines is the idea of an invisible church – 'hope without doctrine' (O'Neill, 1996, p. 287) – in whose moral service the visible church stands ultimately. While religious articulations of practical hope are not to be rejected, other more politically or more historically-oriented articulations are equally permissible. 'We may hope for grace, for progress, or for both, and for each in many forms' – what binds these permissible expressions of practical hope together is the fact that 'behind [them] lies a common commitment to action, which does not vary' (O'Neill, 1996, 304).

Hope: practical and transcendent

Is hope regarding the efficacy of our moral agency equivalent, from a practical standpoint, to faith in God's assistance? On the face of it, this seems unlikely: in the one case we have the idea of morality as a shared human task, in the other the thought of necessary supra-human assistance. In the one case we invoke history, in the other divinity as the object of our hope. In the one case the object of our hope is temporal, in the other atemporal. It seems odd to suggest that one can practically hope either for God's atemporal assistance or for temporal human moral progress so long as one hopes for one or the other. O'Neill may be unconcerned about identifying particular objects of hope; hers may be a conceptual point about the necessary connection between hope and human agency. As agents, we inevitably must hope that we can make a difference to the causal order of things. But how general a point about human agency is this? Must anyone hope who thinks of himself an agent, or must only Kantian agents hope in this way? Must a Humean or an Aristotelian hope for the efficacy of their moral agency? It is not clear to me that the question of hope as O'Neill articulates it must arise for the Humean. The Humean agent confronts no great gulf between nature and freedom. As O'Neill acknowledges, Kant operates with a highly specific conception of free human agency – yet she wants nonetheless to avoid the metaphysical connotations of Kantian freedom. This is a common move. Those uncomfortable with the idea of transcendental freedom as absence of causal determination often insist that

Kantian practical freedom can make do without it: whatever we think of the cogency of transcendental freedom, we must assume deliberative freedom, at least, in relation to action.[8] And yet 'hope' on O'Neill's account has a functional role for Kant, contingent on a gap that opens up when one allows for transcendental freedom. If there is no transcendental freedom, then there is no gap. If there is no gap, then there is no need for 'hope' as a gap-closer. It is hard to see how worries about the great gulf, or about the efficacy of agency within the constraints of a causally ordered world could arise against the background merely of practical, deliberative freedom. If there is a great gulf, underlying it is the metaphysics of transcendental freedom.

In *Kant and the Fate of Autonomy*, Ameriks outlines Reinhold's attempted shift from Kant's thesis of transcendental idealism, with its distinction between things as they are in themselves and appearances, to a version of the primacy of practical reason thesis as one capable of delivering philosophical certainty where Kant, in Reinhold's assessment, leaves us mired by the banks of scepticism (Ameriks, 2000, pp. 96–112). According to Ameriks, the underlying influence of Reinhold's early endeavours remains palpable in current constructivist improvements upon Kant which appeal to versions of the primacy of practical reason thesis as a way of circumnavigating Kant's supposed remnant rationalist commitments. Such circumnavigation overlooks the subtlety of Kant's simultaneous rejection of metaphysical assertability and his acceptance of the intrinsic meaningfulness of perennial metaphysical questions. Acknowledgement of theoretical indemonstrability need not issue in a denial of metaphysical status. To the contrary, acknowledgement of theoretical indemonstrability forms the core of Kant's articulation of the noumenal as negative yet necessary idea of reason – negative in the sense of containing no substantive higher order truths for us; necessary in the sense of preserving the non-empirical status of freedom and morality. Admittedly, the idea of a negative metaphysics will strike many as inherently unstable, not least in the practical domain. Of what practical significance can the acknowledgement be that we can have no theoretical knowledge of God, of the soul, of our transcendental freedom? We either do have an idea of God, or of our transcendental freedom, etc., or we do not. If we do, we will invariably fill this idea with *some* content. Indeed, not even Kant seems able to sustain the notion of mere *negative* idea. On the one hand, Kant thinks us practically warranted in committing ourselves to all manner of quite determinate subjective beliefs about God; on the other hand, he appears at times to subscribe to a version of the view that practical freedom is perfectly intelligible in the absence of the thought of possible transcendental freedom. These seemingly contradictory positions underscore the inherent instability of a negative metaphysics in the practical domain: we seem either to slip into affirmative assertions about God's non-sensible nature, or must content ourselves with a strictly practical interpretation of traditional metaphysical ideas.[9]

I hinted above that hope makes sense only against acknowledged absence of knowledge in relation to the object of one's hope. There is a difference between saying that I believe in God's grace and saying that I know of it. I hinted above that, from a Kantian perspective, my belief in God's grace makes hope in relation to it possible; my knowledge of it renders hope redundant. Hope does not consist in the attempt, practically or otherwise, to overcome or work around lack of knowledge; to the contrary, hope typically embraces lack of knowledge with regard to its object. To hope is in that sense to relinquish a certain kind of (epistemic) control. Oddly, relinquishment of control does not amount to an expression of defeat but counts, to the contrary, as a sign of the refusal to give up. When people continue to hope in the face of overwhelming odds they are not evidently being irrational. It depends, of course, on the nature and context of hope. Hope is not a blind faith akin to a belief in magic, nor is it simply a form of wishful thinking. Belief in and hope for God's grace is not irrational against a background understanding of the radical nature of human evil, for example. O'Neill nonetheless seems to me correct in saying that expressions of hope need not take a religious form. I may reasonably hope that I will survive a potentially terminal illness even if the medical prospects look bleak. God's intervening grace may, but need not, be the object of my hope here. O'Neill views agency itself as a reasoned ground of hope. She claims that insofar as we cannot but act, we must hope. I have already suggested that the plausibility of this claim probably depends on a particular – Kantian – conception of agency. But even within such a Kantian conception of agency it seems important to distinguish mundane hopes from demanding ones. The hope that we can insert our moral intention into a causally ordered world is a highly demanding hope. By contrast my hope that my practising multiplication tables with my son will stand him in good stead is quite mundane in the overall scheme of things. Hope in relation to the latter is not unintelligible. In hoping that practising maths with him will help my son I am not *expecting* that it will do so; even less am I calculating the *probability* that it will. That said, it would not be incoherent of me to adopt, in lieu of hope, an attitude of expectation, or if I were to engage in probabilistic reasoning about input and output, discounting the certain costs of effort involved against the likely benefits to be reaped. If I merely hope that practising with him will make a difference I adopt a less controlling attitude than I would if I were to expect him to profit by it, or were to engage in calculations about the likely difference in outcome. But it would not be unintelligible of me to calculate in lieu of hoping. What about the hope that I can insert my moral intention in the world? Here, it seems to me, it is not intelligible to view hope and expectation – let alone calculation – as interchangeably available possible attitudinal stances. To expect to be able to insert moral intention into the world is precisely to fail to appreciate that here only hope is the appropriate attitude to adopt. In relation to my son's maths skill, I can say 'I could content myself with hoping – but I won't'. If I adopted a similar attitude in relation to the efficacy of my moral agency relative to the causally ordered world I would be missing the point of practical hope as O'Neill understands it. So, not all practical hopes are of the same kind. The hope that I can insert my moral intention in the world seems much more existential than my hope that practising with my son will make a difference. Yet it is not clear to me that O'Neill's radically secular account can account for the qualitative difference between mundane hope and existential hope.

When I hope that practising with my son will make a difference, I put my trust in my son. If, by contrast, I expect practice to make a difference, I precisely do not put my trust in my son – I assume control and seek to bring it about that his maths improves. For Hare, when we hope for God's forgiveness, we put our trust in God. On O'Neill's account, when we hope that our moral agency will make a difference we put our trust in ourselves. O'Neill says that given that we cannot but act, 'we must assume that there is some sort of degree of coordination of nature and freedom' (O'Neill, 1996, p. 283). The implication is that we are warranted in hoping that we can make a moral difference because we in fact must assume that we can.[10] When, in relation to my mundane hope, I place my trust in my son, I, in effect, give expression to my belief that it is ultimately up to him. When, in relation to his existential hope, Hare puts his trust in God, he acknowledges that things are ultimately up to God. When, in relation to her agency hope, O'Neill puts her trust in herself, she believes it is ultimately up to her. If, in trusting, the hopeful person cedes control, then on O'Neill's account it looks as though the hopeful person cedes control to herself: in hoping that her agency can make a moral difference the hopeful agent trusts that she can do it. But it is one thing for me to cede control to my son and for Hare to cede it to God – it is another for O'Neill to cede it to herself: how can a person be hopeful in relation to that of which she must trust herself that she can do it? There is a suspicion of incoherence here that is not dissimilar to Hare's suspicion of incoherence in relation to Kant's translation of theological doctrine into non-doctrinal terms. According to Hare, there is a certain pointlessness about our redeeming ourselves through our own intervention: 'Kant has subtracted from the traditional understanding of God's work in salvation any mediating role for anything that is not already human' (Hare, 2002, p. 65). We either require God's assistance or we do not; if the claim is that we do, there is something fundamentally incoherent about placing ourselves in God's position. There is a similar sense of puzzlement in relation to O'Neill's apparent suggestion that we ourselves must constitute the object of our hope: we either must hope or we need not, but if we must, then for hope to be practically meaningful its object must be something other than ourselves.

Prudence as practical faith

In the end, I am not persuaded that we may hope alternatively either for God's atemporal assistance or for temporal historical progress. I assume that for O'Neill hope for historical progress is an articulation of the hope that we can insert the moral intention in the world. This is not a mundane hope, but an existential one, going to the heart of our very conception of ourselves as agents. O'Neill emphasizes the finitude of rational human agency, and humans' consciousness of their finitude. Human finitude is non-contingent – it is not a shortcoming about ourselves which we can expect to overcome in time. Hope in the face of consciousness of one's constitutive finitude makes a lot of sense. Yet, unless the transcendent connotations of hope thus conceived are explicitly acknowledged, hope in history cannot bear the burden of existential hope. In *Religion* Kant makes an important move from *Kirchenglaube* – doctrinal faith – to *Religionsglaube* – religious faith, a move reiterated in the *Contest of the Faculties*.[11] Whilst according to Hare one cannot shed the former without losing one's grip on the latter, O'Neill commits herself to a further move from religious faith to moral hope as a radically secular kind of faith. The worry is that O'Neill elides Kant's distinction between *Kirchenglaube* and *Religionsglaube*, dismissing both in favour of a radically secular kind of faith. Where *Religionsglaube* as a form of non-doctrinal belief in (the idea of) God comes to be seen as equivalent to a 'this-worldly' faith in our own capacity for moral progress any connotations of transcendence are repudiated. This is not, I believe, Kant's intention: neither *Religion* nor *Contest* amounts to a repudiation of the doctrine of the postulates as practically necessary, subjectively warranted belief in transcendence. The mature Kant does not substitute this-worldly collective hope for historical progress for the earlier other-worldly individual hope for happiness in proportion to virtue. This is not to deny the increasing importance of teleological history in Kant's mature thinking, or the increasing absence of any direct appeal to the idea of God in line with a progressively more political reading of that teleology.[12] That Kant's teleology of human history is entirely this-worldly is nonetheless doubtful. Though direct references to God are increasingly noticeable for their absence, Kant continues to counsel a reading of nature and of nature's moral intentions for us as though guided by 'providential' wisdom (*PP*, AA VIII: 362); he likewise reads into world-historical events the possible manifestation of our non-sensibly grounded moral consciousness in virtue of which we are able to interpret violent political upheavals such as the French Revolution as indicative of humankind's moral progress. Kant's teleological history retains, in other words, the transcendent connotations palpable throughout his practical writings and distinguished from doctrinal faith in *Religion*.

The issue of why God plays, in the end, no role in Kant's political morality when the idea of God continues to be of abiding importance to his ethics is of supreme importance. Though I cannot here enter into a direct discussion of this discrepancy, I do not think absence of reference to God makes Kant's political thinking radically secular or humanistic. I shall press the point indirectly by asking whether one might not plausibly understand the role of prudence in Kant's political morality as a form of transcendently oriented practical faith. The basic question is whether non-doctrinal yet transcendently oriented hope, as articulated in the idea of God in the domain of ethics, can be supplemented by a conception of prudence in the political context. Whilst resisting appeal to divine assistance, prudence as transcendently oriented, practical faith is nonetheless deeply cognizant of theoretically incomprehensible limits to human political agency.

The concept of prudence has not had a good press in modern moral and political thinking. Though the concept's roots go back to Aristotelian *phronēsis*, it is now overwhelmingly associated either with the *virtù* of the Machiavellian prince or with maximizing decision-making by self-interested individuals under conditions of uncertainty. Kant himself is sometimes held responsible for the generally negative reception of prudence in current moral philosophy (Davie, 1973). In *Groundwork* 'counsels of prudence' are presented as a non-moral form of practical reasoning (AA IV: 416). Similarly, in *Perpetual Peace* the *Staatsklugheit* of the political moralist is contrasted unfavourably with the *Staatsweisheit* of the moral politician – in contrast to the latter's practical wisdom, the political moralist appears to bear a strong resemblance to Machiavelli's Prince (AA VIII: 370–81). In fact, Kant's final account of political morality, though rightly seen as a riposte to a certain kind of political brinkmanship, is almost disappointingly sober and dispassionate. The moral ardour that characterizes some of Kant's earlier cosmopolitan writings gives way to a stringent analysis of Right and a correspondingly narrow conception of the politically achievable in the *Doctrine of Right*. It is in the *Doctrine of Right*, too, that one finds allusions to theoretical indemonstrability. I already mentioned the 'postulate of practical reason akin to Right' (*das rechtliche Postulat der praktischen Vernunft* (AA VI: 246)), to which Kant appeals in the justification of rightful external possession, the grounds of which he nevertheless admits 'lose themselves in the intelligible'. The postulate of Right, which asserts the possibility of legitimate external possession, is a theoretically indemonstrable proposition of Right without which rightful external acquisition and the political obligation entailed by such acts would not be conceivable for us. There are other, equally striking examples of acknowledged theoretical limitation. One occurs at the beginning of the text, in the appendix of the introduction to the *Doctrine of Right*. Kant there discusses two kinds of 'ambiguous Right' (AA VI: 234–36), meaning moral claims which, though juridical in nature, are nonetheless juridically non-enforceable. Equity rights are cases in which the injured party advances a justified but unenforceable entitlement claim against the offending party: Kant characterizes these as 'rights without coercion' (*Recht ohne Zwang* (AA VI: 234)). Conversely 'rights of necessity' (*Notrecht*) constitute 'coercion without rights' (*Zwang ohne Recht*): though the offending party has no legal entitlement to act against the victim in the manner proposed nor can he be held legally accountable for so acting. These instances of ambiguous Right draw attention to a conceptual difficulty, not a merely pragmatic one. Kant conceives of the concept of legitimate coercion as analytically 'contained in' the concept of Right in general – Right thus always includes the authority to use coercion (AA VI: 231). In the cases under discussion, entitlement claims and authority to coerce come apart – yet we have no theoretical explanation for why this should be so. Kant's much contested denial of a right to revolution provides another instance where theoretical explanation runs out. We must acknowledge that we cannot coherently conceive a right to revolution (AA VI: 320–23). This is at odds with strongly held convictions about a brutalized people's entitlement to defend itself, by violent means if necessary, against an oppressive tyrant. Contrary to widespread belief, Kant does not deny the unsettling nature of the discrepancy between strongly held moral convictions and theoretical inconceivability: yet we cannot simply declare a (non-conceivable) right to revolution into existence merely on the strength of our moral convictions. A final example concerns the concept of sovereignty, which Kant requires at the level of domestic rights relations, yet necessary endorsement of which at the domestic level confronts him with unaccountable conceptual difficulties at the level of international Right.[13]

One could take the view that these sorts of difficulties, in which moral convictions come up against conceptual limitations, simply reflect flaws in theoretical design. If we are convinced that we must have a right to revolution, then we must undertake the necessary theoretical adjustments. Theoretical accommodation of whatever moral convictions we happen to have is a dominant strategy in much current political theorizing. Apart from encouraging non-rigorous theorizing, the tendency to side-step theoretical inconceivability via appeal to strength of moral conviction can have disastrous effects in political practice: in the context of political morality, ignoring the limits of what is theoretically conceivable can be deeply imprudent.

Although now often presented as such, the normativity of prudence is not reducible to the recommendation of calculative, maximizing behaviour.[14] Prudence shares with hope the feature of constituting a response to acknowledged lack of knowledge in the practical context. Again, one can usefully distinguish between two kinds of prudence – mundane and existential. Mundane prudence is a practical response to insufficient factual information; existential prudence relates to theoretical unknowability in the metaphysical sense set out above. Prudence differs from hope in the precise mode of its practical response to theoretical ignorance. I suggested above that it is a distinguishing feature of hope that it 'embraces' lack of knowledge in relation to its object. To embrace something is to accept, even to welcome it: for hope to be meaningful, epistemic control must be ceded and trust placed in some other party. I do not think prudence similarly amounts to an embracing of ignorance and a willing ceding of epistemic control. Prudence is associated with absence of opportunity to trust. In a sense, the prudent person must be self-reliant precisely because there is no one else to rely upon. The idea here is not the Machiavellian or Hobbesian idea that no one else is trust*worthy* – the thought is rather that responsibility for responding to lack of knowledge falls upon the prudent person herself.

As mentioned, the contemporary literature tends to approach prudence in decision-theoretical terms – often as aiming at rational maximization of advantage under conditions of more or less acute factual ignorance and related uncertainty. In a recent formal analysis of the concept, Philip Bricker defines the prudent person as one who 'acts so as to get what he wants, will want, has wanted'; the prudent person 'must be able to arbitrate the competing claims of past, present, and future selves' (Bricker, 1980, p. 384). Ignorance and uncertainty are here theorized in temporal terms as lack of knowledge of the future, which has repercussions, in turn, upon one's present deliberations and choices. Bricker employs possible-worlds analysis in conjunction with certain maximizing assumptions. A person is ideally prudent 'if the life he had in the world he actualised was better than the life he would have had, had he actualised any other world, by adhering to a different life strategy. More succinctly, A was ideally prudent if he adhered to the best life-strategy that was available to him' (Bricker, 1980, p. 386). The maximizing assumption now standardly associated with the concept of prudence has been criticized by Horsburgh for whom prudence is more properly associated with the attempt to avert or to minimize disaster (Horsburgh, 1962). On this alternative picture, the prudent person adopts the least hazardous strategy of action. On either account, the prudent person is seen as responding strategically to lack of knowledge and related uncertainty. In both cases the condition of ignorance is temporary: eventually the facts of the future will come in and both maximizer and minimizer will find out whether or not they acted prudently.

In the political context, Bricker's individually focused analysis requires twofold modification. First, the possible worlds of Bricker's prudent person represent that person's possible lives – his possible alternative 'conceptions of the good'. A person's conception of the good is standardly conceived as a temporally bounded, internally cohesive, self-contained 'whole'.[15] For the political agent, however, the object of her prudence is not her own life or preferred conception of the good, but the continued survival over an indefinite period of time of her state, or political society. The prudent politician cannot, unlike Bricker's prudent individual, model her preferred conception of the political good as a temporally bounded conception of the world relative to her own preferred life. In contrast to the self-contained world(s) of Bricker's prudent individual, the prudent politician works with a temporally unbounded world which she inherits from her predecessors and passes on to her successors. Second, the politician's world includes more than one agent. Bricker's prudent individual must 'act so as to be maximally satisfied by [his] world'; to achieve such maximal satisfaction he must 'make the world conform to [his] preferences' whilst simultaneously making '[his] preferences conform to the world' (Bricker, 1980, p. 401). By contrast the prudent politician is primarily concerned with anticipating and responding to the actions of others: again, what prudence amounts to for the political agent is not just a matter of her preferences but her assessment of her possible responses to others' likely preferences and actions.

Despite these complications, the basic assumptions of Bricker's analysis do carry over into multi-player game-theoretical analyses of political prudence: under both private and political modelling, the prudent agent is the strategic maximizer (or minimizer) who seeks to reduce uncertainty by way of rational anticipation of a preferred, possible future. There is an interesting attitudinal difference between current and past approaches to uncertainty in relation to political prudence. While current game-theoretical analysis generally seeks to reduce or even eliminate uncertainty by way of strategically rational anticipation, *fortuna* is conceived as an independent player under Machiavellian prudence. The unpredictability of *fortuna* under Machiavelli's analysis compels the prince to act in a more circumspect manner, seizing the opportunities *fortuna* offers and evading the challenges she throws without, in so doing, seeking to control *fortuna* herself. On the one hand, this makes the prince's actions less predictable than they might be under game-theoretical analysis; on the other, acceptance of the uncontrollability of chance dampens temptations of brinkmanship: given *fortuna*'s essential incalculability, Machiavelli's prince must act less recklessly than he is standardly assumed to act and may even seek to give the impression of acting.

In *Perpetual Peace*, Kant's principal objection to Machiavellian political prudence is not to the political moralist's appreciation of chance or contingency as such, but to the manner of his response to it. The political moralist allows chance to dictate principles of political action to him: his is a mere prudentialism (*Klugheitslehre*). The moral politician, by contrast, 'employs the principles of political prudence in such a way as to render them consistent with morality' (AA VIII: 375). Prudence alerts the moral politician to unfavourable contingent circumstances, urging the deferral of intended political or legal reform. The morally prudent politician takes heed of these warnings and does not attempt to push through reform by insisting on point of principle when such insistence is clearly detrimental to long-term success. The prudent politician is not, in other words, a conviction politician. He must not lose sight of his serious intention to introduce reform at the earliest possible moment nor must he introduce reform precipitously. Under no circumstances, however, must the moral politician build his precepts of political agency on the contingency of political circumstance itself. This is what the political moralist tends to do. Kant's remarks here echo those in the *Groundwork* regarding 'counsels of prudence': for the derivation of political principles from contingent political context 'much knowledge of nature is required in order to make use of its mechanism for the end proposed, and yet all of this is uncertain with respect to its result' (AA VIII: 377).[16] The moral politician is guided by a priori principles of Right. These are 'clear to everyone and put all artifice to shame'; they lead 'straight to the end [of perpetual peace], but with the reminder of prudence not to draw to it precipitately by force but to approach it steadily as favourable circumstances arise' (AA VIII: 378). While the political moralist is in the grip of chance precisely because he bases his principles of action upon it, the moral politician can live with chance and contingency because he is able to rely on principles of action which, though not immune to chance at the level of implementation, are independent of it at the level of moral conception.

Chance, contingency, and lack of information are the stuff of everyday politics: they call for prudence in the mundane sense of the term on the part of political agents. Where you cannot be reasonably sure that you have all the relevant information, or where there is great uncertainty about how the other party will react, you had better proceed with circumspection – not least given that what is at stake is not your own conception of the good life but the continued survival of your state. But what about existential prudence – prudence in relation to ignorance that is not circumstantial and contingent but radical and insurmountable? Such radical ignorance is not about the facts of the future, but about the source of moral principles deployed as pillars of steadfastness in the context of contingent ignorance. At one level, Kant commends the a priori character of principles of Right as a moral bulwark against political contingency; yet at another he acknowledges, as we saw above, our radical ignorance regarding the ultimate source of these principles. At least from a theoretical perspective, a priori principles ultimately 'lose themselves in intelligible grounds'. Kant nowhere explicitly discusses the requirements of existential prudence; yet it seems clear that something like Hare's moral gap confronts the moral politician also. In the epigram to this paper, Kant refers to the intelligent politician's awareness of the fact that he has taken on an office – the stewardship of the Right of mankind – that no human being is strictly speaking able to take on. This consciousness of his own constitutive inability with regard to his task should humble the politician and encourage him to act against a background of constant awareness of his possible transgression against this Right.

If, then, consciousness of a priori principles of Right guides the mundanely prudent politician through the perennial contingencies and uncertainties that characterize the domain of politics, the existentially prudent politician is conscious of his severely limited theoretical insight into the grounds of these principles themselves. The question is whether, from Kant's perspective, mundane prudence presupposes existential prudence, that is to say, whether only the political agent who appreciates his necessarily limited theoretical insight into the principles of Right he deploys can in fact deploy them responsibly. I am inclined to believe that, for Kant, mundane prudence must rest on existential prudence: the moral politician must be cognizant not only of his necessary reliance on a priori principles, but also of his necessary ignorance of the ultimate grounds of these principles. In the absence of existential prudence it is not clear to me that the moral politician can acknowledge the demands of his office. But if he cannot acknowledge its demands he will not fail to transgress against the Right of mankind.

The transcendence of practical faith

The implicit aim of this chapter has been to defend a negative conception of transcendence in the context of Kant's practical philosophy. To this end I have argued against both John Hare's theological reconstruction of Kantian practical faith and Onora O'Neill's radically secular reading. Especially in the latter half of the paper I have focused on Kant's political thought. The tendency to attribute a radical secularism to Kant is especially noticeable in that context. Yet although it is the case that, in contrast to Kant's ethics, the idea of God plays little discernible active role in his political philosophy it does not follow that his political thought is radically secularist, humanistic, non-metaphysical. To the contrary, to the extent to which Kant succeeds in translating the insights of *Kirchenglaube* into *Religionsglaube* he shifts focus from the inscrutability of God to the final inscrutability, for us, of our own condition. In a sense, doctrinal belief in God's omnipotence and grace comes to be seen as a reflection of our own inscrutability: we must have faith in God because we cannot know ourselves. This does raise the question of why, given the abiding centrality of the idea of God as a postulate of practical reason in Kant's ethics, his political thought seems in fact concerned to avoid direct appeal to God's assistance. As briefly noted above, Kant's political teleology speaks in rather roundabout ways about the thought of nature's providential wisdom – a thought about nature that we ourselves must entertain when reflecting upon how we might go about instituting principles of Right within the constraints of the causality of nature. Occasional references to God should not here mislead one: if the Right of mankind is the 'apple of God's eye', it is because this right is sacred and God holds it dear because it is sacred. It does not mean that God is ultimately at the helm of the Kantian ship of state. Misguided recent construals of the *Groundwork's* kingdom of ends as a model of the ideal Kantian republic invite such an inference. Yet although God is head of the ethical kingdom of ends, the peculiar problem of a political order is precisely, for Kant, that it can only be headed by fallible man himself.[17] This is why the ruler's acknowledgement of his own deep limitations is especially important in the political context. The ruler has to acknowledge the sanctity of the Right of mankind; he has to acknowledge the dignity of the human person as (part) noumenal being. As Joachim Hruschka has shown (Hruschka, 2002), it is exceedingly hard, perhaps impossible, to make sense of the idea of human dignity or of the sacred Right of mankind in radically secular or humanistic terms – without some appeal, that is, to the idea of the noumenal as indicative of the transcendent connotations of Kantian practical reason.

If the line of interpretation here presented is plausible, it adds weight to Ameriks' contention that early responses to Kant's modest metaphysical commitments by Reinhold and Fichte may have all too precipitously sought to expel the noumenal as negative idea from Kantian philosophical thinking. The present interpretation then also supports Ameriks' further suggestion that the improvements attempted by his early critics have had an extremely important, if insufficiently acknowledged, effect on the reception of Kant even into present times. In the context of political philosophy, the important influence upon John Rawls of Hegel's critique especially of Kant's dualism is increasingly being thematized. Given the stridently anti-metaphysical stance of Rawls-inspired Kantianism it might be worth asking what shape current Kantian political thinking might have taken in the absence of Reinhold's and Fichte's important interventions. In particular, it may be worth asking whether, in the absence of such interventions, a less radically humanistic Kantianism might have survived or whether the broader philosophical spirit of the times would yet have condemned as a non-starter Kant's efforts in behalf of negative transcendence.[18]

Notes

1 (PP, AA VIII: 353, translation amended). Unless otherwise stated, citations from Kant's works are from *The Cambridge Edition of the Works of Immanuel Kant*, Vol. 5, *Practical Philosophy*, translated and edited by Mary Gregor (Cambridge 1996). Page references are to the Prussian Academy Ausgabe included in the Cambridge edition. I use the following abbreviations and acronyms for Kant's works: *Groundwork of the Metaphysics of Morals* (*Groundwork*: GW); *Critique of Practical Reason* (CPR); *Toward Perpetual Peace* (*Perpetual Peace*: PP); *Metaphysics of Morals, Part I: The Metaphysical Elements of Justice* (*Doctrine of Right*: DoR); *Religion within the Limits of Reason Alone* (*Religion*: R).

2 There are of course differences between early post-Kantian and current Kantian appeals to the primacy of practical reason. Reinhold and Fichte's respective strategies as Ameriks describes them take a curiously theoretical approach to practical primacy, culminating in Fichte's attempted deduction of the 'I', and German Idealism's subsequent *Bewusstseinsphilosophie*. Current Kantian appeals to the primacy of practical reason thesis usually start from constructivist assumptions that problems in moral philosophy arise directly from experienced practical contexts such that the principal task of moral theory is seen as finding

solutions to practical problems which we confront. An especially influential position here is Korsgaard (2008). Both early and current exponents of the primacy of practical reason thesis seem nonetheless united in their opposition to Kant's metaphysical commitments, whether in the form of things-in-themselves or in the practical significance of the idea of the noumenal more generally.
3 Contrast, e.g. Beck 1960 and Silber 1959. See also Zeldin 1979.
4 But see Guyer 2002, Flikschuh 2004 and 2007a.
5 Translations of passages from *Religion* are my own.
6 Alternatively, in endowing persons with free will God may have permanently debarred himself from exercising his power of choice in relation to them. In the moral realm, God treats persons as his equals. More carefully: God shares the moral order with all persons. He is head of that order, but his stewardship is non-coercive – a free union of rational wills under the moral law.
7 The conceptual 'two standpoints' interpretation as opposed to the metaphysical 'two worlds' reading is widely attributed to Allison 1983, partly in critical response to Strawson 1966.
8 The influential argument regarding the self-sufficiency of 'mere' practical freedom in relation to Kant was pioneered by Strawson (1974).
9 I discuss the idea of an indeterminate idea of pure practical reason in more detail in Flikschuh 2007a. For a very helpful discussion of the status of subjective practical belief in Kant see Zeldin 1979.
10 On the face of it, O'Neill's dual commitment to 'assumption' and 'hope' is baffling: why hope if we can assume? I take O'Neill's intended meaning to be *not* that we must assume but rather that we must be able to believe, though we can never know, that the gap can be closed. It is because we must be able to so believe that we may hope (rather than assume).
11 R, AA VI: 103–18; CF, AA VII: 49–54.
12 I chart this development to some extent in Flikschuh 2007b.
13 The tension between domestic sovereignty and international Right is especially acute in *Perpetual Peace* (AA VIII: 354–57), in which Kant notoriously dithers between either a coercive federation of states or a non-coercive league of states as appropriate forms of instituting the Right of nations. The conceptual nature of this tension is not usually recognized, but see Kleingeld (2004) for an insightful discussion.
14 For a fine, non-reductivist discussion of the modern concept of prudence see Mabbot (1962). See also the reply by Horsburgh (1962).
15 For Kant-inspired reservations concerning the cogency of the assumption of 'completeness' within the framework of decision theory see Churchman (1970).
16 See also Churchman 1970.
17 This may have to do with the intrinsically coercive morality of Right. While the head of state is authorized to coerce subjects into outward conformity of action with principles of Right, Kant seems to reject the idea of a possible coercively moral relationship between God and *His* subjects.
18 This article was written whilst I was in receipt of a Leverhulme Trust Research Fellowship. I gratefully acknowledge the trust's support. I would also like to thank the organisers and participants at the 2009 British Academy conference in honour of Onora O'Neill for helpful comments on a prior version of the article.

Bibliography

Allison, Henry (1983): *Kant's Transcendental Idealism*, New Haven and London: Yale University Press.

Ameriks, Karl (2000): *Kant and the Fate of Autonomy*, Cambridge: Cambridge University Press.

Beck, Lewis White (1960): *A Commentary on Kant's Critique of Practical Reason*, Chicago and London: University of Chicago Press.

Bricker, Philip (1980): 'Prudence', in: *Journal of Philosophy*, LXXVII, pp. 381–401.

Churchman, C.W. (1970): 'Kant – A Decision Theorist?', in: *Theory and Decision*, 1, pp. 107–17.

Davie, William (1973): 'Being Prudent and Acting Prudently', in: *American Philosophical Quarterly*, 10, pp. 57–60.

Flikschuh, Katrin (2004): 'Ist das rechtliche Postulat ein Postulat der reinen praktischen Vernunft?', in: *Jahrbuch für Recht und Ethik*, 12, pp. 299–330.

——(2007a): 'Kant's Indemonstrable Postulate of Right: A Response to Paul Guyer', in: *Kantian Review*, 12, pp. 1–40.

——(2007b): 'Duty, Nature, Right: Kant's Answer to Mendelssohn in *Theory and Practice III*', in: *Journal of Moral Philosophy*, 4, pp. 223–41.

Guyer, Paul (2002): 'Kant's Deductions of the Principles of Right', in: Timmons, Mark (ed.): *Kant's Metaphysics of Morals. Interpretative Essays*, Oxford: Oxford University Press, pp. 23–64.

Hare, John (2002): *The Moral Gap. Kantian Ethics, Human Limits and God's Assistance*, Oxford: Oxford University Press (first published in 1996).

Horsburgh, H.J.N. (1962): 'Response to Mabbot', in: *Proceedings of the Aristotelian Society*, supplementary volume XXXVI, pp. 66–75.

Hruschka, Joachim (2002): 'Die Würde des Menschen bei Kant', in: *Archiv für Rechts-und Sozialphilosophie*, 88, pp. 463–80.

Kant, Immanuel (1996): *The Cambridge Edition of the Works of Immanuel Kant: Practical Philosophy*, Volume 4, translated and edited by Mary Gregor, Cambridge: Cambridge University Press.

——(1968): *Die Religion innerhalb der Grenzen der bloßen Vernunft*, in: Walter de Gruyter, Kants Werke. Akademie Textausgabe, volume VI, Berlin (photomechanical print of the Prussian Academy Edition started in 1902).

Kleingeld, Pauline (2004): 'Approaching Perpetual Peace: Kant's Defence of a League of States and his Ideal of a World Federation', in: *The European Journal of Philosophy*, 12, pp. 304–25.

Korsgaard, Christine (2008): 'Realism and Constructivism in Twentieth Century Moral Philosophy', in: Korsgaard, *The Constitution of Agency*, Oxford: Oxford University Press, pp. 302–27.

Mabbot, J.D. (1962): 'Prudence', in: *Proceedings of the Aristotelian Society*, Supplementary Volume XXXVI, pp. 51–65.

O'Neill, Onora (1996): *Kant on Reason and Religion*, Tanner Lectures, http://tanner-lectures.utah.edu/lectures/documents/oneill97.pdf (accessed 2 November 2012).

Silber, John (1959): 'Kant's Conception of the Highest Good as Immanent and Transcendent', in: *The Philosophical Review*, 68, pp. 460–92.

Strawson, P.F. (1966): *The Bounds of Sense*, London: Routledge.

——(1974): 'Freedom and Resentment', in: Strawson, *Freedom and Resentment*, London: Routledge, pp. 1–25.

Zeldin, Mary (1979): 'Principles of Reason, Degrees of Judgement, and Kant's Argument for the Existence of God', in: *The Monist*, 54, pp. 285–301.

Part 2

AGENCY, CONSENT AND AUTONOMY

5

INFORMED CONSENT AND REFERENTIAL OPACITY

Neil Manson

It is widely agreed that informed consent is ethically important. It is also evident that there are many problems *with* informed consent. There is a voluminous literature in biomedical ethics addressing problems of competence, levels of disclosure, proxy consent, consent in the very young, the very old, the very tired, and so on.

Onora O'Neill has written a great deal about consent and informed consent. But it would be a mistake to cast O'Neill as another routine worker in the informed consent industry. O'Neill argues that standard ways of thinking about informed consent – even when applied to many seemingly *unproblematic* cases – rest upon a range of false or misguided assumptions. One core element of her critical approach to informed consent is to lay stress on a problem that seems more at home in philosophical logic than ethics: *the problem of referential opacity*. The aim here is to focus on this problem of referential opacity as it features in O'Neill's work on consent and informed consent. Why does she think that referential opacity is such a problem (especially when few others seem to do so)? If referential opacity is a problem for informed consent, is there a solution? If so, what is it? Our answer to these questions will reveal something about the interplay between O'Neill's Kantian philosophy and her work in applied philosophy and biomedical ethics.

The "standard" model of informed consent

It will help if we begin with the "standard" model of informed consent. On the standard model, informed consent – in biomedical ethics at least – is ethically important because respect for persons is ethically important. Clinical practice and medical research involve subjecting the patient or research subject to risk. Informed consent is a way of ensuring that rational agents who seek clinical treatment or who take part in medical research can decide for themselves whether they wish to accept the risks and costs associated with such courses of action. In order for agents to make decisions they will typically need *information* about the nature of the treatment or research; about the various risks, costs and benefits, including the risks and benefits of alternative courses of action or of inaction. Informed consent protects patients from being subjected to risks without their knowledge or approval and allows individuals a degree of control over what is done to them in a clinical or research context.

At first sight it might seem that there is nothing objectionable about this model of informed consent. Surely patients and research subjects need information if they are to make their own decisions about actions that affect them? And, surely respect for persons is something that is, and ought to be, central to important human transactions? What does O'Neill think is wrong with this way of thinking about informed consent?

One useful place to begin is "Between Consenting Adults" (1985). Here O'Neill aims to clarify two central elements of Kant's ethics: the prohibition on *using* one another, and the positive obligation to treat one another as persons, more specifically, to treat them as ends in themselves. One view, easily dismissed, is that treating another as a person is to be friendly and polite to them. A slave owner may be friendly and polite and may have intimate knowledge of, and even an interest in, the personal life of some of his slaves, but he – and it would typically be a "he" – still fails to treat his slaves as persons. What is lacking in the context of slavery, we might now think, is *consent*. So, we might then think that we treat others as persons in an ethically important sense, if, and only if, our interactions with them – employing them to do some task for us, say – are consensual. Other examples suggest that this line of thought has some merit. Consider the difference between consensual sex and prostitution: the former seems to involve treating another as a person, whilst the latter does not. In light of such examples it may seem obvious to conclude that consent is the key to what it is to treat another as a person. Expanding on this line of thought it may then seem that consent is something fundamental, and that the ethical significance of treating another as a person is best understood in terms of individual consent.

But O'Neill rejects the idea that consent is fundamental, and rejects the idea that we can understand what it is to treat another as a person in terms of consent. Consent, she argues, is neither as fundamental, nor as clear, a notion as we might initially think. Why not? It might seem that *some* cases of consent are unclear, but others unproblematic. For example, cases of *tacit* consent might seem to be problematic insofar as they rest upon others' presumptions about what a person's lack of refusal implies: does it imply ignorance or knowledgeable consent? Consent can be made explicit, and in institutional and legal contexts consent can be made explicit in detailed, precise and formalised ways. But even though we do have formal consent procedures in many walks of life O'Neill argues that we are still not clear about what consent is, or about its limits and importance.

In some contexts consent may *appear* to be valid but such consent is defeasible: for example, the giving of consent may rest upon a limited understanding of the proposed course of action. Formal consent procedures may be followed without the various participants *really* giving consent. In some cases social epistemological structures and unjust power relations may create a "false consciousness" where transactions seem to be consensual but only because the participants lack the appropriate epistemic and hermeneutical resources to expose the limits of such apparent consent. Here the external social context of consent defeats what may seem, on the surface, to be consent.

Even in contexts where there are not ideological barriers to consent, there are other obstacles. In medical ethics, proposed courses of action are often complex and may need to be understood without much time in a context where the agent may be anxious, distressed, and perhaps in pain. Formal consent procedures may secure a patient's signature, but it is not clear that this kind of consent is something that is of ethical – rather than of prudential and legal – importance. Our capacity to give consent can be impaired by a wide range of limitations and impairments, none of which would constitute the kind of lack of competence – such as being in a coma – that would justify intervention by others without consent.

Referential opacity

At this point it may seem that these types of problem are familiar ones. Considered in isolation such problems do not, by themselves, call into question the idea that there is a broad set of *unproblematic* consent transactions involving sane, intelligent adults who communicate well with one another. But O'Neill (2001) argues that: "the difficulty of establishing a satisfactory account of informed consent is [...] much deeper than most writing on the subject suggests" (2001, 692). She goes on to add: "Unfortunately I do not believe that we have an account of informed consent that is robust enough to work well in the standard case where individuals 'in the maturity of their faculties' give consent" (2001, 692). That is, unlike the standard approach to consent, O'Neill argues that many of the seemingly unproblematic cases are in fact problematic and, even more strikingly, she holds that one core reason why this is so is because of the problem of *referential opacity*.

Referential opacity is a familiar topic in philosophical logic and philosophy of mind and language. Referentially opaque contexts are those where the substitution, within a sentence, of terms that denote one and the same thing, alters the truth value of that sentence. For example, although the names

"Superman" and "Clark Kent" both refer to a single individual we cannot substitute these names in sentences which ascribe *beliefs* whilst, at the same time, guaranteeing the preservation of truth or falsity. Whilst it is true that "Lois Lane believes that *Superman* can fly" (leaving aside issues about truth in fiction), "Lois Lane believes that *Clark Kent* can fly" is false. Belief statements form a referentially opaque context. Rather than restricting referential opacity to sentences or statements about beliefs, O'Neill makes two moves. First, she glosses the beliefs themselves – and other propositional attitudes – as referentially opaque. Second – and we shall return to this point in more detail below – she casts consent as a propositional attitude. For now, let us follow her usage here. Suppose Lois Lane receives a note from Superman asking her to meet him, and share a night of passion; she gladly consents. Had the letter been signed "Clark Kent" she *would not* have consented.

Such fictional examples of the referential opacity of consent are mirrored by real-life cases. In the early 1970s students were asked to take part in a research trial of lysergic acid diethylamide. Many consented. Of those who consented many would *not* have done so had they realised that lysergic acid diethylamide was LSD (there is less data on those who refused to consent who *would* have consented had they realised that these different terms referred to one and the same substance). More recently, the Alder Hey inquiry revealed confusion over the reference of the term "tissue". Parents of recently deceased babies consented to the removal, storage and use of what was referred to as "tissue". But the clinicians who proposed such actions took "tissue" to refer to a wide range of human biological material, including whole organs, like hearts. Because of an unwitting disagreement about the reference of the term "tissue" there were deep problems with the consent. Some parents argued that *had they known* that whole organs would be removed – had they conceived of the proposed actions in *that* way – they would not have consented.

At first sight it may seem that problems of referential opacity must be relatively rare: our illustrative examples involved one fictional case, a factual one from almost four decades ago, and a more recent one. But O'Neill's view of the problem of opacity is emphatically *not* just that there are some rare occasions involving confusion over the scope or extension of terms. Not only has she continued to stress the problem of referential opacity in papers and books over the years (e.g., 2001, 692; 2002, p. 42; 2003, p. 6; 2007, 12–15, 45), she insists that referential opacity is not merely another specific and local problem to add to the list of problems with informed consent. For example, with regard to the problems which may seem to be problems of consent noted above in O'Neill (1985) – problems of ideology; self-deception; limited competence and so on – O'Neill argues that these problems are "all forms of one underlying problem": the problem of opacity.

Or, consider the following remark from 2001:

> The ethical implications of the *referential opacity of propositional attitudes* are massive. We generally consent in the required, informed and freely chosen way to rather little: so rather little can be legitimated by appeal to consent.
>
> (2001, 692)

Similarly, in *Autonomy and Trust in Bioethics* (2002) O'Neill notes that "there are systematic limitations to the degree of justification that informed consent procedures can offer" and that:

> These arise *because* [emphasis added] informed consent is always given to one or another *descriptions* of a *proposal* for treatment. Consent is a *propositional attitude*: it has as its object not a procedure or treatment, but rather one or another proposition containing a description of the intended procedure or treatment.
>
> (2002, 42)

O'Neill argues, then, that referential opacity is not simply *a* problem for consent and informed consent. In her view it is a *fundamental* problem that is the basis of a wide variety of other problems. This may seem odd for two reasons. First, how can a wide range of problems of consent and informed consent be variants upon, or arise because of, the problem of opacity? The problem of referential opacity, at first sight, merely seems to be a marginal technical problem.

Second, O'Neill's account of the referential opacity of consent seems to rest upon the assumption that consent is a propositional attitude. But consenting is something that we *do* and, in more recent work (e.g., O'Neill 2007), O'Neill herself argues that consent is a *transaction* best understood by focusing upon the communicative actions by which consent and refusal are given. But if consent is a kind of action, does the problem of opacity still apply?

Referential opacity – narrow and broad

Let us deal with the first question: why does O'Neill think that referential opacity is a deep, fundamental problem, rather than a marginal difficulty? It will help if we are a bit clearer about the scope of the problem of referential opacity. In philosophical logic and philosophy of language referential opacity is viewed as a problem that arises when co-referring terms are not substitutable in a sentence in a way that maintains the truth value of the sentence. This readily applies to the "Superman" and "LSD" examples. If this is how we define referential opacity then, strictly speaking, the Alder

Hey "human tissue" example does not involve referential opacity at all. Here there are not two terms that refer to one thing but, rather, a single term – "human tissue" – which is used by different speakers to refer to different things.

But there is an underlying feature that unites the "human tissue" example with the Superman and LSD examples. Lois Lane will not consent to be kissed by Clark Kent because she conceives of that individual in a certain way: he is geeky, awkward, mortal, wears his underwear in the more common fashion (beneath his trousers), and so on. In the Alder Hey example the surgeons think of hearts and organs in a certain way – as being correctly describable as "human tissue"; the parents think of the same bodily parts in a different way (as not being *merely* human tissue). The problem that O'Neill is concerned with is broader than referential opacity as it is conceived by logicians and philosophers of language – as such, it may be that "referential opacity" is a misnomer. O'Neill's appeal to referential opacity is better viewed as a way of highlighting the fact that the inferences and decisions that we make depend upon how things are described or conceived of.

When we view referential opacity in this broad way, it readily subsumes standard examples of many *failures* of consent from the informed consent literature. Take, for example, the landmark legal case in US medical law of *Salgo v. Leland Stanford Jr. University Board of Trustees* (154 Cal.App.2d 560, 1957). Martin Salgo suffered paralysis after operation (translumbar aortography). He argued that he would not have consented had the risks been disclosed. At first sight this seems to be very unlike the Superman, LSD and human tissue examples. There is no issue here about co-referring terms, or about intersubjective disagreement about what certain terms refer to. But *structurally* we have exactly the same kind of problem. There are indefinitely many true descriptions of any action. Our rational deliberation about what to do, about what to consent to or refuse, does not directly engage with situations and actions as they are in themselves: rather, our rational engagement with the world is with the world as *conceived* of, or *described*, in certain ways (but not others). Salgo's complaint was that *had the action been described in a different way, he would not have* consented. This shares something important with the problem of referential opacity in a broader guise, even if it is not the problem of referential opacity as logicians or philosophers of language construe it.

If we expand the scope of referential opacity beyond the narrow definition, then it is clear that referential opacity is not a marginal technical problem in the philosophy of language. O'Neill's talk of referential opacity is a way of directing us towards an unavoidable and very general structural feature of agency and rational deliberation. When we deliberate, when we form beliefs, practical commitments, plans and intentions, and when we act upon them, we do not directly engage with the world under *every* possible description using every possible conceptualisation of the world: we engage with the world in the specific, determinate, and limited, ways that *we* conceive it to be.

It is this broader sense of referential opacity that O'Neill is concerned with. In 2001 she notes:

> Even when consent is well directed to propositional content that is true of a situation (as far as can be judged), and is not economical with the truth, that consent will not automatically transfer to other closely related propositions. In particular, consent will not transfer, and may not be given, to the logical implications, the causal consequences or the more specific aspects of a proposal, situation or action towards which consent has been accurately directed.
>
> (2001, 292)

In 2003 we find her claiming:

> Consent is said to be opaque because it does not shadow logical equivalence or other logical implications: when I consent to a proposition its logical implications need not be transparent to me. Transitivity fails for propositional attitudes.
>
> (2003b, p. 6)

Viewed in this broad way the problem of referential opacity is another way of drawing attention to our rational limitations: what we might think of as our *rational finitude*. If we were not agents our rational finitude might not matter. But we are practical rational beings, who share a world with others. As such there is a standing, structural, problem that different agents may conceive of the world in different ways, yet be required to act in ways that satisfy the needs and interests of different parties. Viewed thus, we can see why it is not a problem that O'Neill now lays stress on consent as a kind of communicative action: the problem of referential opacity remains for any rational activity, insofar as such activities are based upon – indeed, *must* be based upon – our conception of the world.

Is referential opacity simply an informational problem?

With this broader notion of referential opacity in play it is much easier to see why O'Neill thinks that referential opacity underlies a range of problems with consent. Consider the "ideological" limitations on consent, where what seem to be valid consent transactions take place in a context that undermines them. Such cases involve what Miranda Fricker (2007) calls "hermeneutical injustice" where power structures in a society deny agents the conceptual and interpretative resources that they need in order to adequately understand their lives. An agent who consents in such a context may be such that she *would not* consent to one and the same action if a more adequate description were available to her.

Or, take the familiar problems from the bioethics literature about human limitations in understanding complex medical procedures. Here an agent's consent may be directed towards a partial, or misunderstood, description of a proposed course of action even though a sophisticated description was offered.

In every case where consent is given, consent is given on the basis of the agent's conceptualisation of what the proposed course of action is, and there are many reasons why an agent's conceptualisation of the action may fail to connect with some aspects, consequences or entailments of the action in question that *would* be relevant to her decision as to whether or not to consent.

At this point we might simply think that O'Neill has taken a roundabout detour, via philosophical logic and philosophy of language, to reach a familiar and well-trodden part of the contemporary bioethical terrain. Surely all of these problems – *including* the problem of referential opacity – are what we might call *informational problems*? If these are informational problems, won't they have informational solutions?

Take the problem that human beings have limited capacities to understand complex medical procedures. Surely the solution that is required here is that *relevant* information be given in a way that people can understand. This then raises familiar issues about which *standard* should be the measure of relevant information: should it be what the individual patient wants? Should it be what a reasonable doctor would give? Should it be what a reasonable patient wants, or *ought* to want?

But O'Neill rejects these informational solutions (see O'Neill 2007). One difficulty here is that standard ways of thinking about information are themselves problematic. Where information is cast as a kind of stuff that is "disclosed" by one agent and "picked up" by another, this downplays important aspects of thought and communication. Acts of informing are constrained and governed by a wide range of norms and standards including: semantic and epistemic norms that are essential for intelligible communication; pragmatic norms essential for relevant communication in real contexts; and, ethical norms essential for morally sound communication amongst real agents. Worse still, if we implicitly view information as a kind of "stuff" that is "about" things we may ignore the problem of referential opacity altogether: the LSD research subjects were given information *about* LSD, the Alder Hey patients were given information *about* the removal of organs. By focusing on informational solutions that draw upon a thin notion of information and communication we fail to properly understand what consent is, how it works, what its limitations and powers are.

On the standard way of thinking about informed consent, the problem of rational finitude is viewed as a kind of *informational deficit*: something that can be solved or resolved provided that the right kind and amount of information is disclosed to subjects. Rather than acknowledging the limitations of consent – given the broad reach of the problem of referential opacity – informational solutions try to offer a superficial fix. They give the appearance of a solution – if only we can offer more information, or the right amount of information, or the right kind of information, judged against the right standard, then informed consent would be unproblematic. Contemporary biomedical ethics, and professional codes of practice assume what we might call an *informative imperative*: it is assumed that the validity of consent, especially consent to complex interventions with many different risks, demands more and more acts of informing, more and more "disclosure" of "information".[1] But if referential opacity is a problem that arises because of our rational finitude, such an informative imperative may be of little help. Disclosing ever more information, even if presented in "user friendly" ways, will never get *rid of* the problem of referential opacity and, indeed, runs into an immediate problem: given our rational finitude there are limits to the amount of information that we can adequately take on board.

We now have a better grasp of what the problem of referential opacity is for O'Neill: when consent is viewed as ethically fundamental in the way that it is in much bioethical writing, we are, in effect, *building the problem of referential opacity right into the foundations of our ethical thinking*. Informational solutions ignore or avoid the problem of referential opacity and assume that the provision of the right kind or amount of information is all that is required. But now we may still be puzzled. If informational solutions are not the answer, is there any solution to the problem of referential opacity at all?

Two ways of putting consent in its place: with and without Kant

The underlying problem, then, is that a referentially opaque notion – consent – is given a broad and fundamental role in justifying a wide range of actions. There are two kinds of solution that O'Neill has offered to this problem.

One solution is to show that consent does not have as broad or as fundamental a role to play as we might think. This type of solution can be found in *Rethinking Informed Consent* (O'Neill, 2007). The strategy here is to argue that the problem of referential opacity is not something that can be removed, but is something that should be acknowledged. Rather than ridding us of the problem of referential opacity, *consent* itself is downgraded and put in its place. Consent is not an ethically fundamental notion, but is, rather, a procedural device for making, and keeping track of, adjustments in an extant framework of rights and obligations. Consent plays different kinds of *procedural* role. In the formation of contracts, for example, consent involves agents undertaking obligations upon themselves. The consent that is the focus of biomedical ethics is *permissive* consent. Permissive consent operates in a context of conditional rights and obligations. Some obligations and rights have a distinctive kind of conditional status. Many actions are forbidden *unless* certain parties (those to whom the obligation is due) set aside the obligation – in doing so, they waive certain rights. More specifically, consent involves two tiers of rights and obligations. There are first-order rights and obligations: e.g., claim rights against trespass, including bodily trespass. There are second-order derivative rights and obligations: the (liberty) right – typically cast as a privilege – to *waive* one's first-order right against bodily trespass if one wishes. Waivers of this kind constitute a distinctive kind of deontic *power*: a power to bring about a change in rights and obligations. Viewed thus, (permissive) consent cannot be fundamental. Consent merely offers a *procedural* rather than a substantive justification of actions. Consent, by itself, is neither necessary nor sufficient for rightness of action, what does the work is the deeper normative framework *within which* consent operates.

Viewing consent as procedural, rather than substantive and fundamental, does not get rid of the problem of referential opacity. The problems noted above still arise. But in *Rethinking Informed Consent* there is an additional line of argument. We have already noted the tendency to think of information as a kind of "stuff" that is broadcast, picked up, disclosed and so on. This downplays the fact that consent is a *communicative* action, and distorts (or ignores) the distinctive nature of communicative actions.

Consent is a communicative action that takes place in contexts where there are well-established and deeply entrenched norms of communication. If communicators do not adhere to norms of truthfulness and relevance – that is, sufficiently large numbers of communicators, on sufficiently many occasions – then communication is not possible at all. Given that consent is a communicative action, in order for acts of consent to be possible at all, norms of truthfulness and relevance have to *already* be in place. At this point we may object that the existence of such norms does not solve the problem of referential opacity. The Alder Hey surgeons were being truthful when they talked of human tissue. But there is more to good communication than simply being truthful and relevant. Good communication involves a sensitivity to others' interests and limitations, and to one's own interests and limitations too. Good communication in real contexts is, by its nature, finite and limited: it does not, and indeed cannot, presuppose idealised standards of rationality and comprehension. Whilst good communication, rather than the mere disclosure of information, goes some way towards *addressing problems of* our rational finitude, it cannot, however, get *rid of* our rational finitude.

The "solution" in *Rethinking Informed Consent* to the problem of opacity is a measured and contrastive one. The contrast is between two ways of thinking about consent and information. On the standard view, consent is viewed as something of fundamental ethical importance, information is viewed as a kind of stuff that is conveyed amongst agents. Many problems of consent seem to arise because it is unclear how to specify what types of, or how much, information should be given to ensure that this fundamental ethical feature is given due weight. The alternative is to put consent in its place as a procedural device, and to adopt a more appropriate model of communication. With the appropriate model of communication in place we achieve two things: first, some of the work that seems to be done by consent-based ethical norms can be viewed as *already being achieved* by other norms. That is, norms of truthfulness, relevance, and of good communicative practice already do much of the work that we might expect from informed consent regimens. Second, an appropriate model of communication acknowledges our finitude and the problem of referential opacity, but sees it as a ubiquitous problem that is faced by all communicators. The problem of finitude is not solved by speakers and audiences exchanging more and more information, it is solved by the appropriate kind of communicative sensitivity to one another's interests and limitations. The "solution" here is not a direct kind, rather it is to *acknowledge* the problem of opacity and situate it in a broader context where we already deem it to be manageable.

The approach in *Rethinking Informed Consent* is to argue that consent is not as fundamental as may be thought. But it leaves it open as to what the more fundamental ethical notions are in relation to consent. We can extract a second solution to the problem of opacity in O'Neill's writings, one that draws upon her interpretation of Kant. In *Constructions of Reason* (1989) O'Neill offers a distinctive interpretation of the categorical imperative and its authority. Here she interprets Kant as arguing that:

> The Categorical Imperative is a fundamental strategy, not an algorithm; it is the fundamental strategy not just of morality but of all activity that counts as reasoned. The supreme principle of reason is merely the principle of thinking and acting on principles that can (not do!) hold for all.
>
> (1989, 59)

At the heart of this interpretation is the idea that principles of rationality must be *sharable* with others. Not shared with others in the sense of being "broadcast" or "disclosed" to others. A crazy person might attempt to "share" their insane reasoning but without others being able to make any sense of it, and without being able to endorse it. Or, a very powerful person might insist, or bring it about via conditioning or threat, that others "share" his principles of reasoning. But the sense of sharing that Kant requires is a much more robust one: fundamental principles of rationality must be sharable in the sense that we ought only to will a principle (or maxim) if we hold that others could freely and rationally commit themselves to it too. The categorical imperative, so construed, has implications for our *practical* reasoning. In our practical reasoning too, we ought only to commit ourselves to maxims that can be, in principle, freely accepted by others.

The categorical imperative thus has considerable implications for the kinds of action that are prohibited. Actions that are based on deceptive or coercive maxims will fail to meet the standards required. Coercive actions are wrong because they deny others an opportunity to freely endorse or reject the maxim that informs and lies behind the coercive action. Deceptive actions conceal the maxim that lies behind them, and like the coercive action, deny other agents the opportunity to freely endorse or share the maxim in question. These general constraints on action can be framed in terms of a prohibition on certain kinds of *non-consensual* actions. As O'Neill puts it:

> Not to treat others as mere means introduces minimal, but indispensable, requirements for coordinating action in a world shared by autonomous beings, namely that nobody acts in ways others cannot possibly consent to, so in principle precluding their autonomous action.
>
> (1989, 263)

By expanding on the categorical imperative we get a deeper justification of why certain kinds of non-consensual action are wrong. Deception and coercion are wrong, not because people would not consent to being deceived or being coerced, but because the *a priori* argument for the categorical imperative implies that deceptive and coercive fundamental maxims of agency cannot rationally be willed by agents, on pain of contradiction.

The strategy here shares something with the one in *Rethinking Informed Consent*. In each case consent is put in its proper place. In *Rethinking Informed Consent* it is left open just what the deeper ethical framework is. Here Kantian ethics provides the foundation of the normative framework *within which* consent comes to be viewed as important.

Now, there are many questions and issues that arise here. First, the strategy does not seem to tell us much about the role of consent as a *waiver* of rights and obligations. The Kantian prohibition of deception and coercion are not waivable; they stem, rather, from the fact that the maxims that underlie deceptive and coercive actions cannot be shared by others. But this is not a deep problem for O'Neill's account. All that is needed is a richer account of how Kant's fundamental ethical principles can be expanded upon to provide a framework of more specific rights and obligations that pertain to actions in specific contexts. We cannot expand on this here.

The second problem is more challenging. We have been looking at the problem of referential opacity. But drawing upon Kant may seem to simply move the problem of referential opacity back a step, as it were. The problem of referential opacity arose because of our rational finitude: actions can be described in countless different ways, but our communication, deliberation and consent can only operate with *some* descriptions not others. But isn't there an analogous problem with the categorical imperative: the way that a maxim is described matters to whether or not it is universalisable. *Which* description of a maxim is the relevant one for moral evaluation? If Kantian ethics are grounded in the categorical imperative, then the problem of referential opacity seems to be fundamental. But O'Neill, more than anyone perhaps, is well aware of this problem. Indeed, the problem of relevant descriptions is discussed at length in her first monograph *Acting on Principle* (1975). The solution she offers is to argue that the relevant description is in terms of the agent's fundamental maxim. Although O'Neill has revised her view of what maxims are in later work (e.g., 1989), the fundamental thought remains that morally relevant maxims must be, in a sense, *subjective*.

At this point we might wonder how an appeal to subjectivity avoids the problem of opacity. The key point here is that in O'Neill's interpretation of Kant, it is not that Kant somehow avoids, or denies, referential opacity, it is, rather, that a proper understanding of Kant's conception of practical rationality, and thus of his ethics, *fully acknowledges* the inevitability of opacity and subjectivity. Suppose an agent is deliberating about what to do. On O'Neill's view this will involve drawing upon various maxims. But the maxims that an agent draws upon are her own, drawing upon *her* conception of the world. Suppose we seek to evaluate that agent's action. Whilst it is true that her action can be described in countless ways, the *relevant* description will be one that is framed in terms of the agent's (subjective) maxims. The fact that the utterer of the sentence "There is no doubt that Saddam Hussein now has weapons of mass destruction" also utters a sentence of thirteen words in English does not mean that the utterance is somehow permissible, just because the principle "utter sentences of thirteen words in English if asked a question" has nothing to stop it being universalisable. The key to moral deliberation and to moral evaluation is the agent's own fundamental maxims, and the Kantian practical philosophy is framed in terms of ensuring that one only acts on those maxims that pass the test of the categorical imperative.

Now, there is much more that might be said here by way of evaluating O'Neill's interpretation of Kant, and in response to questions about what maxims are, about how we know them and how they both motivate and prescribe action (questions addressed in O'Neill 1975, 1989). The key point here is that O'Neill's ethics has been focused on referential opacity from the start, and her interpretation of Kant is one which, unlike contemporary discussions of consent, fully acknowledges the existence and importance of our rational finitude, manifest in the phenomenon of referential opacity.

Conclusion

What our discussion reveals is that the problem of referential opacity, in O'Neill's writings on consent, is emphatically *not* an additional, specific, problem with informed consent. The underlying problem is much broader than referential opacity as it may be formulated in philosophical logic. The underlying problem is that finite agents engage with the world via their conception of it, or via different descriptions or interpretations of it. This is, of course, a familiar Kantian point. This general point about our rational finitude then features in different ways in O'Neill's work. Obviously, our rational finitude is central to Kantian ethics. But it also poses a problem for interpreting and defending Kant's ethics. The problem of relevant descriptions is that when we turn to the practical problem of trying to identify *which* maxims are the fundamental and relevant ones for feeding into the algorithm of the categorical imperative, we are unclear as to *which* description we ought to employ. But O'Neill, over the past thirty-five years, has argued that not only is there a solution to the problem of relevant descriptions, it is one which, as it were, fully acknowledges referential opacity and our rational finitude.

In her work on consent, and, later, on informed consent in bioethics, these problems of rational finitude resurface and give rise to an interesting interplay between her work in Kantian philosophy and her applied philosophical writings. The Kantian ethics provides her with a framework where consent is not foundational and where our rational finitude is acknowledged from the start. Problems with ethical systems that view consent as fundamental lend indirect support to the Kantian approach. When she turns to applied philosophy and bioethics she adopts a very distinctive approach and, in doing so, gives us an insight into the limitations of a good deal of applied ethics. In applied ethics there is a mode of practice which involves the routine application of a particular kind of ethical theory to unusual or problem cases. For example, consequentialists look at dilemmas to do with reproductive decision making and then the consequentialist machine throws out its answer: the thing to do is to maximise good consequences, whatever they may be. Other bioethicists object: virtue ethics gives us a different answer!

But O'Neill's strategy is not this. She is not simply arguing that if we are deontologists we can generate the correct answer about what to do with regard to the familiar problem cases for informed consent. She is, rather, drawing upon Kant, drawing upon rigorous and abstract critical discussion of Kantian philosophy and Kantian ethics, and then deploying those resources and concepts, not simply to generate a "what would Kant say?" outcome, but to engage thoroughly and systematically with the complex ethical, legal, social, logical and regulatory context that consent operates within. The problem of referential opacity is part of this systematic and multi-faceted engagement with applied philosophical issues, including issues surrounding the role, scope and limitations of informed consent.

Note

1 Peter H. Schwartz critiques what he calls the "quantitative imperative" for clinical consent, where various kinds of "decision aids" are introduced in order to satisfy the joint demand that patients be (massively) informed about risks and that they understand such risks in "Questioning the Quantitative Imperative: Decision Aids, Prevention and the Ethics of Disclosure" *Hastings Center Report* 41, (2011), 30–39. The quantitative imperative is arguably merely a specific variant of the wider informative imperative that O'Neill has targeted in much of her work on informed consent.

Bibliography

O'Neill, Onora (1975) (as Onora Nell) *Acting on Principle*. New York: Columbia University Press.
——(1985) 'Between Consenting Adults' *Philosophy and Public Affairs*, 14, 252–77.
——(1989) *Constructions of Reason*. Cambridge: Cambridge University Press.
——(2001) 'Informed Consent and Genetic Information' *Studies in History and Philosophy of Science Part C: Studies in History and Philosophy of Biological and Biomedical Sciences* 32, 689–704.
——(2002) *Autonomy and Trust in Bioethics*. Cambridge: Cambridge University Press.
——(2003) 'Some Limits of Informed Consent' *Journal of Medical Ethics*, 29, 4–7.
——(2007) (with Neil C. Manson) *Rethinking Informed Consent in Bioethics*. Cambridge: Cambridge University Press.
Fricker, M. (2007) *Epistemic Injustice: Power and the Ethics of Knowing*. Oxford: Oxford University Press.
Schwartz, P. H. (2011) 'Questioning the Quantitative Imperative: Decision Aids, Prevention and the Ethics of Disclosure' *Hastings Center Report* 41, 30–39.

6

RESPECT FOR AUTONOMY IN MEDICAL ETHICS

Suzanne Uniacke

Mr Burke has the degenerative brain condition spino-cerebellar ataxia. By his mid forties he was dependent on a wheelchair for mobility and suffered uncoordinated movements and impaired speech. Some years from now Mr Burke will lose all mobility and eventually he will lose his ability to speak, to gesture and even to swallow. He will then be able to communicate only with the aid of a computerised device and he will need to receive food and water by means of artificial nutrition and hydration (ANH). Mr Burke's mental faculties are unaffected by the disease and will probably so remain until death is imminent. There will come a time at which, although fully conscious and rational, he will be unable to communicate even with a computerised aid. Towards the very end he will become semi-comatose before he dies.

Mr Burke is understandably fearful of the final stages of his disease. In particular, he is concerned about the periods when although conscious he will be able to communicate only by a computerised device and then unable to communicate at all. Mr Burke does not want ANH withdrawn before his death is imminent; he fears this could happen if doctors judge at an earlier point that prolonging his life is no longer worthwhile. His fear is not allayed by the guidance issued to doctors by the General Medical Council of the United Kingdom (GMC), according to which in a case such as Mr Burke's it is the responsibility of the "consultant or general practitioner in charge of a patient's care ... to make the decision about whether to withhold or withdraw a life-prolonging treatment, taking account of the views of the patient or those close to the patient ... "[1] The Guidance further instructs:

> [w]here death is not imminent, it usually will be appropriate to provide artificial nutrition or hydration. However, circumstances may arise where you judge that a patient's condition is so severe, and the prognosis so poor that providing artificial nutrition and hydration may cause suffering, or be too burdensome in relation to

the possible benefits. In these circumstances, as well as consulting the health care team and those close to the patient, you must seek a second or expert opinion from a senior clinician. ... This will ensure that, in a decision of such sensitivity, the patient's interests have been thoroughly considered ... [2]

To be sure these guidelines say that in coming to his or her decision the doctor should *take the patient's views into account* and *assess the patient's best interests* in consultation with others, but they do not refer to the patient's *wishes* in this regard. Mr Burke will be able to make his wishes known by means of a computerised aid for some time after he loses the capacity to communicate by speech or gesture. He might also provide for the period when he will be unable to communicate at all, by making an advance statement that he does not want ANH withdrawn before his death is imminent. But the crucial question for Mr Burke is of course what status his wishes have in this regard. The answer to this question would be relatively straightforward if Mr Burke wanted ANH discontinued at some point. If he were to withdraw his consent to ANH, either while he can still communicate or at a later time by means of an advance statement made while he still has both the capacity to make rational decisions and the ability to communicate those decisions, this would have the force of a directive with which doctors would be obliged to comply. But Mr Burke does not wish to do this; on the contrary, he does not "consent" to the withdrawal of ANH before his death is imminent. Strictly speaking, a patient can either give or withhold consent to particular treatment only if that treatment is offered or provided. Here it might seem appropriate to invoke a distinction between a patient's either *accepting* or *refusing* treatment on offer, as opposed to his *requesting* treatment. However, the characterisation of Mr Burke's wish that ANH not be withdrawn before his death is imminent as (merely) a *request* for treatment on his part strikes at the heart of his concern.

In 2004 Mr. Burke sought clarification of the circumstances in which ANH could lawfully be withdrawn.[3] He asked for declarative relief: that his wish that ANH not be withdrawn before his death is imminent should be enacted.[4] The High Court decided in his favour. In a lengthy and detailed judgment that addressed a number of related matters, Mr Justice Munby ruled that on the specific issue of the continuation of ANH, Mr Burke's wishes could have the same force as a refusal of treatment. This judgment was widely regarded as a strong defence of the view that the medical law and the human rights principles relevant to Mr Burke's circumstances are grounded in the moral value of patient autonomy.[5] But, if this was indeed a victory for the view that a competent patient can have a right to require the provision of particular medical treatment in specific circumstances, then it was short-lived.[6] In 2005 the GMC brought an appeal which was upheld and the decision in *Burke* [2004] reversed.[7] Nevertheless, the Court of Appeal sought to assure Mr Burke that his fears are unfounded, declaring that:

> [w]here a competent patient indicates his or her wish to be kept alive by the provision of ANH any doctor who deliberately brings that patient's life to an end by discontinuing the supply of ANH will not merely be in breach of duty but guilty of murder. Where life depends upon the continued provision of ANH there can be no question of the supply of ANH not being clinically indicated unless a clinical decision has been taken that the life in question should come to an end. That is not a decision that can lawfully be taken in the case of a competent patient who expresses the wish to remain alive.[8]

This proffered assurance is unconvincing, it seems to me, even if we set aside that it ignores Mr Burke's fears about the period in which although conscious and rational he will be legally incompetent due to his inability to communicate. Under current law in the United Kingdom a doctor will be guilty of murder if she deliberately (i.e. intentionally) brings a patient's life to an end *by whatever means*. But if the relevant sections of the GMC's Guidance are lawful (as the Court of Appeal held them to be), then a doctor who withdraws ANH before a patient's death is imminent on the basis of her judgment that "providing artificial nutrition and hydration may cause suffering, or be too burdensome in relation to the possible benefits" does not "deliberately bring the patient's life to an end by discontinuing ANH". This is so even if the patient's life depends upon the continued provision of ANH; it is so independent of the wishes of the patient one way or the other.[9]

The withdrawal of ANH before Mr Burke's death is imminent might be objectionable for other reasons of course. For instance, if Mr Burke were to experience the painful and distressing effects of malnutrition and dehydration this would be cruel. However, presumably he could be spared these effects by heavy sedation. Mr Burke could refuse sedation while he is still competent and perhaps he could use an advance statement to refuse sedation at a later stage. But would he want to do so in these circumstances? The point is that Mr Burke does not wish simply to obliterate any pain or distress that he might suffer in the event that ANH is withdrawn before his death is imminent. He wants to remain conscious as long as possible and he does not want to die of malnutrition and dehydration.

Mr Burke's case draws attention in a particularly stark way to the question of the status of a patient's wishes in the provision, as opposed to the refusal of, medical treatment. In this chapter I focus on several aspects of this question in the context of thinking about some examples that involve decisions by competent patients about the provision of treatment for illness or injury. Mr Burke's is an actual case that was addressed as a matter of law. His circumstances are also unusual and extreme. The other examples that I shall introduce are based on real life and represent what I take to be reasonably common situations in which competent patients make decisions about treatment from a limited range of options. The issues that motivate the paper are primarily conceptual and ethical. They are raised by the following questions: What is it for a doctor to respect a competent patient's wishes in relation to the provision of treatment for significant illness or injury? What bearing do a competent patient's wishes have on a doctor's obligations in relation to the provision of treatment? What is the relevance of individual (patient) autonomy in this regard?

These questions are prompted by Onora O'Neill's discussion in *Autonomy and Trust in Bioethics* of individual (patient) autonomy in relation to medical treatment for serious illness or injury.[10] In this connection, O'Neill distinguishes between a conception of autonomy as an attribute of individual persons having to do with independent choice (individual autonomy), as opposed to a Kantian conception of autonomy as "a matter of acting on certain sorts of principles, and specifically on principles of obligation".[11] Within a conception of individual autonomy, O'Neill further contrasts a minimalist sense in which individual autonomy might amount to "mere sheer choice", with a more robust Millian sense in which autonomy has to do with personal independence, self-direction and self-expression and involves individual persons "reflecting on and selecting among [their desires] in distinctive ways".[12] O'Neill says that autonomy in medical ethics is generally seen as individual autonomy, as "a matter of *independence*, or at least as a *capacity for independent decision and action*".[13] Moreover, she maintains that it is the minimalist interpretation of individual autonomy that is mostly in play, since "the practices that are proposed for securing or respecting autonomy in medical contexts are in fact generally no more than informed consent requirements",[14] which in turn need not represent patient autonomy in anything like a robust sense, as opposed to constituting important constraints on deception and coercion.[15] I do not wish to take issue with these claims. Nonetheless, in addressing the questions that I have posed above about a doctor's obligation to respect a competent patient's wishes about the provision of treatment and the relevance of patient autonomy in this regard, I hope to show that a relatively robust conception of individual autonomy has a greater and a more fundamental role in medical decision-making in contexts of serious illness or injury than O'Neill suggests when she says that a "limited focus on informed consent, rather than on any more extensive conception of autonomy, serves reasonably well in medical ethics because it suits the real context of illness and injury".[16] The exercise of individual autonomy in a more-than-minimalist sense is, I think, highly significant to reasonably common cases in which patients make decisions about the provision of treatment for serious illness or injury from a very limited range of options. Respect for individual (patient) autonomy in a relatively robust sense can also shape the obligations of medical professionals in such cases, in that appropriate respect for patients and their rights can require a doctor positively to engage with the patient's values and priorities, *qua* the patient's values and priorities, in relation to the provision of treatment. I shall couch my defence of these claims in a somewhat wider, critical examination of the notion of respect for a patient's wishes, since in medical ethics respect for individual (patient) autonomy is often expressed in these terms.

Respecting a patient's wishes

The dictum "a patient's wishes should be respected" is very familiar in medico-legal contexts. It is, however, frequently unreflectively invoked.[17] The term "respect" admits of a number of senses and respect for a person's wishes – what he or she wants to happen – falls under the wide category of *recognition* respect, as opposed to *appraisal* respect.[18] In respecting a person's wishes I recognise them as having a certain purchase in relation to my own deliberations or conduct.[19] But what does respecting a patient's wishes about the provision of medical treatment require in the form of recognition, and why? In answering this question we can contrast two general ways in which a person's wishes are commonly thought to be respected.

The first I shall call "compliance respect". Compliance respect for a person's wishes is a strong type of recognition that regards the person's wishes as determinative: compliance respect for a person's wishes requires that one carry them out. Moreover, compliance respect requires that one carry out this person's wishes *qua* her wishes, irrespective of one's own evaluation of them. For this latter reason, compliance respect is also thin recognition in that it does not imply that in carrying out a person's wishes one regards her wishes as having any intrinsic merit. Rather, her wishes receive compliance respect in virtue of her role or status as, e.g., the person in authority, the property owner, or simply as a competent adult. Everyday examples of compliance respect spring readily to mind: when a customer declines the better offer that is entirely her prerogative; when she selects the better offer that too is entirely her prerogative. Compliance respect for a person's wishes does not involve one's taking his wishes into account in one's deliberations about how to act: on the contrary, it requires that one enact his wishes *qua* his wishes. Compliance respect can thus be distinguished from the second general way that a person's wishes might be respected, which I shall call "consideration respect".[20] Respect for a person's wishes is often acknowledged to consist in giving her wishes serious consideration, in taking them into account in coming to one's own decision based on a balance of reasons. Again, we can think of everyday examples: a friend asks me not to tell others about something that he finds embarrassing; a neighbour wants me to prune a tree in my garden in order to enhance the view from her property. Whether I convey the information or prune my tree is up to me, but in considering what to do in these cases I can take these people's wishes into account. Consideration respect for a person's wishes is consistent with acting in accordance with his wishes, but unlike compliance respect, it does not require this.

If one might be said to respect a person's wishes in either of these different ways, what determines which type of respect (if any) might be appropriate in a particular context? The answer to this question will depend upon the relevant evaluative norms. These cannot be identified in simple terms. For instance, it would be wrong to say that compliance respect can be appropriate only in relation to a person's wish for non-interference, the relevant norms being those of non-coercion, non-deception and non-maleficence, and that a person's request for assistance, on the other hand, can only ever warrant consideration respect, the relevant norm being that of benevolence. Compliance respect can sometimes be appropriate when a person requests assistance that another person has an obligation to provide on request.[21] We can think of non-medical examples in which a request for assistance carries a strong presumption of compliance respect; in requesting assistance from someone else a person might be invoking a role-related duty to provide such assistance, or calling upon a debt of gratitude, for instance. This means that in identifying the type of respect for a person's wishes that might be appropriate in a particular context, we need to look beneath very general categories such as whether a person is requiring non-interference, as opposed to requesting assistance, and consider carefully and critically the relevant evaluative norms. These will include the rights and obligations of the parties concerned, both as persons and also in their role-related capacities. Such considerations can go very deep; they can influence the way in which we characterise the conduct in question. For instance, whether discontinuation of ANH before Mr Burke's death is imminent would constitute interference, as opposed to a withdrawal of assistance, could depend on what we take Mr Burke's rights, and his doctor's obligations to be.[22]

The prevailing view about provision of medical treatment is that compliance respect is always appropriate where a competent patient refuses treatment for illness or injury, whereas only consideration respect can be appropriate when a competent patient requests treatment. (For example, if a competent patient declines surgery on the basis of views or priorities that the doctor regards as mistaken or foolish the doctor must comply with the patient's wishes nonetheless, but if a competent patient requests a course of antibiotics the doctor may or may not take this into account in deciding what treatment, if any, to provide.) Both compliance respect and also consideration respect for a patient's wishes are frequently said to be grounded in respect for patient autonomy. The idea that respect for patient autonomy could give rise to compliance respect in one context, and be confined to consideration respect in the other, should alert us to the relevance of other evaluative norms.

In thinking critically about the basis of compliance respect for a competent patient's refusal of treatment, it is instructive to consider O'Neill's claim that such a refusal might involve little or no exercise of individual autonomy in a sense that implies reflection and self-determination. If compliance respect for a patient's refusal of treatment is based on respect for patient autonomy, then as O'Neill claims, this need be autonomy only in a very minimalist sense.[23] All the same, it is significant that compliance respect for a patient's refusal of treatment requires recognition of the patient's wishes as determinative *qua* the patient's wishes: it is *her* prerogative. This is so even if, as O'Neill maintains, compliance respect for a patient's refusal of treatment can be grounded in a more general commitment to a universal, impersonal principle of non-coercion.[24]

It is widely held that a patient's request for the provision of treatment could require only consideration respect. Why is compliance respect inappropriate? Why is consideration respect appropriate, when it is? The answer to the first of these questions concerns the domain of patient choice in relation to the provision of medical treatment for illness or injury. According to the prevailing view, patient choice can legitimately be exercised only within a range of options that are clinically indicated; this means that a doctor must make her own professional, clinical judgment about a patient's request for the provision of treatment. According to this view, the underlying norm in the provision of treatment is the doctor's obligation to provide treatment that is in her professional judgment clinically indicated. This suggests a particular model for the provision of medical treatment, one which the Court of Appeal in *Burke* [2005] explicitly set out and endorsed in reversing the decision in *Burke* [2004].[25] I shall comment on this in the next section of the paper.

On what basis might a patient's wishes in relation to provision of treatment receive consideration respect? I shall approach this question by distinguishing two ways in which a doctor might take a patient's wishes into account within a range of options that are clinically indicated.[26] The first way involves the doctor assessing the patient's wishes entirely on their own merits, so to speak; here the doctor makes an independent judgment about the reasons and the values on which the patient's wishes are based, without affording any significance to the position or role of the person whose reasons and values these are. The second way involves the doctor giving the patient's wishes weight or purchase in her own deliberations *as the patient's wishes*, in addition to her independent evaluation of the reasons and priorities on which they are based. An example will illustrate this difference. A scan reveals a small asymptomatic cerebral aneurysm in a seventy-year-old man, Mr A. The aneurysm can be monitored and there is presently no particular reason to suggest it will rupture. Chances are that Mr A could die of old age with the aneurysm intact. Because of the aneurysm's location, surgery to remove it would cause significant post-operative debilitation lasting twelve months or more; the surgery itself would also carry risk of brain damage. This is explained to Mr A and he requests surgery to remove the aneurysm. His doctor then considers the reasons why Mr A wants the surgery and she asks herself whether these are good and sufficient reasons to go ahead: in so doing she makes an independent judgment about whether, on the basis of these reasons, the possible benefits of the surgery are worth the side-effects and the risks. This is the first way in which the doctor might be said to take Mr A's wishes into account. The second way involves the doctor also affording significance to the reasons why Mr A wants the surgery as the *patient's* reasons, that is to say, as considerations that reflect the values and priorities of the person who would suffer the side-effects of the surgery and who wishes to assume the risks to his own wellbeing.[27]

Does the doctor give appropriate consideration to Mr A's wishes if she takes them into account only in the first way? In my view the answer is no. Obviously one reason why a competent patient's request for treatment can merit consideration respect is epistemic: careful consideration of the reasons on which a particular patient's request for treatment is based can reveal relevant factors that might otherwise elude the doctor. (These might include the real extent of a patient's pain, discomfort or fear, for instance.) But this is not the only, nor perhaps even the central reason why consideration respect for a patient's wishes is important. A competent patient also has a particular status in relation to decisions that affect *his own* life and health that deliberation about the provision of treatment needs to include. Some non-medical contrast examples can help illustrate the point.

Say a fellow train passenger asks me to exchange seats with him because he wants to sit by the window. In this case, affording my fellow passenger's wishes appropriate consideration respect would simply involve deciding whether, impartially speaking, there are good and sufficient reasons for my doing what he asks. My deliberation about this can of course include my considering the seating arrangements from his perspective as well as from my own. (For instance: He wants to see the countryside. Would I particularly mind an aisle seat? Is there reason to be generous?) It is decent that I consider his request and perhaps it is right that I do so; nonetheless, simply as a fellow passenger his wishes have no particular status in relation to my giving him my seat and in deciding to do as he asks I would be doing him a favour. We can contrast this example with another, different one in which my friends' children are in my care for a few days. It is my responsibility to feed the children nutritious meals but exactly what I feed them is up to me. Their parents have asked (not instructed) me to give the children fruit with their breakfast if possible. Here my taking the parents' wishes into account in deciding what to feed the children does require affording them significance *qua* their parents' wishes. Although the children are in my care, they are my friends' children after all. Subject to familiar constraints, their parents have a particular status, based on considerations of responsibility and authority, in relation to what their children eat.

Appropriate consideration respect for a patient's wishes in the provision of treatment that is clinically indicated is like the second of these examples. Just as the children's parents' wishes are significant *qua* their parents' wishes to what I feed the children, in similar fashion a competent patient's wishes are significant, *qua* the patient's wishes about his own life and health, to a doctor's provision of treatment. In the case of the patient, like that of the parents, appropriate consideration respect for their wishes involves recognition of that person's particular status in relation to what they want to happen.

Consideration respect for a patient's wishes is distinguishable from compliance respect in significant ways. Consideration respect requires the doctor to take the patient's wishes into account in coming to her own decision on the balance of reasons; compliance respect does not require this.[28] Compliance respect requires the doctor to carry out the patient's wishes; consideration respect is consistent with an independent decision not to do what the patient wants. However, compliance respect and appropriate consideration respect for a patient's wishes (that is, consideration respect in the second way) also share an important feature, namely that respecting a patient's wishes in both of these senses involves recognition of the significance of a patient's wishes *qua* the patient's wishes.

In the next section I focus on what bearing a competent patient's wishes might have on a doctor's obligations in relation to the provision of treatment, and on the relevance of individual patient autonomy in this regard. So far I have gone along with the prevailing view that a patient's request for treatment for illness or injury can merit consideration respect only within a range of treatments that are clinically indicated, the underlying norm being a doctor's obligation to provide treatment that is, in her professional judgment, clinically indicated. I do not intend to challenge this view. Nonetheless, I shall try to show that appropriate consideration respect for a patient's wishes must complicate what a doctor's basic obligation in the provision of treatment can reasonably be taken to be and that this involves respect for individual (patient) autonomy in a more-than-minimalist sense.

The doctor's obligation and the patient's choice

The Court of Appeal in *Burke* [2005] accepted the view of *Burke* [2004] that the underlying norm in the provision of medical treatment is a doctor's duty of care, more specifically a doctor's obligation to act in her patient's best interests. However, the Court of Appeal disagreed with the earlier judgment in its view about the relationship between the doctor's obligation and the patient's wishes in a case such as Mr Burke's. In *Burke* [2004] Munby J maintained that what is in Mr Burke's best interests in relation to the continuation of ANH is very closely tied to Mr Burke's own wishes on this matter, based on Mr Burke's own view about the stage at which he would find continuation of life-prolonging treatment intolerable. If this is right, then a doctor's judgment about whether continuation of ANH would be in Mr Burke's best interests is largely determined by Mr Burke's wishes in this regard. An upshot of this view is that Mr Burke's request that ANH not be withdrawn before his death is imminent could be determinative. This would not be an instance of compliance respect, however, since Mr Burke's wishes would be carried out not *qua* his wishes, but rather because the doctor's obligation is to act in Mr Burke's best interests and on *this* matter Mr Burke's wishes and his best interests happen to coincide.[29]

In reversing the judgment in *Burke* [2004] the Court of Appeal adopted a somewhat different conception of the norm underlying the provision of medical treatment. It took the view (at least initially) that the doctor's obligation is to act in, what is in her professional clinical judgment, the best interests of her patient. So described, this obligation *could* conflict with a patient's request for treatment in a case such as Mr Burke's (as Mr Burke fears) where in the doctor's clinical judgment continuation of requested treatment is no longer in the patient's best interests.[30] As part of its broader rulings, the Court of Appeal set out and endorsed the following procedural model for the provision of medical treatment to a competent patient:

i) The doctor, exercising his professional clinical judgment, decides what treatment options are clinically indicated (i.e. will provide overall clinical benefit) for his patient.

ii) He then offers those treatment options to the patient in the course of which he explains to him/her the risks, benefits, side effects, etc. involved in each of the treatment options.

iii) The patient then decides whether he wishes to accept any of those treatment options and, if so, which one. In the vast majority of cases he will, of course, decide which treatment option he considers to be in his best interests and, in doing so, he will or may take into account other, non-clinical factors. However, he can, if he wishes, decide to accept (or refuse) the treatment option on the basis of reasons which are irrational or for no reasons at all.

iv) If he chooses one of the treatment options offered to him, the doctor will then proceed to provide it.

v) If, however, he refuses all of the treatment options offered to him and instead informs the doctor that he wants a form of treatment which the doctor has not offered him, the doctor will, no doubt, discuss that form of treatment with him (assuming that it is a form of treatment known to him) but if the doctor concludes that this treatment is not clinically indicated he is not required (i.e. he is under no legal obligation) to provide it to the patient although he should offer to arrange a second opinion.[31]

This model is consistent with the prevailing view that consideration respect for a patient's request for treatment is appropriate within a range of treatments that are clinically indicated. It also represents a subtle but significant shift in the way in which the Court of Appeal regarded the relationship between the doctor's obligation and the patient's wishes. This shift is apparent in the paragraph following, in which the court went on to say:

> ... In truth the right to choose is no more than a reflection of the fact that it is the doctor's duty to provide treatment that he considers to be in the interests of the patient and that the patient is prepared to accept.

According to this statement a doctor's obligation is not to provide treatment that in her professional clinical judgment is in her patient's best interests; rather, she has a duty to provide treatment that she considers to be in the patient's interests (note, not best interests) *and* that the patient is prepared to accept. If we adopt this latter view, then the doctor's obligation includes compliance respect for patient autonomy at least in what O'Neill calls the minimalist sense of individual autonomy. I want to suggest, however, that in practice a doctor's obligation of care in the *provision* of treatment will commonly also include consideration respect for individual (patient) autonomy in a fuller sense that involves genuine engagement with the patient's wishes as based on the patient's own values and priorities. O'Neill may well be right that in "contemporary medical practice patient autonomy is often no more than a right to refuse treatment",[32] and that "[t]ypically a diagnosis is followed with an indication of prognosis and suggestions for treatment to be undertaken. Patients are typically asked to choose from a smallish menu." But I do not think we should generalise from this that "[t]he minimalist interpretation of individual or personal autonomy in medical ethics in fact fits rather well with medical practice (in cases of illness or injury)."[33] O'Neill makes the important point that a patient's informed consent to treatment is necessary but not sufficient for autonomous choice. Nonetheless there are also reasonably common cases in contemporary medical practice in which patient autonomy is significantly more than a right to accept or refuse treatment. In the kinds of cases I have in mind, a restricted choice of options does not thereby restrict the scope of patient autonomy to little more than a right to refuse treatment on offer. Here are two examples:

A fifty-eight-year-old man, Mr C, is diagnosed with prostate cancer. The cancer is localised and with appropriate treatment the prognosis is very good. Surgical prostatectomy is an option in early-stage prostate cancer. However, this is not recommended in Mr C's case because of the particular location of the cancer and the high risk of damaging adjacent tissue. The alternative treatment is radiotherapy. Acceptance of the radiotherapy option is relatively straightforward as far as Mr C is concerned. However, his specialist also recommends a course of hormone treatment over a number of months prior to and during the radiotherapy. This will decrease the cancer by starving it of testosterone, thereby increasing the likelihood that the radiotherapy will eliminate all of the remaining cancerous cells. The loss of testosterone causes side effects in almost all men but the degree and extent of the side effects of hormone therapy in a patient with prostate cancer are impossible to predict. Mr C is informed of the possible side effects, which include hot flushes, decreased sexual desire, erectile dysfunction, fatigue, weight gain, osteoporosis, decreased muscle mass, and memory loss. He can have targeted radiotherapy without the prior hormone treatment but this is not what his doctor recommends. It is important not to delay his treatment. In the next year Mr C has important personal and professional commitments which he cannot postpone; they would be seriously impeded by some of the possible side effects of the hormone therapy.

Ms D, a woman in her mid thirties, suffers from endometriosis which seriously affects the quality of her personal and professional life. The symptoms of the endometriosis might be partly relieved by drug treatment; conservative surgery to remove endometriosis deposits is also a possibility. However, her doctor believes that at this stage a hysterectomy offers the best chance of relief and that in postponing this Ms D would only continue to suffer in order to "put off the inevitable". A hysterectomy is something that Ms D is reluctant to accept at this stage. Endometriosis can adversely affect fertility but it does not do so in 60–70% of patients with the condition. Although Ms D has unsuccessfully tried to conceive during the past four years she hopes that she can still become pregnant.[34] Her doctor believes on the basis of Ms D's medical history and the severity of her endometriosis that the chances of this are negligible.

What conception of individual (patient) autonomy is applicable to these two examples? Given these patients' medical conditions and the limited range of options available to each of them, arguably it is not the fully robust sense that O'Neill reminds us concerns "individuality or character, [and is] about self-mastery, or reflective endorsement, or self-control, or rational reflection, or second-order desires, or about any of the other specific ways in which autonomous choices supposedly are to be distinguished from other, mere choices."[35] But neither is it individual autonomy only in a minimalist sense that amounts simply to the (possibly unreflective) acceptance or refusal of treatment on offer. In deciding whether or not to undertake the hormone therapy, Mr C must engage in rational reflection and he must make very important, possibly life-shaping decisions based upon his considered values and priorities.[36] Ms D must consider whether the significant physical, emotional and professional costs of postponing the recommended hysterectomy are "worth it" in order to preserve what is at best a very slim chance of pregnancy that may well come to nothing. Ms D's decision, too, will reflect her values and priorities and possibly change the course of the rest of her life.

If Mr C decides against the hormone treatment, and Ms D decides against the hysterectomy, in the professional, clinical judgments of their respective doctors both Mr C and Ms D are not acting in their own best interests. (Their doctors might also believe that these patients are not acting in their own best interests more broadly construed, since if things don't work out as they hope, both Mr C and Ms D might later regret their decisions.) Their doctors must treat Mr C's and Ms D's refusals of particular treatments with compliance respect, irrespective of their own evaluations of their patient's reasons. However, we should not lose sight of the fact that Mr C and Ms D have not simply *refused* particular treatment; both of them have also made a positive decision *for* alternative treatment.

The procedural model endorsed by the Court of Appeal in *Burke* [2005] is a streamlined specification that omits significant discussions and deliberations that are appropriate at and between the various steps in the procedure. For instance, the move from step (ii) to step (iii) can require, as part of the doctor's duty of care, her engagement with the patient's deliberations, and this might include discussion of non-clinical factors that are relevant to the patient's decision. What can occur at step (iv) is also very compressed in the procedural model. The treatments that Mr C and Ms D request are, to be sure, within a range of treatments that are said to be "clinically indicated" for their conditions. But a treatment is clinically indicated provided it will offer "overall clinical benefit" and this is a broad and relative notion.[37] A treatment that is clinically indicated for a patient's condition might provide minimal overall benefit compared with an alternative treatment, for instance. In fulfilling her obligation of care, it can be a matter of judgment on the doctor's part in what way to provide treatment that is clinically indicated, and for how long.

Appropriate consideration respect for a patient's wishes requires the doctor to take the patient's wishes into account as the *patient's* wishes, in her own deliberations about the provision of treatment. The risk Mr C decides to take by opting for radiotherapy without the hormone treatment may not work out as Mr C hopes, but it is a risk that Mr C wants to take on the basis of reasons that his doctor might well need to take into account in her deliberations as the *patient's* reasons. Her doing so might significantly influence how Mr C's treatment is delivered. (Is Mr C's doctor obliged to schedule the radiotherapy to commence as soon as possible, or is it permissible for her (is she obliged to?) delay it a little in the hope that Mr C will reconsider having the hormone treatment?) Similarly, Ms D's request for treatment that aims to relieve some of the symptoms of endometriosis might well be a mistake, but her doctor can recognise that it is based on the patient's reasons and that it can be appropriate to take this into account in deciding, e.g., for how long to persevere with drug treatment or at what point to call a halt to conservative surgery. Appropriate consideration respect for a patient's wishes in relation to the provision of treatment can significantly influence both the way in which, and also the extent to which, a doctor discharges her duty of care.

O'Neill's claim that "[w]hat is rather grandly called 'patient autonomy' often amounts simply to a right to choose or refuse treatment on offer, and the corresponding obligations of practitioners not to proceed without patients' consent" is probably true of most *acute* cases in which a competent patient can either accept or refuse medical treatment. But in cases like those of Mr C and Ms D this claim draws attention away from the way in which patient choice can often engage more-than-minimal individual autonomy even in circumstances where there are quite limited treatment options. O'Neill notes that "[o]f course, some patients may use this liberty [the right to choose or refuse treatment on offer] to accept or refuse treatment with a high degree of reflection and individuality, hence (on some accounts) with a high degree of personal autonomy. But this need not generally be the case."[38] Indeed it need not generally be the case. But examples in which it is the case are not unusual.[39]

In light of the preceding discussion, we might now consider Mr. Burke's request that ANH not be withdrawn before his death is imminent. The withdrawal of ANH contrary to Mr Burke's wishes would not constitute coercion. Might lack of consideration respect for Mr Burke's wishes be said to show disrespect for individual (patient) autonomy in a more robust sense? Arguably it is simply inappropriate to invoke the notion of respect for individual autonomy in relation to Mr Burke's circumstances. By the time ANH might be withdrawn against Mr Burke's wishes, Mr Burke will be completely dependent on others for his survival; he will be incapable of any action other than mental action, and eventually he will lose the ability to communicate any "decisions" he might make. What Mr Burke sought from the High Court was, as Munby J said, *protection* from lack of treatment which would result in him dying in avoidably distressing circumstances.[40] And perhaps respect for Mr Burke's wishes can best be defended in these terms.

On the other hand, in seeking legal protection, Mr Burke also sought to exert his own independent decision about something that is very important to him, namely "how he passes the closing days and moments of his life". Within the very strict limitations for choice that his illness will inevitably impose on him, Mr Burke seeks to manage his own death. And it is crucial for Mr Burke that he reflects very carefully on his request that ANH not be withdrawn before his death is imminent, in the knowledge that if he were to change his mind he will be unable to revise his request once he can no longer communicate.[41]

Notes

1 "Withholding and Withdrawing Life-Prolonging Treatments: Good Practice in Decision-making" (2002), Paragraph 32. (Hereafter referred to in the text as the Guidance.)
2 Ibid., Paragraph 81.
3 R (on the application of Oliver Leslie Burke) v The General Medical Council Rev 1 [2004] E.W.H.C. Admin 1879 (30 July 2004).
4 This was the core of Mr Burke's application to the High Court. He also sought to establish that relevant sections of the Guidance were incompatible with his rights under various Articles of the European Convention for the Protection of Human Rights and Fundamental Freedoms.
5 David Gurnham, "Losing the Wood for the Trees: Burke and the Court of Appeal", Medical Law Review, 14, (2006): 253.
6 Munby J was not concerned with the extent to which, in general, a patient has a right to insist on particular treatment, but rather with a patient's choice of whether or not to receive life-prolonging treatment and with the right to decide "how one chooses to pass the closing days and moments of one's life and how one manages one's own death" (Burke [2004] 63).
7 R (on the Application of Oliver Leslie Burke) v The General Medical Council [2005] E.W.C.A. Civ. 1003 (28 July 2005).
8 Burke [2005] 53.
9 The general law of murder holds that a person intends to kill if she foresees someone's death as a morally certain outcome of her action. (Thus a person who plants a bomb in a railway carriage with the aim of killing a particular person can also be guilty of murdering other people in the carriage who die from the blast.) However, the law relating to withholding or withdrawing medical treatment invokes a stricter notion of intention, whereby in withholding or discontinuing life-prolonging treatment a doctor can foresee but does not thereby intend a patient's death.
10 Onora O'Neill, Autonomy and Trust in Bioethics (Cambridge: Cambridge University Press, 2002).
11 Ibid., p. 84 and, more generally, chapters 2 and 4.
12 Ibid., p. 31.
13 Ibid., p. 23, emphasis original.
14 Ibid., p. 37.
15 "In contemporary medical practice patient autonomy is often no more than a right to refuse treatment. This right is important. Insofar as patients are protected by informed consent procedures that are scrupulously used, they will be protected against coercive or deceptive medical treatment. However, by themselves informed consent procedures neither assume nor ensure that patients are autonomous in any more demanding sense." Ibid., p. 49.
16 Ibid., p. 49.
17 We might ask, for instance, what the judges took respecting a person's wishes to imply in Re A (Children) (Conjoined Twins) [2000] 4 All E.R. 961, which ruled on the surgical separation of infant conjoined twins against their parents' explicit wishes. The Court of Appeal emphasised that the parents' wishes deserved great

respect. Yet it rejected and overrode the parents' refusal of consent and permitted the hospital to do what the parents did not want.
18 S. Darwall, "Two Kinds of Respect", *Ethics* 88 (1977): 36–49. For a discussion of this distinction and other types of respect see http://plato.stanford.edy/entries/respect/.
19 We do not recognise some wishes as having any such status of course, e.g., a busybody's wish to know your business or a thief's wish to have your wallet.
20 Several writers use the term "consideration respect" more broadly than the sense that I contrast with compliance respect. See, e.g. William Frankena, "The Ethics of Respect for Persons", *Philosophical Topics* 14 (1986): 149–67.
21 In making a will, a person requests the assistance of others in distributing her assets after her death in accordance with her wishes. As executor of a friend's will, for example, I must ensure that her nephew receives her legacy, as she wished, even though the nephew is a wastrel and her assets would be better given to Oxfam. Wills can sometimes be overturned of course. However, in the case of wills the presumption is clearly one of compliance respect unless it can be shown that in making the will the person was coerced or deceived, or else incompetent. Wills can also be overturned on other grounds, e.g., if they are manifestly unjust. But a presumption of compliance respect for a person's wishes can, more generally, sometimes give way to other types of considerations.
22 For more general discussions relevant to this issue see Jeff McMahan, "Killing, Letting Die and Withdrawing Aid", *Ethics* 103 (1993): 250–79, and Suzanne Uniacke, "Absolutely Clean Hands: responsibility for what's allowed in refraining from what's not allowed", *International Journal of Philosophical Studies*, 7, 2 (1999): 189–209.
23 O'Neill (2002), chapter 2.
24 Ibid., chapter 4.
25 *Burke* [2005] 50.
26 A further question is whether it can be appropriate to take into account a competent patient's request for treatment that is *not* clinically indicated. In many cases the answer will be no (as when, e.g., a patient requests antibiotics for a virus). The answer to this question can be complicated, however, by the fact that a treatment that is not directly clinically indicated might work effectively as a placebo, because of the particular patient's (false) beliefs about its efficacy, and hence be indirectly "clinically indicated". In such a case, in providing the requested treatment, the doctor would not, I think, be affording the patient's *wishes* consideration respect, as opposed to taking the efficacy of the patient's false beliefs into account.
27 Either way of showing consideration respect for a patient's wish that *x* happen (in this case, that he receives the surgery) will involve taking into account the reasons why the patient wants *x* to happen. Whether the second way of showing consideration respect for a patient's wishes, which affords significance to these wishes *as the patient's wishes*, would also give additional weight to a patient's *express* wish (that is, to his explicit request), is not something I explore here.
28 On the contrary, for the doctor, compliance respect for a patient's wishes constitutes what Joseph Raz has identified as an exclusionary reason (Joseph Raz, *Practical Reason and Norms*, 2nd edition (Princeton: Princeton University Press, 1990), pp. 38–43.
29 If Mr. Burke's request were to merit compliance respect (exactly the same type of respect as is appropriate for a refusal of treatment) then a doctor would need to enact Mr Burke's request *irrespective* of whether or not what he requests is in his interests.

30 The Court of Appeal nonetheless sought to assure Mr Burke that where ANH is necessary to a competent patient's survival, there can be no such clinical judgment contrary to the patient's wish that ANH be continued. I question this reassurance above (text accompanying footnote 8).
31 *Burke* [2005] 50.
32 O'Neill (2002), p. 49.
33 Ibid., p. 38.
34 Hormone treatment aimed to reduce the endometriosis would need to be stopped should Ms D intend to conceive, however.
35 O'Neill (2002), p. 37.
36 Within the U.K. healthcare system Mr C would be strongly encouraged to consider carefully how his disease is managed (http://www.nhs.uk/prostatecancer).
37 The so-called "Bolam" test refers to a form of treatment that is recognised as clinically appropriate for a particular condition by a large body of responsible and competent relevant professional opinion.
38 O'Neill (2002), p. 37.
39 Prostate cancer is the most common cancer in men in England, causing about one in four of all new male cancers. Endometriosis is said to affect 15% of pre-menopausal women in the United Kingdom.
40 The relevant part of Munby J's ruling is as follows: "Personal autonomy – the right of self-determination – and dignity are fundamental rights, recognised by the common law and protected by Articles 3 and 8 of the Convention. (8) The personal autonomy which is protected by Article 8 embraces such matters as how one chooses to pass the closing days and moments of one's life and how one manages one's death. (9) The dignity interests protected by the Convention include, under Article 8, the preservation of mental stability and, under Article 3, the right to die with dignity and the right to be protected from treatment, or from a lack of treatment, which will result in one dying in avoidably distressing circumstances. (10) An enhanced degree of protection is called for under Articles 3 and 8 in the case of the vulnerable." *Burke* [2004]: 116.
41 My thanks are due to participants in the British Academy conference, "Ethics and Politics Beyond Borders: the work of Onora O'Neill" (24–26 September, 2009), to philosophers at the University of Glasgow, and to Antony Hatzistavrou, David Archard and Neil Manson for helpful comments on earlier versions of this paper.

7

INDEPENDENCE, DEPENDENCE, AND THE LIBERAL SUBJECT

Marilyn Friedman

Independence sounds like a great idea. It has a positive resonance for many people and is the subject of important historical "Declarations." How could anyone be opposed to independence? Yet recently independence has become a target of some critical discussions.

Some recent work in feminist philosophy raises doubt about the value of independence. Independence is criticized as either a faulty aim, one that is bad in some way, or a false aim, one that in practice promotes what is not independence *sans phrase* but only a limited or distorted manifestation of it. Either way, the emphasis on independence is said to obscure a range of related phenomena that are equally if not more valuable. These include especially dependence, or dependency, and the work of caring for those who are dependent. These values, according to the critique, have been underestimated or ignored altogether and should instead be esteemed in the understanding of interpersonal relationships.

This feminist criticism of independence has made important contributions to moral, social, and political theory. It has inspired new approaches to thinking about character, interpersonal relationships, and political ideals. It has contributed significantly to the discourse on disabilities and their place in liberal political theory. However, the pendulum may have swung too far in this critical literature. Onora O'Neill has discussed independence and dependency in suggestive ways that point us toward worthwhile meanings of independence. Her comments provide a useful starting point for reclaiming the worthwhile meanings and for understanding how to combine them with the more recent critical insights. The aim of this paper is to build on O'Neill's suggestions. We can appreciate the valuable consequences of dependence without having to jettison all notions or ideals of independence. In particular, independence, with suitable qualifications, has been and still remains a crucial ideal for women globally in their quests to overcome the various practices of female subordination and oppression that are maintained in part by the vulnerabilities generated by enforced forms of female dependency.

Independence and dependence can be defined for several distinct sociopolitical areas of life that overlap in practice but can be distinguished conceptually.[1] Drawing on O'Neill's writings, I shall focus on two contexts in which to delve into the concepts of independence and dependency: first, the realm of character as exhibited in interpersonal relationships, and, second, the realm of liberal theorizing about citizenship.

Independence as an ideal of character in interpersonal relationships

There are various lines of thought that comprise the critique of independence in the context of interpersonal relationships; they include the following. First, independence is humanly impossible. Second, an idealization of independence obscures other values that are equally, if not more, important than independence, especially the value of dependency. Third, dependence has been unfairly disparaged and is much more valuable than has been previously realized. Fourth, the value of dependency is of special concern because of its close connection with women's traditional social roles. These lines of thought are often intertwined but can be conceptually distinguished.

First, independence is humanly impossible. It is a fiction or myth. Eva Kittay writes that "independence, except in some particular actions and functions, is a fiction. ... "[2] Martha Albertson Fineman explores what she calls "the myth of individual autonomy" in the United States, which is "spun out in very individualistic terms" such as "independence" and "self-sufficiency," terms that are supposed to identify traits of "the ideal citizen."[3] Fineman states that independence is central "to the construction of individual American identity" as "reflected in the mythic and foundational document the Declaration of Independence."[4] Yet the assumptions involved in the related concepts of independence and autonomy are "unrealizable."[5] Independence is mythic in part because "some individuals are subsidized and supported in their 'independence'."[6] She claims also that: "Independence from subsidy and support is not attainable, nor is it desirable; we want and need the webs of economic and social relationships that sustain us."[7] Fineman writes that we are deluded if we think that "many (perhaps any) endeavors in our complex modern society can be undertaken in an autonomous and independent manner."[8]

Second, the idealization of independence obscures other values that are equally, if not more, important than independence, especially the value of dependency. Thus, Ellen Feder and Eva Kittay write that a project of independence is "impossible" if "it both relies on and masks the inevitability of human dependency and the work of giving care to dependents."[9]

INDEPENDENCE, DEPENDENCE, AND THE SUBJECT

Dependency can involve relying on others "to meet essential needs [one is] unable to meet [oneself]."[10]

Fineman argues that autonomy, which today subsumes the ideal of independence, is invoked to "stigmatize and punish those among us labeled dependent." Dependency is thereby regarded as a "societal problem" requiring "drastic measures to remedy."[11]

Third, dependence has been unfairly disparaged and is much more valuable than has previously been realized. Kittay, for example, writes that the fiction of independence "turns those whose dependence cannot be masked into pariahs, or makes them objects of distain [sic] or pity."[12] Instead, dependence should be regarded in a more positive light. Here again is Kittay: "In acknowledging dependency we respect the fact that as individuals our dependency relations are constitutive of who we are and that, as a society, we are inextricably dependent on one another."[13]

Kittay reminds us that everyone goes through the extreme dependency of early childhood. Nearly everyone goes through occasional dependent periods of illness or injury across their lifetimes. Many people live long enough to enter a period of gradually increasing dependency in old age. And some people experience extended or lifelong disabilities that make them continually dependent on ongoing care by others.

Relationships of dependency often give rise to emotional bonds between dependent and caregiver that become especially important in the lives of both. These relationships can give meaning to human life, shape the goals and values of a lifetime, and define who we are. Without the needs that make people dependent on care by others, it is not obvious that such relationships would form or endure across time. Thus dependency can have valued and valuable consequences. As noted above, Fineman claims that "we want and need the webs of economic and social relationships that sustain us."[14]

Fourth, the value of dependency is of special concern because of its close connection with women's traditional social roles. Most of the people who do the daily caretaking that dependents require are women. When we disregard dependency, we at the same time, disregard crucial social work done mainly by women. We disregard some of the profound social contributions that women make, often for no wages, to provide the care we all need in order to survive through our dependencies. A positive regard for dependency carries with it both a positive valuing of the work of meeting the needs of dependents and a high regard for those who do the work of caring for dependents.[15]

One context particularly related to women's traditional social roles, in which "dependency" is disparaged as a character failing, is that of state welfare provision. In this context, dependency is disparaged as a personal failure and a character flaw. It is the failure of some mothers (in the U.S., often young and black), namely those who have children they cannot afford to raise with men to whom they are not married and who do not contribute child support. These mothers have no income-earning jobs by which to sustain themselves or their dependent children. Dependency of this sort is widely considered to be shameful and the women who are dependent in those ways are regarded as moral failures. Feminists such as Nancy Fraser and Linda Gordon, and Iris Young have tried to undermine this negative use of the term "dependency" in the context of welfare programs.[16]

The third and fourth lines of criticism seem especially apt and they will not be challenged in this context. Dependence is often unfairly disparaged and often in connection to women's traditional social roles. What seems less clear is that independence is a fiction or that the values realized by dependency are obscured by a focus on independence in particular. O'Neill's discussion of independence indicates especially how to address the first criticism, that independence is a myth. Regarding the second criticism, O'Neill indicates some ways of thinking about the value of independence so as to balance it against values related to dependence. The remainder of this section will combine discussion of these two concerns.

How can we understand independence in a non-mythical fashion, one that is humanly possible to achieve? We might first ask why we should seek such an understanding. Part of the answer is that there are many contexts in which the term is used as if it genuinely applied to people. This would be hard to explain if people thought they were describing a character trait or a set of interpersonal arrangements that was humanly impossible to achieve, such as absolute self-sufficiency. We could suppose that ordinary people are, for the most part, deluded about independence. However, it seems more charitable to look first for alternative meanings that make sense of the way the term is applied by real human beings in practice.

O'Neill provides the relevant articulation. She states that the meaning of independence, especially in the context of interpreting autonomy, is specified in relation to something else and admits of degrees. In this way, "independence is *from* something or other and may be *more or less complete*."[17] Thus, independence is a qualified notion. Even when the qualifications are not stated explicitly, it is not too far-fetched to suppose they are implicitly understood. Let us add one more qualification to O'Neill's list of two. Independence is also generally understood in relation to a specific sphere of activity, such as income-earning. An independent person might be one who "lives within her means" (she is free from debt, meeting her financial needs with income of her own), "takes care of herself" (she is free from, say, health problems because she eats nourishing food, exercises, and monitors her health), or "thinks for herself" (she does not defer uncritically to the opinions or commands of others but generally reflects critically on them before making decisions).

Iris Young concurs in finding the popular notion of independence to be a partial and graduated one. She refers to William Galston's idea that independence is a liberal virtue.[18] However, Young carefully interprets this character ideal in terms of "having a well-paid job sufficient to support oneself and one's children. ... "[19] On this account, the real battle over, say, welfare programs is not that opponents believe welfare recipients should attain an impossible degree of absolute self-reliance. The real battle is over the belief by welfare opponents that taxpayers do not have an obligation to provide even modest income support for those persons who lack income-earning jobs.

O'Neill's articulation brings out the way in which independence is a feature of someone's circumstances or interrelationships with others. Independence from someone or something is a matter of someone's being self-governing, free, liberated, nonaligned, unconstrained, uncontrolled, or unregimented.[20] This range of meanings points largely to the absence of external controls. External controls could take the form of dominating persons who have the power to regulate someone's actions or they could take the form of a tyrannical political regime that unjustly controls someone's life. Independence as a matter of socio-political circumstances contrasts with the situation of someone who is dominated, enslaved, or otherwise under the overarching control of others.

Underneath this qualified usage lies the unstated assumption that no human being is independent in all humanly possible ways to the highest degree humanly possible in each way. Thus calling someone "independent" means implicitly that they are free of some influence or control to act in some specific area to some comparatively high but still humanly possible degree. In this way, independence is a relative and comparative notion. It is to be above average in freedom from controlling factors in some specific way(s) that is(are) regarded as noteworthy by the one who uses the term. A person can be very independent in some ways but much less so or not at all in others. Someone who sews her own clothes may buy cloth at the store. Yet she is more independent in that respect than someone who simply buys ready-made clothes. Every conscious human being probably combines degrees of independence in some ways with degrees of dependence in other ways.

To understand fully what someone means when she calls someone "independent," we would have to know the particular activities or conditions she had in mind, the controlling factors she believes are absent, and her thoughts about what is humanly average along the continuum in that activity. This articulated understanding shows that "independence" can easily be meaningful and need not be a myth or fiction.

O'Neill associates current cultural esteem for independence with twentieth century events in which (some form and degree of relative) independence is correlated with what appears to have been the morally right or better side of those events. Thus, independence was associated with those who resisted Nazism, those who survived in death camps, those who had democratic rather than authoritarian personalities,[21] those who resisted administering electric shocks to other research subjects in the infamous Milgram experiments,[22] and those who reached the supposedly highest levels of moral reasoning in studies by Lawrence Kohlberg.[23]

However, this alone does not show that independence is valuable in any important way, either for the person who lives it or for others who might be affected by it. O'Neill reminds us that independence can be for good or ill.[24] Independent action can include "deviant and criminal activity."[25] O'Neill writes that "independence *per se* does not seem to be either necessary or sufficient for an act to be morally valuable or an agent to be excellent."[26] She urges that "there is no reason to admire action merely because it is independent of something else."[27] O'Neill notes that independent-mindedness is not necessarily good or bad; it depends on the nature of the beliefs, values, traditions, or decrees from which one deviates.

Thus, the merits of "mere/sheer independence" are "highly variable."[28] O'Neill notes that "independent people may be self-centred, selfish, lacking in fellow-feeling or solidarity with others."[29] Independent action "can be important or trivial, heroic or brutal, helpful or selfish, admired or distressing to others."[30] O'Neill writes that:

> The fact that individual independence in the face of evil, or of temptation, is admirable does not show that individual independence in the face of others' needs or in the context of family or professional relationships will be good or right.[31]

However, O'Neill's survey of these moral possibilities does leave a place for valuable independence. To be sure, the value would be *derivative* from the goodness or rightness of what was done. The crucial point for this context is that independence can be instrumentally valuable if carried out in pursuit of valuable ends. Such derivatively valuable independence needs no apology.

O'Neill suggests that Kant's approach to autonomy "provides a framework for judging when and why specific sorts of independence are valuable, and for criticizing some but not other relations of power and dependence. Kantian autonomy ... neither mindlessly endorses ideals of self-sufficiency nor devalues all forms of dependence and interdependence."[32] What is distinctive about Kant's account of autonomy is that it combines the notion of independence with that of "rationality or coherence."[33] Kant's conception of the independence required for autonomy is that of "negative freedom," that is, "independence from alien causes."[34] This independence is an underlying presumption of the standpoint human beings must take up when they reason practically, a standpoint that is ineliminable to the extent that "we take ourselves to be agents," that is "if we are to judge and deliberate, reason and argue. ... "[35] The resulting moral framework does not involve idolizing "self-sufficiency or ... mere sheer independence" nor does it "conflate autonomy. ... with independence *sans phrase*."[36] Instead it provides a basis for evaluating "the innumerable specific types of dependence and independence which human lives and practices may produce" and discerning which ones are morally valuable.[37]

Independence as a presumption of the practical standpoint is independence from alien causes. However, this is not the notion of independence at issue in the feminist critiques. What matters there are what O'Neill calls the "innumerable specific types of dependence and independence" in human life. O'Neill's Kantian account leaves open the possibility of valuable forms of dependence and interdependence as well of independence. There may be specific interpersonal relationships, in which someone is independent from (or dependent on) something or someone in certain specific ways to some particular degree. O'Neill provides some helpful remarks about how to identify these possibilities in relation to women's lives and how to evaluate them.

Thus, O'Neill writes about the value of independence for women and vulnerabilities to which dependence gives rise for women. For example, she recognizes that "Institutional arrangements can disable agency" by "limiting capacities to reason and act independently. ... "[38] One problematic type of dependence is "disadvantageous dependence on those who provide credit"; another type consists of "disadvantageous patterns of entitlement within the family."[39]

O'Neill writes that "the most dependent women" are those who are dominated by economically powerful others in market transactions or family arrangements.[40] Reduced independence can come about when women are "isolated, secluded, barred from education or wage-earning, or have access to information only via the filter of more powerful family members." Women whose independence is reduced in these ways become vulnerable to "coercion and domination."[41] O'Neill observes that women are easier to coerce when their "effective independence" is restricted by family responsibilities, or denial of their entitlements or shares in family property.[42] These forms of *dependence* have to do with the social subordination of women within the family.

One sort of independence mentioned by O'Neill is that of having means that are "adequate" for oneself and one's "dependents."[43] The "means" in question need not come from paid employment. O'Neill does not state or imply that someone must have a paying job. She does not presuppose a work ethic. Someone's means might consist of a proper share of family property. Also, this conception of independence can be specified in a way that does not blame dependent persons for their marginalization or exclusion. The ideal living arrangement for a woman (as for anyone) is a situation that avoids impoverishment. Impoverishment reduces someone's "effective capacities and their opportunities for action" and constrains her "possibilities for refusal and negotiation."[44]

It is helpful to distinguish between two different sorts of ideals for which human beings may strive. On one hand, there are virtues and moral character ideals. Galston's notion of independence as a virtue of citizens fits into this broad category. On the other hand, there are prudential ideals, character ideals that are neither morally required nor morally prohibited, but are advantageous for persons to have in pursuing their goals and living their lives. Prudential ideals can be especially important for people whose subordinated social position makes them vulnerable to abuse and oppression. Independence is an ideal in this prudential sense. In particular contexts (such as family and wage-earning), independence from specific sorts of controlling factors (such as financial dependence on those who would dominate, abuse, or oppress one) can be the key that allows one to seek one's well-being and that of loved ones. Thus a prudential ideal of independence illuminates the effective agency and available opportunities that help someone to avoid being vulnerable to domination by more powerful others.

O'Neill is aware that a focus on women's ways of being independent by itself does not necessarily reveal the whole story about such women's lives. This restricted focus can obscure women's continuing dependencies and the problems created by these. She writes that women's "dependence on husbands and fathers can seem acceptable if they are after all wage-earning individuals and so not dangerously dependent." In this same vein, women's "low wages can seem unworrying if the women are wives for whom others provide. ... "[45] Here the problem is the vulnerability involved in being dependent on another person's income support, a vulnerability that is masked if one does happen to earn wages of one's own.

O'Neill's sensible conclusion is not that women's ways of being independent should be disregarded or that the ideal of independence is flawed. Rather, O'Neill draws attention to the way an awareness of women's ways of being (to some significant degree) independent should be combined with an awareness of women's ways of continuing to be dependent (to some significant degree). For O'Neill, one reason to consider the ways in which women's interrelationships continue to make them dependent is to recognize the risks and harms to which these dependencies subject them. Celebrating dependency overly much, and the ways that it grounds meaningful and rewarding relationships, might obscure its disadvantages and the ways it sometimes disadvantages the (relatively more) dependent partners in relationships. Women's historical situations have traditionally included various forms of dependency on others that were detrimental to women's lives. There seem to be many ways in which women would be better off if they had a wider range of morally acceptable options for agency that allowed them to promote better their own well-being and the well-being of those for whom they care.

O'Neill's expression "mere/sheer independence," suggests a useful contrary notion, "mere/sheer *dependence*." Just as O'Neill holds that mere/sheer independence has no inherent value of its own, we can say in parallel fashion that *mere/sheer dependence* is not intrinsically valuable either. Kinds and degrees of dependency are certainly pervasive features of the human condition. They arise in infancy, declining old age, and in all the illnesses, injuries, and chronic impairments that afflict human beings throughout life. Dependency makes the dependent party vulnerable to the risk of harm by the party on whom she depends. This possibility seems to be an inherent part of any dependency relationship. If the risk of harm is inherently part of dependency relationships, then such relationships are morally good or valuable only to the extent that harm is minimal and both parties, but especially the dependent one, benefit overall from the relationship.

Does the cultural emphasis on independence, even as a prudential ideal, obscure the benefits of dependency? If so, there might be an advantage to emphasizing the potential valuable effects of dependency rather than those of independence at particular historical time periods in which this rhetorical imbalance occurs. However, at any time period, the cultural appreciation of either independence or dependency need not add up to a zero sum game. Cultural appreciation of the contingent importance of dependency could increase without necessarily devaluing independence. The reason for continuing to value some forms of independence, as O'Neill's work suggests, is that specific forms of prudential independence for women within their social arrangements and relationships, for example income-earning and educational opportunities, position women better than otherwise to protect themselves and their loved ones from various threats of harm.

Independence in liberal theory

Liberal theorizing supposes an ideal liberal citizen for the purpose, among other things, of working out conditions of governmental legitimacy and principles of justice. The liberal citizen is ideally an autonomous person and "independence" is either a synonym for "autonomy" or close to it in meaning. On consent-based versions of liberal theory, the consent of ideal, independent or autonomous citizens to political principles is one criterion of the legitimacy of those principles.

However, the conception of an ideal citizen as independent serves to marginalize or exclude altogether those citizens who lack the abilities to be independent in the requisite sense. The requisite sense usually centers around the cognitive ability to reflect on political principles or arrangements, deliberate about them with others, and consent to them or find them justified from the agent's own perspective. It is as if, from the liberal standpoint, the legitimacy of coercive political power, grounded in appropriate principles of justice, is conceptualized in a way that takes no account of the severely cognitively disabled persons who must also live under liberal principles. The question of how the liberal political order is legitimate for the severely cognitively disabled does not traditionally arise. The severely cognitively disabled are simply ignored by traditional theories of liberal legitimacy.

A preliminary note about this issue is in order. The critique of independence is especially a critique of liberal theory. Political theorists such as John Rawls offer liberal theoretic interpretations of the conceptual and normative foundations and justifications of liberal-democratic societies that become dominant among intellectuals as reconstructive rationales for the practices of actual so-called liberal-democratic political systems. It is important, however, to distinguish theory from practice. Whether, and to what extent, those theoretical reconstructions really correspond to the actual workings of liberal-democratic societies in practice is an open, empirical question. Rawls's "difference principle," for example, has never been implemented in the United States, where economic conditions conform much more to the old adage that "the rich get richer and the poor get poorer."

The critics of independence concentrate their criticism on liberal theory. However, showing that a particular liberal theory rests on a misguided idealization of independent citizens tells us nothing yet about whether any actual liberal-democratic system is marred in the same way in practice. To make that case, we would need empirical evidence about actual institutions, policies, or practices in a particular, functioning liberal-democratic system. Even in that case, there is probably always room for competing interpretations about what conception of the person or principles of justice are being presupposed by the actual workings of the institutions, policies, or practices in question. Since liberal-democratic societies usually harbor different and competing political parties and perspectives, it is always an open question how best to interpret the array of actual practices.

For the sake of this discussion, I restrict my focus to theoretical work pertaining to the conceptual and normative foundations of liberal-democratic societies, with the understanding that liberal-democratic theory may tell us very little about any particular, actual liberal-democratic system. There may be something drastically wrong with John Rawls's conception of the ideal liberal-democratic citizen, but that alone does not tell us that, say, the United States in particular denies all citizenship privileges to those persons who cannot measure up to Rawls's ideal. Showing the latter requires empirical evidence, which is beyond the scope of this discussion.

Eva Kittay has criticized independence as an ideal of liberal citizenship that excludes the severely mentally disabled.[46] Independence and rationality are features a human being must have, according to liberal theory, in order to qualify for citizenship and rights. As Kittay puts it, in the "reigning liberal understanding of justice," those with "severe or profound cognitive disabilities" can "never be citizens" and "have no rights associated with their needs."[47] Kittay writes that the cognitively disabled "have rarely been seen as subjects, as citizens, as persons with equal entitlement to fulfillment."[48]

Thus liberal political theory fails to accord the status or privileges of citizenship to cognitively impaired members of society. Kittay continues:

> Liberalism invokes a notion of political participation in which one makes one's voice heard. It depends on a conception of the person as independent, rational, and capable of self-sufficiency. And it holds to a conception of society as an association of such independent equals.[49]

In this regard, Kittay argues that liberal democratic nations have a "self-understanding" as an "association of free and independent equals." The notion of equality, however, is a "fiction" that Kittay challenges.

The assumption of equality, in Kittay's view, masks human dependencies, the needs of dependents, and women's role in tending to those needs. As well, the assumption of equality masks asymmetries in human interactions. Women's dependency work has historically been tied to women's subordination. Dependency work makes someone vulnerable to domination and excludes them from the class of equals. Kittay sets out a goal of ending domination in a way that is compatible with equality concerns.[50]

O'Neill's comments on the concepts of independence and dependence in theories of justice are relevant to these concerns and help to make progress in thinking about them. However, O'Neill's suggestions also need to be developed more fully. O'Neill is concerned especially with the way many theories of justice marginalize *women*, whose relationships of "dependence and interdependence" leave them with "relatively little control over the circumstances" of their lives.[51] O'Neill and Kittay agree that one problem with most theories of justice is that they "idealize": they presume conceptions of human agents that do not fit any actual human agents.[52] In O'Neill's view, an idealization of independence might fit certain human beings but not all of them and, in particular, "covert gender chauvinism" can thereby enter the account, thus excluding women indirectly.[53]

O'Neill argues that liberal theories do not have to begin by presuming individuals who "meet some ideal standard of rationality and independence." They could consider what political principles could be accepted by non-ideal persons. There is no need for a "fiction" of ideal independence.[54] The goal, she argues, is to find principles of justice that represent a middle ground between that to which "ideally rational and mutually independent beings *would consent*" and the arrangements to which possibly oppressed persons do consent.[55]

O'Neill's words could encompass the cognitively impaired but her later discussion suggests that her thinking here is instead about persons who are oppressed but not cognitively impaired. They are the consenting oppressed.

The challenge they pose is that their consent is suspect because it is given under coercive conditions. O'Neill suggests a test for determining the legitimacy of arrangements to which the consenting oppressed consent. Arrangements are legitimate if the oppressed can "refuse or renegotiate" those arrangements.[56] O'Neill recognizes that as "capacities to act are less developed and more vulnerable" and "opportunities for independent action are restricted," it becomes harder for the oppressed to dissent.[57]

These suggestions are important for the consenting oppressed and also the oppressed who have not actually consented but do have the capacity to do so. O'Neill writes that "Institutional arrangements can disable agency ... by limiting capacities to reason and act independently...."[58] Women are vulnerable to "coercion and domination" when "their judgment is weakened and their independence stunted" because they are "isolated, secluded, barred from education or wage-earning, or have access to information only via the filter of more powerful family members."[59] O'Neill continues that women are easier to coerce when their "effective independence is restricted" by family responsibilities, denial of their entitlements or shares in family property.[60]

O'Neill argues that:

> Relations of dependence are not always or overtly coercive; but they provide structures of subordination within which it is all too easy to silence or trivialize the articulation of dissent. ... Institutionalized dependence tends to make dissent hard or impossible.[61]

O'Neill is here discussing women's vulnerabilities within the family and the marketplace. However, these remarks are also relevant to liberal theorizing. Someone lacks the political independence of being able to accept or refuse political principles if she is immersed in relationships that make her subordinate to others who can use coercion to influence her choices.

Autonomy is regarded by most liberal political theorists as part of a standard that political systems should meet in order to be legitimate. A government exercising coercive power over people does so legitimately only to the extent that the people consent to it and do so autonomously. The independence called for by these ideas is that of being independent-minded. A citizen's consent to governing authority should, in some sense, be her own, that is, based on her own perspective in some deep sense. Most accounts of autonomous independent-mindedness are compatible with human socialization, the embodied and social nature of selves, and the social nature of human selves.

However, independent-mindedness, even in humanly possible degrees of it, requires certain minimal cognitive capacities, such as the capacity to understand political norms and issues, engage in political dialogue over those norms and issues, and express a position on them. There is still no room in O'Neill's expanded citizenry for the liberal conception of legitimacy to take account of the severely cognitively disabled.

Martha Nussbaum suggests that to change liberal theory to recognize the importance of dependency relations and the entitlements of dependent persons would not change liberal theory in the radical way Kittay thinks.[62] Nussbaum's resolution of the debate is for liberalism to revise its notion of the person and be "more attentive to need and its material and institutional conditions."[63] Nussbaum thinks liberal theory can recognize that persons are "both capable and needy."[64] Liberal theory can give: "all citizens the chance to develop the full range of human powers, at whatever level their condition allows, and to enjoy the sort of liberty and independence their condition allows."[65] The image of the citizen should include dependency. But this is not a "sufficient image for the citizen in a just society." Instead, writes Nussbaum, "I think we need a lot more: liberty and opportunity, the chance to form a plan of life, the chance to learn and imagine on one's own."[66] Yes, mentally disabled people have "dependencies [that] must be understood and supported." But all persons have a need to be "distinct and an individual" as well as a need for the "support required to be free-choosing adults, each in his or her own way."[67]

However Nussbaum's imagery of "free-choosing adults" still excludes profoundly cognitively impaired people such as Kittay's daughter, Sesha. From Kittay's description, it does not seem that Sesha could ever form a plan of life or be "free-choosing" across a wide range of choices.[68] It seems that Nussbaum falls back on the same unqualified image of the citizen with which liberalism started, a citizen who is within the statistically "normal" range of human abilities for cognition and agency, a range that is perhaps widened a bit. This is a person who can seize opportunities, take liberties, and actively learn and imagine in a variety of ways. This is close to the standard image of the citizen. Nussbaum's proposal to keep these traditional liberal values in the conception of the citizen seems to continue ignoring the severely cognitively disabled.

Thus, liberal theorists traditionally assumed that all citizens are equal in terms of the cognitive abilities needed to consent to political rule. If there is a developmental threshold that someone must cross in order to be addressed by liberal theory as a moral equal to other human beings and a potential citizen of a just political order, this is likely to be, as Kittay suggests, someone who can communicate in political processes and can express a political perspective of her own.

In this spirit, Kittay makes two suggestions toward modifying the liberal conception of the person. One suggestion is to add another moral power to the famous Rawlsian conception of the person. Rawls famously conceives of persons as having two moral powers, the capacity for a sense of justice and the capacity for a conception of the good. Kittay recommends adding a third moral power to Rawls's conception of the citizen, namely the capacity to "respond to vulnerability with care."[69] Kittay's other suggestion reflects an attempt to better conceive of citizens as equals. She recommends basing this idea on "the inevitability of human interdependence."[70] Kittay represents this notion with the metaphor that "we are all some mother's child."[71]

Asha Bhandary thinks that neither of these suggestions is satisfactory. She notes that the capacity to respond to vulnerability with care is not equal among all human beings. "Utter dependents" who are extremely cognitively impaired lack this.[72] Bhandary rejects the proposed metaphor of each being "some mother's child" on the grounds that someone's status as claim-maker should not be based solely on relation to some other person.[73] Bhandary seems to recommend a dual conception of citizenship: the status of "self-authenticator of claims" for those who "are not utterly dependent" and, for the utterly dependent, the status of having someone to "discern, stand for, and fulfill her needs."[74]

These suggestions point to a revised conception of liberal legitimacy. O'Neill can help us at this point. She asserts that theories of justice must "begin with the thought of a plurality of potentially interacting and diverse agents."[75] This rules out theories of justice that would ground their principles on "an assumed ideal convergence between persons or an assumed actual social or historical convergence between them."[76]

However, at this point, O'Neill makes a move that continues to exclude the severely cognitively disabled. She claims that justice requires that its "most basic principles be ones that could be adopted by all."[77] O'Neill is worried about narrowly drawn boundaries that exclude people such as women who are *capable* of giving meaningful consent. She maintains that theorists should not exclude "anybody with whom interaction is to be undertaken or held possible." More strongly, no one should be excluded if we can depend on their having capacities to reason and "act independently," however limited these may be.[78] O'Neill claims that "justice is then in the first place a matter of keeping to principles that can be adopted by all members of any plurality of potentially interacting beings."[79] O'Neill reiterates that theories of justice should encompass those otherwise excluded persons who do have the capacities to understand and consent to political principles. This continues to leave the severely cognitively impaired out of the scope of her theoretical recommendations.

O'Neill's notion of "interaction" is not sufficient to effect the needed inclusion. Caretakers do interact with the severely cognitively impaired persons for whom they care. Yet the impaired persons still cannot participate in processes of liberal legitimation because they are unable to understand and consent to political principles.

Thus, the consent of independent or autonomous citizens is not a sufficient condition of the legitimacy of a governing order because there are always citizens who fall under its governing power but who lack the capacity to consent. This includes persons with severe cognitive impairments, as we have been discussing, and also children, those with senile dementia, and those with temporarily impaired cognitive functioning due to illness. Whether a political order is legitimate for all those citizens who are unable to consent to it, permanently or temporarily, has to depend in part on something other than the consent of the governed.

The obvious adaptation of liberal theory is to rest legitimacy on a two-pronged approach: consent for those who are able to understand and give (genuinely uncoerced) consent and some other criterion for those who are unable to understand or give (genuinely uncoerced) consent. Each criterion by itself would be considered necessary but not sufficient for the legitimacy of a political order. A possible and plausible criterion for those who cannot give consent on their own behalves is the proxy consent of those who represent the interests of the non-consenters. This is Asha Bhandary's suggestion.

Why adopt this strategy? This question has at least two parts. First, why retain the criterion of consent for those capable of giving non-coerced consent in a context in which not all can consent? Second, why require proxy consent by others for those citizens not able to give consent on their own behalves? Let us consider first why we might want to retain consent by those capable of consent as one necessary but not sufficient criterion of legitimacy for a political order. Consent is valuable for those who have sufficient cognitive capacity to enact it. The political order should be satisfactory to those who are capable of understanding it and either accepting or rejecting it. From their perspectives, they should regard the political order as acceptable. The idea of consent of the governed incorporates an invaluable assumption, namely, that what can be thought and reasoned about a political system matters to its legitimacy.

The alternative would be a political order that is *not* accepted by some, many, or all of those who are capable of understanding and consenting to political order. Such a political order would be *imposed* on some or all of those who can understand and consent to political order. In regard to such persons, the governing order would be tyrannical. Liberalism rejects governing by tyranny. The consent of those who can understand and consent to political order should remain a necessary condition of liberal legitimacy. It is important to preserve as much critical citizen reflection on government as possible, even if some citizens cannot share in this process. Those who can do so can represent the interests of those who cannot do so.

There is, to be sure, the possibility that, within a consent-based political framework, those who lack the abilities to participate in processes of reflecting on political principles will be disparaged as second-class citizens. This attitude should be resisted, but there may be no way to prevent this outcome in practice. However, critical political reflection by those citizens who can do so is overwhelmingly important, so much so, I believe, as to outweigh the harms of demeaning attitudes toward citizens who cannot participate in critical political reflection. Although not a guarantee against tyranny, citizen reflection is the best way to prevent governing abuses and tyranny. Were these harms to occur, they would endanger all citizens, both those who are capable of political reflection and those who are not. Eliminating the requirement of critical reflection and consent by citizens from the conception of liberal legitimacy does nothing to protect those citizens who are incapable of reflecting or consenting and might make them much worse off under a tyranny imposed on all.

This brings us to the second part of our question: why require proxy consent by others for those citizens not able to give consent on their own behalves? The very regrettable fact that some people are incapable of the cognitive activity required for understanding the political order or giving consent to it means that the legitimacy of the order for them must depend on its doing well for them even though they are not capable of recognizing it. The political order should promote the well-being of the severely cognitively disabled even if they cannot express the comprehension that it is doing so.

Other persons – those who can understand and consent to the political order – have the responsibility of ensuring that the political order promotes the well-being of all those who *cannot* understand it or consent to it. How should we imagine the role of these proxies in relation to the severely cognitively impaired? The ideal would be to suppose persons whose concern for the impaired is as close as possible to self-concern. We should especially imagine proxies who are the loving caregivers for the severely cognitively impaired. They are the ones who have the well-being of the impaired at heart. They are the ones best positioned to decide on behalf of the impaired whether the governing order meets the needs of the impaired. The proxies should want the well-being of the impaired as much as liberal theory supposes any ordinary citizen wants her own well-being. The proxies should decide whether to consent to the governing order on behalf of the impaired based on whether the governing order provides for that well-being in a just manner.

However, this approach is second best. First, we appear to have created a category of second-class citizen. This charge still needs to be dispelled. Second, we should not suppose that proxies, even with their fiduciary responsibilities to act as trustees for the severely cognitively impaired, hold the same standing as citizens who act on their own behalves. Proxies are always ineliminably other persons. They interrelate with the impaired in ways that involve asymmetrical dependency with the attendant vulnerability, risks of harm, and potential for abuse that affect the ones cared for. These dangers are, I have tried to suggest, outweighed by the importance of giving the privilege of consent to those citizens at all capable of understanding and consenting to political principles. However, the outweighed harms should not be set aside as if they did not exist. They remain complicating factors at the core of liberal legitimacy.

The overall result is that any citizen who is capable of understanding and consenting to political principles remains central to the liberal conception of political legitimacy. However, this citizen is not to be considered impossibly "ideal." She is simply anyone above a minimal threshold of cognitive capacity; she is anyone capable of understanding political order, reflecting on it, and deciding whether to consent to it or not. She is also part of a group that includes those who stand in for citizens incapable of giving meaningful consent to political processes. If such a citizen is not convinced that a particular political order is worthy of consent after considering how that political order treats all its citizens, including those who cannot understand or consent to political order, then this matters to liberal legitimacy.[80]

This proposal can be formulated so as to require two different sorts of citizens with rational competence, one who reflects on whether the governing order promotes her own well-being justly and one who reflects on whether the governing order promotes justly the well-being of a cognitively impaired person for whom she cares as much as she cares for herself. In this way, the legitimation process encompasses consideration of how the political order treats those citizens who cannot speak for themselves or cannot understand or consent to political order. Because these citizens cannot represent their own perspectives in political deliberation, it is crucial that their perspectives and needs be represented or expressed by those citizens who do cross the cognitive threshold for participating in the reflective legitimation process.

In this paper, drawing on the work of Onora O'Neill, I have dealt with two sets of issues regarding independence and dependence. First, I defended the meaningfulness and instrumental value of the concept of independence in the realm of interpersonal relationships and suggested some ways to balance it against the instrumental value of dependence. Second, I argued that the independent, or autonomous, liberal citizen should still be part of the standard for establishing the legitimacy of political principles such as those of justice. However, a liberal account should also accommodate those citizens who cannot engage in critical political reflection and I proposed a way of conceptualizing this addition to liberal theory.

Notes

1 See Nancy Fraser and Linda Gordon, "A Genealogy of *Dependency*: Tracing a Keyword of the U.S. Welfare State," in *The Subject of Care: Feminist Perspectives on Dependency*, eds., Eva Feder Kittay & Ellen K. Feder (Lanham, MD: Rowman & Littlefield, 2002), pp. 14–39, for a discussion of four different but overlapping meanings of "dependency" over the course of U.S. history.

2 Eva Feder Kittay, "When Caring Is Just and Justice Is Caring," in *The Subject of Care*, p. 268.
3 Martha Albertson Fineman, *The Autonomy Myth: A Theory of Dependency* (New York: The New Press, 2004), p. 22.
4 Fineman, p. 18.
5 Fineman, p. 25.
6 Fineman, p. 3.
7 Fineman, p. 28.
8 Fineman, p. 33.
9 Ellen K. Feder and Eva Feder Kittay, "Introduction," in *The Subject of Care*, p. 2.
10 Feder and Kittay, p. 2.
11 Fineman, p. 31.
12 Kittay, p. 268.
13 Kittay, p. 268.
14 Fineman, p. 28.
15 Eva Feder Kittay, *Love's Labor: Essays on Women, Equality, and Dependency* (New York: Routledge, 1999), Ch. 1.
16 Fraser and Gordon, "Genealogy of Dependency"; and Iris Young, "Mothers, Citizenship, and Independence: A Critique of Pure Family Values," in *Intersecting Voices: Dilemmas of Gender, Political Philosophy, and Policy* (Princeton: Princeton University Press, 1997), pp. 114–33.
17 Onora O'Neill, "Agency and Autonomy," in Onora O'Neill, *Bounds of Justice* (Cambridge: Cambridge University Press, 2000), p. 29.
18 William Galston, *Liberal Purposes* (Cambridge: Cambridge University Press, 1991), p. 222.
19 Young, "Mothers, Citizenship, and Independence," p. 121.
20 Barbara Ann Kipfer, ed., *Roget's 21st Century Thesaurus* (New York: Dell, 1992), pp. 461–62.
21 O'Neill cites Theodor W. Adorno, *The Authoritarian Personality* (Harper & Bros., 1950); see Onora O'Neill, *Autonomy and Trust in Bioethics*, The Gifford Lectures (Cambridge: Cambridge University Press, 2002), p. 23.
22 O'Neill cites Stanley Milgram, *Obedience to Authority: An Experimental View* (Tavistock Publications, 1974); O'Neill, *Autonomy and Trust in Bioethics*, p. 24.
23 O'Neill cites Lawrence Kohlberg, *The Philosophy of Moral Development* (Harper & Row, 1981); O'Neill, *Autonomy and Trust in Bioethics*, p. 24.
24 O'Neill, "Agency and Autonomy," pp. 30–31.
25 O'Neill, "Agency and Autonomy," p. 31.
26 O'Neill, "Agency and Autonomy," p. 31.
27 O'Neill, "Agency and Autonomy," p. 39.
28 O'Neill, *Bioethics*, p. 25.
29 O'Neill, *Bioethics*, p. 24.
30 O'Neill, *Bioethics*, p. 25.
31 O'Neill, *Bioethics*, p. 25.
32 O'Neill, "Agency and Autonomy," p. 32.
33 O'Neill, "Agency and Autonomy," p. 41.
34 O'Neill, "Agency and Autonomy," p. 44.
35 O'Neill, "Agency and Autonomy," p. 45.
36 O'Neill, "Agency and Autonomy," p. 49.
37 O'Neill, "Agency and Autonomy," p. 49.
38 O'Neill, "Justice, Gender, and International Boundaries," in *Bounds of Justice*, p. 163.
39 O'Neill, "Justice, Gender, and International Boundaries," p. 164.

40 O'Neill, "Justice, Gender, and International Boundaries," p. 164. This comment obviously focuses on those who are not cognitively impaired.
41 O'Neill, "Justice, Gender, and International Boundaries," p. 165.
42 O'Neill, "Justice, Gender, and International Boundaries," p. 165.
43 O'Neill, "Justice, Gender, and International Boundaries," p. 166.
44 O'Neill, "Justice, Gender, and International Boundaries," p. 166.
45 O'Neill, "Justice, Gender, and International Boundaries," p. 161.
46 Kittay, "When Caring Is Just," p. 262.
47 Kittay, "When Caring Is Just," p. 270.
48 Kittay, "When Caring Is Just," p. 257.
49 Kittay, "When Caring Is Just," p. 258.
50 Kittay, *Love's Labor*, pp. 14–15.
51 O'Neill, "Justice, Gender, and International Boundaries," p. 143.
52 O'Neill, "Justice, Gender, and International Boundaries," p. 151.
53 O'Neill, "Justice, Gender, and International Boundaries," pp. 152, 155.
54 O'Neill, "Justice, Gender, and International Boundaries," p. 156.
55 O'Neill, "Justice, Gender, and International Boundaries," p. 162. Italics in original.
56 O'Neill, "Justice, Gender, and International Boundaries," p. 163.
57 O'Neill, "Justice, Gender, and International Boundaries," p. 163.
58 O'Neill, "Justice, Gender, and International Boundaries," p. 163.
59 O'Neill, "Justice, Gender, and International Boundaries," p. 165.
60 O'Neill, "Justice, Gender, and International Boundaries," p. 165.
61 O'Neill, "Justice, Gender, and International Boundaries," p. 166.
62 Martha C. Nussbaum, "The Future of Feminist Liberalism," in *The Subject of Care*, p. 196.
63 Nussbaum, "The Future of Feminist Liberalism," p. 196.
64 Nussbaum, "The Future of Feminist Liberalism," p. 194.
65 Nussbaum, "The Future of Feminist Liberalism," p. 195.
66 Nussbaum, "The Future of Feminist Liberalism," p. 196.
67 Nussbaum, "The Future of Feminist Liberalism," p. 196.
68 Kittay, *Love's Labor*, Ch. 6.
69 Kittay, *Love's Labor*, p. 102.
70 Kittay, *Love's Labor*, p. 50.
71 Kittay, *Love's Labor*, p. 50.
72 Asha Bhandary, "Dependency in Justice: Can Rawlsian Liberalism Accommodate Kittay's Dependency Critique," *Hypatia*, vol. 25, no. 1 (Winter 2010), p. 147.
73 Bhandary, "Dependency in Justice," pp. 152–53.
74 Bhandary, "Dependency in Justice," pp. 153–54.
75 O'Neill, "Justice, Gender, and International Boundaries," p. 156.
76 O'Neill, "Justice, Gender, and International Boundaries," p. 156.
77 O'Neill, "Justice, Gender, and International Boundaries," p. 157.
78 O'Neill, "Justice, Gender, and International Boundaries," p. 157.
79 O'Neill, "Justice, Gender, and International Boundaries," p. 158.
80 The question of how to determine legitimacy based on the actual consent or refusal of consent of the many members of an actual political system is a huge, thorny question that lies beyond the scope of the present discussion.

Part 3

SOME PRACTICAL QUESTIONS

8

AGENTS OF GLOBAL JUSTICE[1]

Simon Caney

> Any discussion of transnational economic justice needs to take account of the diversity of capacities and scope for action of these various agents and agencies, and of the possibility and limits of their transformation. Yet discussions of economic justice have often been conducted on the basis of very incomplete views of agency. Some writers assume that the only relevant agents are individuals; others that they also include 'sovereign' states
>
> *Bounds of Justice* (Cambridge: Cambridge University Press, 2000), pp. 117–18.

Onora O'Neill has for many years been one of the foremost philosophers writing on morality and international politics. In a series of articles and in three books – *Faces of Hunger*, *Towards Justice and Virtue*, and *Bounds of Justice* – she has developed and defended a distinctive perspective on global justice.[2] One of the longstanding themes of O'Neill's work has been an emphasis on the centrality of obligations. This emphasis on obligations is at the heart of many of her criticisms of those approaches which are grounded in a commitment to individual rights; and, it is also the central feature of her own positive account of global principles of justice and virtue.[3]

In this chapter I shall focus on one aspect of O'Neill's analysis of obligations, namely her treatment of what she terms 'the agents of justice'. Who are the bearers of the duty to bring about a just world? What kinds of duties are they under? As O'Neill has rightly noted, questions surrounding the agents of justice have not received the attention they merit. I shall analyze O'Neill's own answers to some of these questions, and, building on it, hope to provide a normative account of the rights, roles, and sources of legitimacy of the agents of justice. In doing so I will be at pains to bring out the ways in which different agents of justice differ from one another in a number of morally relevant respects.

The paper is organized as follows. I begin by outlining O'Neill's account of the agents of justice (Section I). The following three sections then examine O'Neill's concept of a 'primary' agent of justice, and explore who ought to perform this role (Sections II–IV). I then suggest a more comprehensive framework for thinking about agents of justice, before turning to explore the ways that primary agents of justice may differ from one another (Sections V–VI).

I: O'Neill on the agents of justice

§1. In *Towards Justice and Virtue* O'Neill examines the scope of justice, arguing that there are global principles of justice. Agents, she argues, are under duties of justice to those whom they presuppose in their actions. To explain: whenever we act we make assumptions about others – about what they have done, about how they are affected by our actions, about what they will do in the future, and so on. When I buy a shirt, I recognize that some have produced the raw materials, others have produced the shirt, still others have transported it, some store it in my home country, others sell it and so on. In each case, my actions are, thus, predicated on assumptions about a series of other people (e.g., cotton farmers and pickers; those working in a garment factory; those engaged in transportation), and in particular, about their agency. Given this, I cannot coherently deny that their condition is connected to me. My actions presuppose that they exist and that they are agents. As such I am under duties of justice to them. Furthermore, given the extent to which we are living in a globally integrated world, O'Neill observes that her approach would justify a cosmopolitan account of the scope of justice.[4]

At this point, however, it is important to note that there is a significant difference between the following two questions:

(i) Who is subject to duties of justice to whom? and
(ii) Who should be responsible for ensuring that persons comply with the duties of justice that apply to them?

The argument outlined in the previous paragraph presents O'Neill's answer to (i). But our answers to (i) do not necessarily provide an answer to question (ii). Consider an institution (state or firm or individual) who has committed a heinous injustice. In such a case we would say that it is 'subject to duties of justice' (a type (i) claim). It is obligated to make appropriate reparations and compensation. However, it does not follow from this that it should be what O'Neill terms an 'agent of justice' (a type (ii) claim). On my understanding, 'agents of justice', for O'Neill, refer to those actors whose job it is to build and maintain a fairer world.

§2. Who then are the agents of (global) justice? O'Neill addresses this most fully in two papers – the first simply entitled 'Agents of Justice' and the second 'Global Justice: Whose Obligations?'[5] In these two papers she provides a subtle and sophisticated analysis of who can be an agent of justice. O'Neill begins her analysis by distinguishing between primary and secondary agents of justice. She introduces the distinction as follows:

A plausible initial view of agents of justice might distinguish *primary agents of justice*, with capacities to determine how principles of justice are to be institutionalised within a certain domain, from other, *secondary agents of justice*. Primary agents of justice may construct other agents or agencies with specific competencies: they may assign powers to and build capacities in individual agents, or they may build institutions – agencies – with certain powers and capacities to act. Sometimes they may, so to speak, build from scratch; more often they reassign or adjust tasks and responsibilities among existing agents and agencies, and control and limit the ways in which they may act without incurring sanctions. Primary agents of justice typically have some means of coercion, by which they at least partially control the action of other agents and agencies, which can therefore at most be secondary agents of justice. Typically, secondary agents of justice are thought to contribute to justice mainly by meeting the demands of primary agents, most evidently by conforming to any legal requirements they establish.[6]

Drawing on this passage, we may say that primary agents of justice perform both a *legislative* and an *executive* role. They perform a *legislative* role because they decide who does what (they 'construct other agents' and 'assign powers', and they may assign or 'reassign ... tasks and responsibilities among existing agents'). They also appear to perform an *executive* role for they 'at least partially control the action of others'.

Secondary agents of justice do not perform either a legislative or an executive function: their role is to comply with the tasks set out for them by primary agents. (This raises the question of whether secondary agents of justice are permitted, or required, not to comply with primary agents of justice if and when the latter err. Primary agents of justice are not infallible. So should secondary agents of justice always simply follow orders? Or may they (should they) exercise their own judgement?)

This distinction is an extremely fruitful one for a number of reasons. It is important to note that the realization of a just world (or even simply a world that is more just than the current one) involves several quite different kinds of responsibility. To illustrate this consider global environmental degradation, and problems such as climate change, biodiversity loss, the over-use of renewable resources, and the depletion of nonrenewable natural resources. When faced with the problems these phenomena raise we want to know who may permissibly engage in what kinds of activities. How many environmental resources may particular agents use? How much greenhouse gas may given agents emit? How much of a rare natural resource can be used and how should that use be distributed? But, we need to know more than this. It is also vitally important that some create and maintain a political and legal architecture that ensures that others conform to these principles. In particular, what is crucial is that some take a lead – that they play a leadership role. One aspect of being a primary agent of justice, as O'Neill defines it, is to be a leader: such agents must, under certain circumstances, create new legal and political structures and help sustain them.[7]

The skills and resources needed to play a leadership role are, however, quite different to those that are needed to comply with other kinds of responsibility (for example, the responsibility to comply with a just distribution of burdens and to adhere to fair climate agreements).[8] Consider three features. First, those who take on the responsibility to play a leadership role may require a different set of dispositions and character traits. For example, they (more than other duty-bearers) will need to possess good negotiating skills and a capacity and willingness to persuade others (*psychological dispositions and skills*). Whereas other kinds of duty-bearer will simply need to stick to their obligations, primary agents of justice need to be able to bring people together and facilitate cooperation. In addition to this, leaders will also (again, by contrast with other duty-bearers) need to be able to offer 'carrots' and 'sticks' to motivate compliance (*political resources*). In addition to this, leaders will likely need to possess a certain kind of authority and command respect from others (*moral authority*). An agent that lacks this respect from others must, of course, honour the principles of justice that apply to it. But, if it is to perform a leadership role, an agent must normally have more than this: it must enjoy a certain standing and trust. Without these, it may in fact bring the system it is seeking to promote into disrepute. Leaders, thus, will generally need these psychological, political and social attributes. Other duty-bearers, by contrast, will not necessarily need to possess these particular attributes, but must simply possess those necessary for conscientious adherence to the principles. These properties of leadership will have important implications for the ascription of responsibilities for they entail that some agents (those who lack the relevant attributes) cannot be expected to play that kind of role, whereas they can, of course, be expected to play other kinds of roles (such as being a secondary agent of justice and complying with the principles of justice that apply to them).

O'Neill's distinction is thus important on both a *theoretical* level (it enables a deeper understanding of the different kinds of responsibility involved *and* who should perform which kind) and on a *practical* level (it makes clear that the realization of a fairer world depends vitally on primary agents of justice playing their role).

Several further points about O'Neill's distinction should, however, be noted. First, it is, I submit, better to distinguish between primary and secondary *roles* rather than between primary and secondary *agents*. One reason for doing so is that some agents may perform both primary and secondary roles. A political institution may, for example, act in a primary capacity in some domain (it may, for example, determine and enforce rules governing the extraction of minerals) but act in a secondary capacity in other domains (for example, complying with rules on gender equality or child labour). Thus, while it is useful to distinguish between primary and secondary ways in which agents can and do act, it would be misleading to think that there are always primary and secondary *agents of justice*.

Second, the distinction between primary and secondary roles/agents is not clear-cut and can become fuzzy in practice.[9] For example, there may be a lengthy chain of command. One institution (A1) may assign some responsibilities to another agent (A2), who may in turn assign them to several other bodies (A3 and A4) and may check whether they comply with their responsibilities.[10] A1 is a primary agent of justice and A3 and A4 are secondary agents but A2 has some features of both primary and secondary agents. It is, for example, complying with the roles given to it by A1, but at the same time it is assigning roles to A3 and A4 and exercising some control over them. We might, then, see the distinction between primary and secondary agents/roles as representing a continuum rather than a sharp categorical distinction.

Third, as O'Neill notes, the distinction between primary and secondary agents/roles of justice is also not exhaustive.[11] Consider the following situation: an NGO lobbies a government and provides it with appropriate legal advice.[12] Suppose then that, partly on this basis, the government passes a certain bill that imposes duties on certain secondary agents. Now the NGO in this case is not (simply) a secondary agent – for its action is not simply that of complying with demands assigned to it by primary agents. But it is not a primary agent of justice in O'Neill's terms because it is not coercively determining how duties are to be assigned. Nonetheless it is acting as an agent of justice and an important one at that.[13]

Fourth, we need to address the question: What properties must an actor have to be a primary agent of justice (or, as I prefer, for an agent to act in a primary role)? O'Neill does not provide a list of jointly necessary and sufficient conditions to be a primary agent of justice. She does, however, repeatedly stress that an actor can be a primary agent of justice only if they have the capability to do so.[14] This is certainly a plausible candidate for a necessary property, but is it sufficient? This is a question I will address subsequently.

§3. With all this in mind, let us now turn to O'Neill's analysis of the primary agents of justice. O'Neill's analysis has both a critical and a positive component. Let us consider the critique first.

O'Neill targets two positions for criticism. One simply holds that all actors are bound by some universal obligations of justice. O'Neill discusses both a utilitarian and a rights-based version of this approach and she rejects them both for the same reason. A system of universal obligations is insufficient. What is required is an account specifying exactly who should do what. Positing a theory that simply contains universal obligations does not help us to achieve the requisite level of specificity.[15]

Consider now O'Neill's second target. This second view treats states as the (sole) primary agents of justice. O'Neill writes that one can find this approach in the Universal Declaration of Human Rights.[16] It is also, she argues, the approach ultimately taken by Rawls in *The Law of Peoples*. Rawls himself says that the agents of justice are what he terms 'peoples' and he explicitly eschews 'states'.[17] However, as O'Neill points out, Rawlsian peoples are very state-like in their properties.[18] Rawls simply uses a rather restrictive notion of a state.

O'Neill makes three criticisms of the assumption that states should be the only primary agents of justice. First, some states are evidently unjust. They lack the appropriate motivation.[19] Second, some states are too weak to fulfil the task.[20] They are what Robert Jackson has termed 'quasi-states' – entities that have the formal status of states but which do not have the power to govern.[21] They lack the power to set in place and enforce principles of justice on secondary agents, and, as such, fail the 'capability' condition. Third, even states that are not 'quasi-states' have had their power weakened by the processes of globalization.[22] In short, to treat states as the only primary agents of justice has 'gigantic costs'.[23]

It is worth elaborating on O'Neill's first point about states. Her claim about governments with unjust motivations is not that that exempts them from having responsibilities. Consider an unjust government (G). O'Neill can (and, I assume, would) say that (i) G ought to be motivated to act in just ways; and (ii) as an agent with the capacity to implement principles of justice, G ought, in one sense, to act as a primary agent of justice. (That is, G ought to cease being corrupt and should use its power to further the cause of justice.) She can, moreover, add that (iii) primary agents of justice may, under certain conditions, legitimately make G comply with principles of justice. O'Neill can grant all of these. Her central point is simply that (iv) *given* the motivations of some governments we cannot rely on governments to be the sole primary agents of justice. It would be reckless and irresponsible – given the motivations of some states – simply to regard states as the primary agents of justice and look no further afield. A wholly statist account of the primary agents of justice is thus inappropriate.

§4. What then should be done? O'Neill's response is to suggest that we should broaden our horizons and consider other actors as primary agents of justice.[24] She singles out transnational companies (TNCs) and non-governmental organizations (NGOs) as potential primary agents of justice.[25] She writes that in normal circumstances one might expect them to act as secondary agents of justice. However, when the state is too weak or is improperly motivated then other actors may step in. Both kinds of organization can, O'Neill argues, play a constructive role. TNCs can, for example, refuse to comply with attempts at bribery. They can establish safe working conditions and respect labour rights. By doing so they can have knock-on effects and help cultivate a culture in which bribery is regarded as unacceptable and in which environmental and labour concerns are respected more than would otherwise be the case.[26] O'Neill further argues that NGOs may be less powerful than TNCs but maintains that they may still perform an important role. They may, to give one of her examples, play a major role in the provision of health care.[27] In addition to this, they can provide badly needed technical and legal advice for international negotiations on trade or climate change.

To all this, O'Neill then makes the interesting and important point that if one ascribes a greater role to TNCs and/or NGOs then this might affect the powers and exemptions one applies to them. One may, for example, exempt them from rules that one might otherwise require of them if they were merely secondary agents of justice. For example, O'Neill floats the idea that some NGOs and TNCs that act to help secure justice might be exempt from a general prohibition on hoarding food in the same way that we exempt states from this prohibition.[28] As well as enjoying exemptions, one might, O'Neill argues, grant them various powers that one would not grant to them if they worked in a well-functioning state.[29]

Having outlined O'Neill's treatment of the primary agents of justice I now wish to discuss three questions concerning who may be a primary agent of justice before proposing an expanded account of the normative issues surrounding agents of justice.

II: Question 1: International institutions as agents of justice?

As noted above, O'Neill discusses the possibility of Nongovernmental Organizations (NGOs) and transnational companies (TNCs) acting as agents of justice. However, she says relatively little about international institutions like the International Monetary Fund, the World Bank, the World Trade Organization and the European Union. In this section I discuss the potential of such institutions. It is, of course, important to note at the start that international institutions vary enormously. There are differences in the roles they perform (the World Trade Organization (WTO) regulates global trade, whereas the World Bank grants loans). They differ in the powers at their disposal and the extent of their power (compare the European Union (EU) with the International Labour Organization (ILO)). International institutions also vary in the number of states that belong to them, and the number of people they affect (the WTO has a membership of 153, whereas the EU currently has 27 member states).[30] International institutions are, then, highly heterogeneous and this should be reflected in any normative analysis of their potential as agents of justice who can act in a primary capacity.

Why should we think of some/all of them as primary agents of justice? I think they can perform a number of important roles. First, they can exercise power by imposing 'conditions' on other actors. Some examples illustrate the point. The European Union, for example, specifies various conditions for accession to the EU. Most notably in 1993 the European Council outlined what have come to be known as the 'Copenhagen criteria'. These state that:

> Membership requires that the candidate country has achieved stability of institutions guaranteeing democracy, the rule of law, human rights and respect for and protection of minorities, the existence of a functioning market economy as well as the capacity to cope with competitive pressure and market forces within the Union. Membership presupposes the candidate's ability to take on the obligations of membership including adherence to the aims of political, economic and monetary union.[31]

Since membership is very beneficial, this enables the EU to exercise considerable power over would-be members. This has been reflected in the recent history of EU expansion, specifically the accessions of 2004 and 2007, and is reflected in ongoing negotiations about future accession. The EU can also exert power in other ways, through its policies with non-member states. To give one example, following a report into human rights abuses in Sri Lanka (including detaining just under 300,000 Tamils with no freedom of movement) the EU withdrew beneficial trade regulations – what is known as 'GSP+' – from its trade relations with Sri Lanka.[32]

A second case where international institutions enjoy this kind of power is the Bretton Woods institutions (the International Monetary Fund and the World Bank). These have the capacity to impose conditions on the loans they make and, as such, they too can have the capacity to incentivize elites to comply with principles of justice. As Ngaire Woods points out, '[t]he powers of the IMF and World Bank to require governments to reform are significant. They do not lend large proportions of global development financing but the timing of their loans gives them considerable leverage because they lend at times when governments have few alternative sources of finance'.[33] The WTO is a further case in point: membership in the WTO is often seen as desirable. Given this, existing members of the WTO have the capacity to encourage greater compliance with just rules.

The first kind of mechanism refers to cases where one agent can get others to comply with certain kinds of behaviour. International institutions can, however, sometimes exercise power in a more far-reaching way, namely, through the production and diffusion of norms. As a substantial body of international relations analysis brings out, international institutions can socialize members. This can occur in relation to the first point: states may initially comply with norms because of the conditions imposed. However, after time they may come to internalize the norms. Elites from participant states may, for example, be socialized into the underlying norms.[34] Given these two reasons, I suggest that international institutions already have the capacity (certainly greater in some contexts than those of NGOs or TNCs) to act as primary agents of justice.

III: Question 2: transnational companies as primary agents of justice?

Some might make an argument that pushes in the opposite direction. Some, for example, may challenge O'Neill's claim that TNCs should, in some circumstances, take on some of the roles of a primary agent of justice. Whereas I have just argued that another kind of actor should be included, I suspect that many might argue that one of her proposed actors should be excluded. This kind of critic may argue along the following very familiar lines:

> Different institutions have different ultimate aims. The point of a firm, for example, is to make a profit (or increase its market share or maximize revenue – depending on one's theory of the firm). The central point is that managers of economic corporations are under role obligations to their shareholders. One might extend the same reasoning to some international organizations and argue that their responsibility is to serve the interests of the members of the organization and fulfill their mandate as specified in the original terms of agreement. Their job is not to serve global justice: as contractually created institutions it is to comply with the terms of the contract.

Note, moreover, that a sophisticated proponent of this view can also add:

> I accept that institutions like firms must not violate principles of justice. So I concur with the claim that all agents must observe negative duties of justice. TNCs should thus pursue the interests of their shareholders within these moral parameters. However, I fail to see why they have, in addition to this, a moral duty to take on any of the extra roles associated with being a primary agent of justice.[35]

O'Neill has commented on this line of reasoning and in particular on the claim that economic enterprises may only pursue profit. In response she argues that it is 'sociologically simplistic' to assume that TNCs are motivated solely by the pursuit of profit. Businessmen and women may have other objectives, and it is not more plausible to assume that they are concerned only with profit than it is to assume that states are concerned only with their power.[36] Furthermore, even a casual knowledge of the business world reveals that there have been some philanthropically minded owners and managers of companies.

However, to argue that TNCs will sometimes be concerned with moral principles does not, of course, provide any support for the claim that they have a duty to do so. The question remains: Why do they have a *duty* to take on some of the roles of primary agents of justice? One initial thought might be: 'In *some* circumstances, with power comes responsibility'. I think that this is along the right lines but it invites the question: 'In what circumstances?' For example, just because a private entrepreneur like Bill Gates has the capacity to promote justice in a country does not necessarily entail that it is his job. We might naturally think, for example, that the responsibility falls to others – most notably their elected government (assuming that one exists). In many circumstances, this seems right. To accommodate this, then, we might reformulate the initial suggestion so that it reads:

> When an agent (such as a government) is either unable or unwilling to protect the entitlements of those to whom it has a responsibility to protect (their citizens and the citizens of other states), then other agents who have the capacity to protect those entitlements have a *pro tanto* reason to do so.

This, I think, is O'Neill's position in 'Global Justice: Whose Obligations?'[37] This second version reflects the principle that agents may have a responsibility in virtue of their capacity to further the cause of justice, but it also recognizes that it is a *remedial* responsibility, one that comes into play when others have failed to do their bit.[38] This formulation is still, of course, incomplete because it leaves open just how much they should do. The answer to this must depend, in part, on (i) what their capacity is and how much good they could do; but also (ii) what costs would be incurred and whether the benefits realized justify these costs; and (iii) whether the agents have other obligations to others that might be more morally weighty. On this proposal, then, TNCs *can* serve as primary agents when others have failed to perform their role and when they can play a valuable role without imposing unfair costs on themselves or others.

A similar kind of reasoning applies to international institutions. Consider, for example, the WTO. It is sometimes proposed that the WTO should construct trade laws so as to protect the environment or to help realize labour rights. Some strongly resist such linkages, arguing that the point of the WTO is simply to further trade. Arthur Dunkel, Peter Sutherland and Renato Ruggiero give a crisp formulation of this view in their 'Joint

Statement on the Multilateral Trading System'. They write there that '[t]he WTO cannot be used as a Christmas tree on which to hang any and every good cause that might be secured by exercising trade power.[39] They thus reject the claim that the WTO should seek to address global poverty or should combat exploitative labour laws. The problem with this view, however, is that the WTO is *not* simply an institution that governs trade, for it has unavoidable impacts on other domains of human life, such as health, the environment, workplace conditions, and poverty. These are inextricably linked with trade relations. As such, it is not plausible to say that the WTO has no responsibilities with respect to labour rights or poverty. Whatever it does, it will exert a major and unavoidable impact on these and, as such, it has some responsibility to construct trade relations that acknowledge these implications.

IV: Question 3: 'the unjustly treated' as primary agents of justice?

Let us turn now to consider who else might act as an agent of justice. Much, if not all, of the literature on global justice looks at the distribution of wealth, resources and environmental burdens from the perspective of the advantaged. It asks: What principles should 'we' (members of affluent societies) adopt and comply with? However, it is also important to consider what actions those who suffer from injustice can undertake to prevent that injustice being inflicted on them. My claim here, then, is simply that the victims of injustice may also act as agents of justice. If they are subject to unjust laws or unjust treatment by others they are entitled to take steps to rectify that situation.

Someone might dispute this on the grounds that those who suffer injustice are always helpless and powerless. This seems to me not borne out by the facts. Their actions are, of course, often greatly restricted by poverty and coercion, but the history of social and political transformation (such as national revolutions, or decolonization, or the collapse of the Soviet bloc, or resisting occupation and indeed recent events in the Middle East) makes clear that those who suffer from injustice possess some agency.

Of course, my claim that those suffering from injustice may act as agents of justice leaves a great deal unsaid. Space precludes the much fuller analysis that would need to be undertaken. Here I shall just indicate four key issues that would need to be addressed.

1. First, we would need to provide an account of why breaking the rules can be justified. What justifies such noncompliance? One can distinguish between, at least, two different grounds one might have for engaging in some illegal activity – what I shall call 'Self-preservation' and 'Reform'. Self-preservation refers to a case where someone faces such serious injustice

that his or her capacity for a minimally acceptable human life is jeopardized. According to Self-preservation, persons or groups of persons are entitled to take steps, including breaking the law, in order to acquire resources needed for themselves or others to attain a minimally acceptable human life. This is, of course, a claim that has been advanced by earlier social contract thinkers, like Hobbes and Locke.[40] Under the heading of Self-preservation one might, then, justify the actions of agents who steal necessary medicines that have been overpriced; or those who violate border controls to smuggle themselves into another country; or those who take vital foodstuffs or access to water. Self-preservation gives agents one reason to break laws. It is not, however, the only reason, and it cannot be a long run solution. According to what I am terming 'Reform', victims of injustice (or potential victims of injustice) are entitled to take steps, including breaking the law, to protest against the injustice of the order they are living under and to campaign for a fairer set of political arrangements.

2. Moral Limits. To say that victims of injustice have rights to break laws in order to preserve themselves and/or to reform the unjust institutions governing their lives is not, of course, to say that there are no moral restraints on what they can do in their pursuit of Self-preservation or Reform. A second key question, then, would be what moral limits there are on what those suffering from injustice can do to bring about a fairer world. Hobbes, notoriously, writes in *Leviathan* that a person is entitled to do 'any thing, which in his own Judgement, and Reason, hee shall conceive to be the aptest means thereunto [of securing his self-preservation]'.[41] Such a drastic view is unsustainable. Most people would accept that there are moral constraints on what people may do in the name of Self-preservation and Reform. What is required, then, is an account of what these moral limits are.

3. Against Whom? A third important issue concerns who is a legitimate object of the efforts by those suffering from injustice to secure their entitlements. Against whom may victims of injustice direct their action? For example, consider those suffering from terrible destitution and malnutrition. May they simply take from those who have more than enough? Who should bear the costs of their actions?

4. When? Fourth, and finally, an adequate account of justified resistance must address the question: When may victims of injustice pursue this path as opposed to others?

Thus, much more needs to be said. The main point I wish to convey, however, is simply this: if we are to take seriously the idea (affirmed by O'Neill) that there are some universal principles of justice then when others (including states, international organizations, TNCs and NGOs) fail to prevent injustice (or even act to foster injustice) we need to take seriously the idea that those who bear the brunt of injustice are entitled to act to secure what is rightfully theirs.

V: Towards an analysis of the normative character of agents of justice

The previous three sections have all focused on the issues surrounding O'Neill's account of who should be a primary agent of justice. A comprehensive normative analysis of the primary and secondary agents of justice needs, however, to say more than this. There are, I suggest, at least five key questions, namely:

Q1: Who are the primary and secondary agents of justice, and why? [the *membership*]
Q2: What kinds of responsibility do they have? [the *types* of duties]
Q3: What sorts of powers may they use? [the *powers* at their disposal]
Q4: What sort of moral norms should govern their decisions and policies? [their *binding norms*]
Q5: How much should they do? [the *extent* or *magnitude* of their duties].[42]

Let me consider each of these in turn. Q1 is hopefully straightforward and we have already examined it at some length. Consider now Q2. Here we may note two kinds of distinction. The first is O'Neill's distinction between primary and secondary agents of justice. It is also important, however, to draw attention to a second distinction: that is, we may distinguish between what I shall term *first-order duty-bearers*, on the one hand, and *second-order* (and *third-order, fourth-order*, and so on) duty-bearers, on the other. A first-order duty-bearer is a duty-bearer who should in the first instance perform the duty. First-order duty-bearers, however, sometimes do not do what they are supposed to do. They may be incompetent, say, or negligent. Where there has been a failure to act by a first-order duty-bearer, there needs to be a back-up to step into their place and fulfill the role that the original duty-bearer should have performed. This process can then be iterated if the second-order duty-bearer fails to do their job, and so on.[43] This second distinction should not be confused with the first. The first refers to a distinction between different ways in which agents can act to realize principles of justice. The second refers to what should be done in non-ideal circumstances and thus to who is first in turn to be a (primary or secondary) agent, who is second, third and so on. (I have already implicitly invoked this second distinction between discussing the responsibilities of TNCs above.)

Consider now Q3. Different agents of justice may have different powers, including passing binding laws and regulations, vetoing laws and regulations, imposing sanctions, levying taxes, being able to require information, compelling disclosure of key facts, summoning officials and personnel, initiating a review process, triggering a referendum, and so on. Furthermore, as O'Neill points out, if some primary agents of justice fail to perform their allotted task we may then grant further powers to some other agent that we would not otherwise do. Or we may exempt them from restrictions that they would otherwise be bound by.[44]

Turn now to Q4. What I mean by 'binding norms' are those norms that should govern the way that an agent of justice discharges its role. Many, for example, think that political institutions – states, international institutions – should observe the norm of transparency. This is, of course, a popular view from Bentham and Kant to many contemporary theorists. As we shall see later, one might also propose other binding norms.

This leaves Q5. I take this to be fairly self-explanatory. Agents may differ in just how much they are required to do. Our analysis of Q1–Q5 thus provides our analysis of agents of justice.

O'Neill has provided a valuable framework. My suggestion, here, is that we need to build on it further and address additional issues surrounding the agents of justice. In what follows, I want to focus on Q4: What are the norms that should govern their conduct and the discharge of their duties? It often appears to be assumed that agents of justice are subject to the same norms. A more plausible view, I think, is a 'pluralist' view that holds that different agents of justice are subject to different norms, have different sources of political legitimacy, and are subject to different kinds of competing responsibility.[45] We can see this by examining several considerations.

§1. The first holds that:

> Thesis I: The Differential Responsibilities Thesis: The nature, and extent, of an institution's obligations depends, in part, on that institution's underlying purposes.

Consider a firm. O'Neill argues (and I have agreed above) that firms can, in some circumstances, take on some of the roles of primary agents of justice. Many invoke the point that firms have fiduciary obligations to shareholders and others. O'Neill, I think, is right to argue that this does not entail that they do not have other responsibilities – including responsibilities to act as primary agents of justice.[46] However, this does not mean that those fiduciary obligations have no weight. That would be a non sequitur. Firms have responsibilities to their shareholders and their employees. Given this, it seems reasonable to say that they should always comply with duties of justice *and*, moreover, that they may sometimes be required to act as primary agents of justice *but* that when discharging the latter they must also take into account other responsibilities (for example to their employees). It might often be that those responsibilities to employees are trumped by their responsibility to take on the role of a primary agent of justice; my point is only the modest one that they are nonetheless subject to other obligations too and this might make a moral difference.

§2. Consider now a second way in which agents of justice differ from one another. Agents of (global) justice differ not only in the purposes that they pursue but also the means that they employ. Whereas some (such as NGOs or individuals) do not employ coercion over others, others (such as states and also, to a lesser extent, international institutions) do. International institutions, as we have just seen, exercise some coercion over their members. States may coerce two different bodies of people. Consider a state that levies taxes in order to fund a humanitarian intervention. It coerces both its own citizens and also members of other states.

What difference does the use of coercion make? In what follows, I shall argue that agents of justice that use coercive methods are subject to importantly different binding norms than other agents of justice. To make my case I shall first present a general thesis about legitimacy. This articulates the core notion that I wish to defend. I shall then try to illustrate this more fully by presenting more specific accounts of what it might entail for different actors. The general thesis about legitimacy that I wish to advance can be stated as follows:

> Thesis II: The Legitimacy Thesis (general version): Agents of justice that employ the use of coercion in order to realize a fairer world must meet certain demanding standards of *political legitimacy* – standards that we do not apply to actors that do not employ coercion.

The underlying idea is that where agents exercise coercion over others then there needs to be some account of what entitles them to exercise this coercion. What legitimizes their conduct? In the case of actors who do not use coercion but seek only to persuade others, there is no similar requirement. So long as they do not violate other people's rights they are free to act as they please and need not provide some account of their political legitimacy. If this is right, then private individuals and NGOs are subject to different binding norms than coercive bodies like states or the EU or the World Bank.[47]

Thesis II is, however, deliberately phrased in a rather vague and unspecific way. I do so to show that even people who subscribe to very different accounts of political legitimacy can accept the core idea of the position that I am defending. Thus, even those who reject the more specific accounts of political legitimacy that I outline below may accept the general idea that different agents of justice must satisfy different standards of political legitimacy. With this in mind we may now examine more specific accounts of the demands of political legitimacy as it applies to the agents of global justice.

One model starts by considering liberal discussions of political legitimacy in pluralistic societies. John Rawls has, for example, famously argued that states should eschew comprehensive doctrines when constructing constitutional essentials and matters of basic justice. He holds that it would be unreasonable to employ coercion to impose one's comprehensive doctrines on other persons. Citizens may seek to persuade others of their own comprehensive doctrine and use their private funds to promote it, but they may not use coercion to promote that ideal.[48] Now drawing on such reasoning, one might propose:

> Interpretation 1 of the Legitimacy Thesis: Agents of justice that employ the use of coercion in order to realize a fairer world must eschew considerations on which there is reasonable disagreement. Agents of justice must be neutral between competing controversial ideals [the neutralist version].[49]

What might neutrality entail here? First, as we have just seen there is the familiar liberal idea of (a) neutrality towards conceptions of the good. Second, there is (b) neutrality towards principles of justice (egalitarian, libertarian, prioritarian, sufficientarian, and so on). Third, and distinctly, there is (c) neutrality towards political systems (capitalism, socialism, social democracy). The World Bank, for example, is bound by this kind of constraint. Article 4 section 10 of the Articles of Agreement of the International Bank for Reconstruction and Development (IBRD) states that:

> The Bank and its officers shall not interfere in the political affairs of any member; nor shall they be influenced in their decisions by the political character of the member or members concerned. Only economic considerations shall be relevant to their decisions, and these considerations shall be weighed impartially in order to achieve the purposes stated in Article I.[50]

Consider now a second model. This holds that:

> Interpretation 2 of the Legitimacy Thesis: Agents of justice that employ the use of coercion in order to realize a fairer world must, (a) do so on the basis of political procedures which treat legitimate parties as free and equal, and they should also (b) adopt certain norms of respect, civility and a willingness to seek agreement. Agents of justice need not be neutral between competing controversial ideals, but any decisions must be made in a maximally fair decision-making process [the proceduralist version].[51]

This is a second way of using coercion whilst being respectful of the existence of reasonable disagreement about justice and the good life.

I believe that the second version is more plausible, but, as stated above, I do not have space to argue for that here. However, the key point I wish to drive home is this: that whichever conception one adopts, coercive primary agents of justice are constrained in ways that do not apply to non-coercive primary agents. Not all primary agents of justice are therefore the same. The situation of states and international institutions can be contrasted with NGOs, private individuals and firms. None of the last three actors is normally entitled to use coercion. (We might allow some exceptions in extreme situations. Individuals, for example, may perform a citizen's arrest. But the normal expectation would be that these should not employ coercion in the pursuit of global justice.) As such, they are not bound by the strictures that bind coercive actors. They may then, for example, draw on comprehensive doctrines that some reasonable people reject. To give some examples: on the analysis I have given here NGOs may draw on religious ideas to ground and motivate their views on debt cancellation (as was the case with Jubilee 2000). There is nothing remiss about organizations such as CAFOD or Christian Aid or some other NGOs being motivated by religious considerations if by doing so they serve ideals of global justice. Their position can, however, be contrasted with international organizations which must *either* adopt a stance of neutrality *or* implement a system of legitimate political procedures (or both). And states and NGOs can be contrasted with states. For states must legitimize themselves both to their own citizens[52] as well as to others they coerce.

§3. Some further points are in order. First, my claim above is that coercive actors are under a particular duty to eschew controversial ideals (version 1) or adopt fair political procedures (version 2). In making this claim I do not deny that coercive and non-coercive agents might also, for example, have other good reasons to adopt a broadly neutral approach. For example, one might adopt a neutral approach to controversial ideals for purely pragmatic reasons. Many NGOs, for example, adopt principles of neutrality and impartiality. One might justify this simply on the consequentialist grounds that employing controversial considerations would alienate others and, as such, undermine the likelihood of their success.

Second, it is worth considering the claim, advanced by some, that NGOs also need to be legitimized. It is sometimes said in criticism of some NGOs that they are not really legitimate. Does this undermine my claim about the link between coercion and legitimacy? I do not think so. I think that there are two explanations of this phenomenon – both of which are compatible with Thesis II. First, many of these NGOs claim to represent people from developing countries and, as such, it is appropriate to ask how 'representative' they are. Can they plausibly claim to be acting as voices for the marginalized and oppressed of the world if they are in fact drawn entirely from wealthy first world backgrounds? Second, one might argue, on purely instrumental grounds, that unless NGOs are comprised of members of developing countries they are less likely successfully to promote the interests of those in the developing country. For these two reasons, NGOs might also be subject to criticism if they are not inclusive and representative. This, though, is quite compatible with my argument above. My claim above is not that non-coercive actors are not subject to some binding norms. It is rather, more positively, that coercive actors are bound to some particular binding norms.

Third, it is important to stress that I am not claiming that all agents of justice that employ coercion are subject to exactly the same binding norms. States may be subject to different legitimation standards to the IMF, and both of those may be subject to different norms when compared to the EU.

§4. Thus far I have adduced two reasons for thinking that different agents of justice are subject to different norms and requirements. To further support this case, I now introduce a third claim, namely:

> Thesis III: The International Law Thesis: the principles of global justice that should inform international law may legitimately differ from those that inform the actions of those operating within the constraints set by international law.[53]

With some notable exceptions, current analyses of global justice do not discuss international law and therefore do not discuss the principles that should inform international law as opposed to those that inform actors like NGOs or members of civil society.[54] Three reasons support Thesis III.

R1: Consequences and the General Nature of Law. The first arises because law of any kind involves institutionalizing general rules. These rules will have incentive effects and because law is necessarily couched in general terms it is not always possible to design them only to allow the particular phenomena one wants to allow. This is familiar from municipal law. To give a well-known example, consider euthanasia. One might think both (a) that in a given case it is morally appropriate for one person to assist someone else to commit suicide, but also (b) the law should not allow people to assist others to commit suicide. I am not saying that either (a) or (b) is correct. My point here is simply that one can consistently affirm both – because one may reasonably think that one cannot design laws in such a way as to allow it only in those cases where one thinks it permissible.[55] Laws are blunt instruments and even laws created with the best of intentions can be abused by unjust opportunists. Thus, the norms that go into international law may legitimately differ from those that might morally bind individual agents.

To illustrate the kind of reasoning I have in mind, and to see the implications this might have for international law and morality, consider two examples. One obvious example is humanitarian intervention. It would be quite coherent to argue that a particular state is morally justified in intervening in a given case and yet also hold that international law should generally prohibit intervention (fearing that more permissive formulations would be abused by states with imperial ambitions).[56] A second example comes from the work of Jeff McMahan. McMahan argues that the assumption that combatants have moral equality is unwarranted. At the same time, he maintains – on instrumental grounds – that international law should not seek to mirror the moral inequality of combatants.[57]

This first rationale arises from the blunt and uncontrollable effects of legalizing/criminalizing activity. If law were not so blunt and one could design it in such a way as to only allow the cases one thinks should be allowed then this discrepancy would not arise. However, given normal assumptions about human behaviour and the history of legal regulation Thesis II rests on solid ground.[58]

R2. Impartiality and Discretion. A second consideration in support of Thesis III concerns not the bluntness of the law but its special function. It is universally accepted that law – whether municipal or international – should be impartial. International law must show no favourites, and should not act on discretionary grounds. Compare this, however, with agents like states or NGOs. Here it is reasonable to suggest that they may exercise a (qualified) discretion. Suppose, for example, that one adheres (as I think one should) to some robust principles of global justice and that one thinks that people's *entitlements* should not be determined by national boundaries. It is quite compatible with this to hold that some agents may seek to concentrate on upholding the cosmopolitan rights of some persons rather than others. Agents may, thus, show discretion in a way that the institutions of international law may not. To give an example: a cosmopolitan may hold that all persons have a right to a fair trial. However, they may also hold that a state may legitimately focus on ensuring that its own citizens abroad have their right to a fair trial honoured. In this way we combine a cosmopolitan conception of entitlements with an acceptance of special responsibilities.[59] Private actors may thus act with discretion in ways that the underlying legal structure may not.

R3. Effectiveness and the Credibility of International Law. A third reason for affirming Thesis III runs as follows: there are some principles which, though they may be morally compelling, would be routinely flouted if they were embodied in international law. Furthermore, the effect of introducing them into international law would be not simply that the contentious new law would not be successfully implemented but that international law as a whole would lose credibility and therefore that the other values served by the law would be undermined. Attempting to incorporate such contentious ideals could thus be counter-productive. At the same time it may be perfectly sensible for NGOs, social movements, states, and private individuals to campaign vigorously in support of these currently contentious ideals. That an international law affirming a controversial ideal (e.g. that there is a human right to democracy) is unenforceable does not mean *either* that other agents that have coercive powers at their disposal (e.g. the EU) would be similarly incapable of advancing this ideal *or* that other agents that do not seek to enforce their ideals (e.g. NGOs or faith communities) should abstain from attempting to canvass these ideals.

For all these reasons, then, we should accept Thesis III. One might ask at this point what this has to do with agents of global justice. The answer is that it bears on the way that states perform their role as primary agents of justice when they shape the content of international law. When they are acting in this legislative capacity, states should take on board the three points made above. However, other actors – those working within the framework of international law – are not thus confined. This is, of course, not to say that they have carte blanche; they too may be primary agents of justice. It is just that when discharging their responsibilities they operate with a different set of normative principles than do those who shape the legal framework.

It is time to conclude this section. I have argued for three separate theses. The underlying argument is that when analyzing the agents of justice, it is crucial to be sensitive to the ways in which they differ from one another. They differ in terms of their self-given purposes and hence in terms of their responsibilities; they differ in the standards of legitimation they must meet and to whom they owe justification; and they differ depending on whether they help form international law or whether they act solely within its confines.

VI: Concluding remarks

O'Neill has written that 'much of the cosmopolitan rhetoric of contemporary discussions of justice says little about the agents and agencies on which the burdens of justice are to fall.'[60] I agree entirely that too little has been said – and not only by cosmopolitans – on these critical issues. O'Neill has provided a valuable framework within which one can address these questions. In this paper I have sought to build on her pioneering work in this domain and to examine the normative foundations underlying her concept of a primary agent of justice. Drawing on this I have argued that O'Neill's account of the primary agents of justice should also include international institutions, and, moreover, that we should not overlook the role that those who bear the brunt of injustice can play as agents of justice. Finally, I have suggested that we should not focus just on who is a primary agent of justice; we should also note the morally relevant differences between different agents of justice. What we should *not* do – as O'Neill has forcefully brought out – is continue to evade the question about who should be a primary agent of justice or to put our faith simply in states.

Notes

1 I wrote this paper while holding an ESRC Climate Change Leadership Fellowship. I am grateful to the ESRC for its support. The paper was presented at

the conference 'Ethics and Politics Beyond Borders: The Work of Onora O'Neill' held at the British Academy on 24–26 September 2009. I am grateful to members of the audience for their questions. I am also very grateful to O'Neill, both for the inspiration provided by her work and for her support and encouragement.
2 See Onora O'Neill, *Faces of Hunger: An Essay on Poverty, Justice and Development* (London: Allen and Unwin, 1986); *Towards Justice and Virtue: A Constructive Account of Practical Reasoning* (Cambridge: Cambridge University Press, 1996); and *Bounds of Justice* (Cambridge: Cambridge University Press, 2000). See also the following important papers: O'Neill, 'Bounded and Cosmopolitan Justice', *Review of International Studies* vol. 26 no. 5 (2000), pp. 45–60; 'Agents of Justice', *Metaphilosophy*, vol. 32 nos. 1/2 (2001), pp. 180–95; 'Global Justice: Whose Obligations?' in *The Ethics of Assistance: Morality and the Distant Needy* (Cambridge: Cambridge University Press, 2004) edited by Deen K. Chatterjee, pp. 242–59; and 'The Dark Side of Human Rights', *International Affairs* vol. 81 no. 2 (2005), pp. 427–39.
3 See, for example, *Faces of Hunger*, chapter 6 and *Towards Justice and Virtue*, pp. 129–36.
4 *Towards Justice and Virtue*, pp. 100–121, especially pp. 113–21.
5 See 'Agents of Justice', and 'Global Justice: Whose Obligations?' in *Bounds of Justice*.
6 'Agents of Justice', p. 181.
7 'Agents of Justice', p. 181.
8 I am indebted to Robyn Eckersley and Henry Shue for helpful discussions of leadership and to Eckersley for an illuminating paper ('Moving Forward in the Climate Negotiations: Multilateralism or Minilateralism?') presented at a conference on 'Justice and Climate Change' (Oxford, 2011).
9 O'Neill herself writes that the distinction between primary and secondary agents of justice can become less clear and straightforward when states are weak, 'Agents of Justice', p. 194.
10 A state (A1) may, for example, assign some responsibilities to a hospital (A2) and the hospital may outsource some of these responsibilities to private bodies (A3) (e.g. catering may be delegated to a private company).
11 As O'Neill writes: '[a]lthough INGOs cannot themselves become primary agents of justice, they can contribute to justice in specific ways in specific domains', 'Agents of Justice', pp. 191–92. The example that follows in the text illustrates exactly this point.
12 This example is based on an account of Oxfam's policies in Malawi. Duncan Green, Head of Research for Oxfam GB, claims that Oxfam played a critical role in getting the Prevention of Domestic Violence Bill passed in Malawi in April 2006. Among other things, Oxfam publicized the issue, lobbied key actors and helped mobilize support. See http://www.oxfamblogs.org/fp2p/?p=313.
13 See 'Global Justice: Whose Obligations?', p. 254.
14 'Agents of Justice', pp. 189–90 and 'Global Justice: Whose Obligations?', pp. 250–51.
15 'Global Justice: Whose Obligations?', pp. 244–45.
16 'Agents of Justice', p. 183.
17 See John Rawls, *The Law of Peoples with 'The Idea of Public Reason Revisited'* (Cambridge, MA: Harvard University Press, 1999), pp. 23–30.
18 For O'Neill's discussion of Rawlsian 'peoples' and how state-like they are see 'Agents of Justice', pp. 186–88 and 'Bounded and Cosmopolitan Justice', pp. 50–51.
19 'Agents of Justice', p. 182 and 'Global Justice: Whose Obligations?', p. 246.
20 See 'Agents of Justice', p. 182 and 'Global Justice: Whose Obligations?', pp. 246–47.

21 Robert Jackson, *Quasi-States: Sovereignty, International Relations, and the Third World* (Cambridge: Cambridge University Press, 1990). O'Neill cites Jackson's book in 'Agents of Justice', p. 182 (fn3).
22 See 'Global Justice: Whose Obligations?', p. 247.
23 'Global Justice: Whose Obligations?', p. 244. For more on the deficiencies of states, see *Bounds of Justice*, pp. 180–81.
24 See O'Neill, 'Bounded and Cosmopolitan Justice', p. 60.
25 'Agents of Justice', pp. 191–94 and 'Global Justice: Whose Obligations?', pp. 252–56.
26 'Agents of Justice', pp. 192–94 and 'Global Justice: Whose Obligations?', pp. 253ff.
27 'Global Justice: Whose Obligations?', pp. 254–55.
28 'Global Justice: Whose Obligations?', p. 255.
29 'Global Justice: Whose Obligations?', p. 255.
30 For this information see http://www.wto.org/english/thewto_e/whatis_e/tif_e/org6_e.htm and http://ec.europa.eu/enlargement/the-policy/from-6-to-27-members/index_en.htm.
31 See Para 7.A iii) of the European Council's meeting in Copenhagen. This is available at: http://europa.eu/rapid/pressReleasesAction.do?reference=DOC/93/3& format=HTML& aged=1& language=EN& guiLanguage=en.
32 For the decision of the Council of the European Union implementing Regulation (EU) No 143/2010 of the Council of 15 February 2010 see: http://eur-lex.europa.eu/LexUriServ/LexUriServ.do?uri=OJ:L:2010:045:0001:0002:EN:PDF. For background information see 'EU temporarily withdraws GSP+ trade benefits from Sri Lanka' (at http://trade.ec.europa.eu/doclib/press/index.cfm?id=515) and Randeep Ramesh 'Sri Lanka's Top Envoy hits out at EU as Cut in £1bn Trade Concession Looms', *The Guardian*, 10 September 2009 (available at http://www.guardian.co.uk/world/2009/sep/10/sri-lanka-eu-trade-cut).
33 Ngaire Woods, *The Globalizers: The IMF, the World Bank, and their Borrowers* (Ithaca and London: Cornell University Press, 2006), p. 71.
34 For discussion of the process of socialization see G. John Ikenberry and Charles A. Kupchan, 'Socialization and Hegemonic Power', *International Organization* vol. 44 no. 3 (1990), pp. 283–315; Jeffrey T. Checkel, 'International Institutions and Socialization in Europe: Introduction and Framework', *International Organization* vol. 59 no. 4 (2005) pp. 801–26.
35 The point that all must honour negative duties of justice (and do so without discrimination on grounds of nationality or citizenship) is of course a key theme of the work of Thomas Pogge (cf. for example, Thomas Pogge, *World Poverty and Human Rights: Cosmopolitan Responsibilities and Reforms* (Cambridge: Polity, 2008) second edition).
36 'Agents of Justice', p. 192.
37 'Global Justice: Whose Obligations?', especially pp. 252–55 and 258.
38 For a discussion of remedial responsibilities, including a principle similar (but not identical) to that in the text, see David Miller, *National Responsibility and Global Justice* (Oxford: Oxford University Press, 2007), chapter 4, especially pp. 103–4.
39 See http://www.wto.org/English/news_e/news01_e/jointstatdavos_jan01_e.htm.
40 Thomas Hobbes, *Leviathan* (London and Melbourne: Dent, 1983) with an introduction by K. R. Minogue, chapter XIV, p. 66 and John Locke, *Two Treatises of Government* (London and Melbourne: Dent, 1986) with an introduction by W. S. Carpenter, second treatise, chapter 5 'Of Property', section 25, p. 129.
41 Hobbes, *Leviathan*, chapter XIV, p. 66.
42 I do not think that this list is complete. Another key question would be: What systems of accountability should regulate the behaviour of primary agents of

justice? Primary agents of justice might be required to put in place charters and other regulatory frameworks which bind them and monitor the extent to which they promote justice rather than injustice.

43 See Henry Shue's discussion of 'default duties' in *Basic Rights: Subsistence, Affluence, and U.S. Foreign Policy* (Princeton: Princeton University Press, 1996) second edition with a new afterword, pp. 171–73 and 178.
44 O'Neill, 'Global Justice: Whose Obligations?', p. 255.
45 For an earlier statement see Simon Caney, 'Cosmopolitan Justice and Institutional Design: An Egalitarian Liberal Conception of Global Governance', *Social Theory and Practice*, vol. 32 no. 4 (2006), pp. 753–54 and 'The Responsibilities and Legitimacy of Economic International Institutions' in *Justice, Legitimacy and Public International Law* (Cambridge: Cambridge University Press, 2009), edited by Lukas Meyer, pp. 97–98.
46 'Agents of Justice', p. 192.
47 Note that this analysis of the normative significance of coercion should be distinguished from the kinds of claims recently advanced by Michael Blake and Thomas Nagel. Blake and Nagel both maintain (albeit in different ways) that there is a link between coercion and *distributive justice*. My proposal here is quite different to this: the Legitimacy Thesis holds that there is a link between coercion and *political legitimacy*. See Michael Blake, 'Distributive Justice, State Coercion, and Autonomy', *Philosophy and Public Affairs*, vol. 30 no. 3 (2001), pp. 257–96 and Thomas Nagel, 'The Problem of Global Justice', *Philosophy and Public Affairs*, vol. 33 no. 2 (2005), pp. 113–47.
48 John Rawls, *Political Liberalism* (New York: Columbia University Press, 1993).
49 One version of this is, of course, Rawls's, *The Law of Peoples*. I agree with Leif Wenar that the key idea motivating *The Law of Peoples* is a commitment to legitimacy (and the ideas associated with *Political Liberalism*). See Leif Wenar, 'Why Rawls is Not a Cosmopolitan Egalitarian' in *Rawls's Law of Peoples: A Realistic Utopia?* (Oxford: Blackwell, 2006) edited by Rex Martin and David A. Reidy, pp. 95–113.
50 See the IBRD's Articles of Agreement at: http://web.worldbank.org/WBSITE/EXTERNAL/EXTABOUTUS/0,contentMDK:20049603~pagePK:43912~piPK:36602,00.html#I11.
51 This is, for example, how some think that the state should respond to reasonable disagreement within the state. See, for example, Kurt Baier, 'Justice and the Aims of Political Philosophy', *Ethics*, vol. 99 no. 4 (1989), especially pp. 775–76; Amy Gutmann and Dennis Thompson, 'Moral Conflict and Political Consensus', *Ethics*, vol. 101 no. 1 (1990), pp. 64–88; and Simon Caney, 'Anti-Perfectionism and Rawlsian Liberalism', *Political Studies* vol. 43 no. 2 (1995), pp. 248–64, especially pp. 255–56.
52 See Allen Buchanan, 'The Internal Legitimacy of Humanitarian Intervention', *Journal of Political Philosophy* vol. 7 no. 1 (1999), pp. 71–87.
53 For an earlier statement of this view see Simon Caney, 'Cosmopolitan Justice and Equalizing Opportunities', *Metaphilosophy* vol. 32 nos. 1/2 (2001), pp. 128–29. The distinction employed is similar, but not identical, to Pogge's distinction between 'interactional' and 'institutional' approaches: *World Poverty and Human Rights*, pp. 176ff. The central difference is that Pogge's 'institutional' approach covers much more than international law.
54 For two notable and important exceptions see Allen Buchanan's book-length treatment of the morality of international law, *Justice, Legitimacy, and Self-Determination: Moral Foundations for International Law* (Oxford: Oxford University Press, 2004), especially chapter 7, and Thomas Pogge's analyses of what

he terms the 'international resource privilege' and 'international borrowing privilege', *World Poverty and Human Rights*, pp. 118–21.

55 This example is also used by Buchanan to show why international law may legitimately differ from international morality: *Justice, Legitimacy, and Self-Determination*, pp. 22–23. See more generally his discussion of 'institutional moral reasoning', *Justice, Legitimacy, and Self-Determination*, pp. 22–27.

56 For discussion see Simon Caney, *Justice Beyond Borders: A Global Political Theory* (Oxford: Oxford University Press, 2005), pp. 255–56.

57 See Jeff McMahan, 'The Morality of War and the Law of War' in *Just and Unjust Warriors: The Moral and Legal Status of Soldiers* (Oxford: Oxford University Press, 2008) edited by David Rodin and Henry Shue, pp. 19–43. See also Jeff McMahan, *Killing in War* (Oxford: Oxford University Press, 2009), pp. 104–10, especially pp. 109–10.

58 For further support consider a third example. It is, I think, quite possible to judge that a specific case for secession is morally justified while at the same time rejecting the proposal that international law should adopt any provision permitting secession. Note, though, that this view is rejected by Buchanan in his important treatment of secession and the morality of international law. See Buchanan, *Justice, Legitimacy, and Self-Determination*, pp. 345–48, especially his discussion on p. 347 of what he terms 'the dualist position'.

59 See Caney, 'Global Distributive Justice and the State', pp. 511–12.

60 'Agents of Justice', p. 183.

9

PROCREATIVE RIGHTS AND PROCREATIVE DUTIES

David Archard

Having Children: Philosophical and Legal Reflections on Parenthood co-edited by Onora O'Neill and William Ruddick was published in 1979 (O'Neill and Ruddick 1979). It was one of the first serious works of English-speaking philosophy to address the ethics of procreation, of child care, and of the formation of families. Along with the collection edited by Aiken and LaFollette, *Whose Child? Children's Rights, Parental Authority and State Power* (Aiken and LaFollette 1980), *Having Children* played an important role in identifying the status of parenthood and of the child as proper topics for normative philosophy. Their publication can also be seen as contributing to the impressive corpus of philosophical writing devoted to matters of applied or practical significance which dates from the 1970s and 1980s. O'Neill has expressed reservations about a simple-minded view of 'applied' philosophy, and has sought to clarify the proper role that normative philosophy can play in informing public policy (O'Neill 2009). Nevertheless, she has herself produced important and influential work in subject areas relevant to the formulation of law and policy. The pieces devoted to reproductive autonomy and children's rights (O'Neill 1988) are exemplary in this regard. They represent a small part of her life work. However, they have helped significantly to shape subsequent philosophical treatment of their subject matter. No-one writing as a philosopher about the rights of the child or about the moral responsibilities of a procreator can ignore these pieces.

O'Neill's contribution to the edited collection is 'Begetting, Bearing, and Rearing' (O'Neill 1979). In it she addresses themes to which she returns thirty years later in Chapter 3 of her *Autonomy and Trust* (O'Neill 2008). In both places she is concerned to deny that there is an unrestricted right to procreate; instead she insists upon a duty or responsibility to create new persons only if adequate provision can be made for their care. Such a claim stands in stark contrast to a prevailing orthodoxy in bioethics which maintains, in simple terms, that no wrong is done in procreating so long as any child created enjoys a life that is at least (but not necessarily any much) better than non-existence. I have considerable sympathy with the view she defends. However, I also recognise the real problems in defending it. In what follows I want to set out the view she defends, indicate the problems in defending it against the orthodox position, and suggest in what ways the debate might be further advanced.

I think it fair to say that her view can be defended independently of any of those other broader philosophical commitments that O'Neill endorses. I have chiefly in mind her subscription to a suitably interpreted Kant. Nevertheless, her unwillingness to accept that there is a right to procreate, or at least any unrestricted right to procreate, echoes a familiar theme in her work, namely a preference in the overall configuration of moral discourse for the language of duties over that of rights.

O'Neill opens her 1979 chapter by citing disapprovingly the behaviour of Jean-Jacques Rousseau and his mistress, Thérèse. Rousseau and Thérèse produced five infants and left them all at the gates of the local foundling hospital. The example chosen is felicitous since its target is a celebrated Enlightenment philosopher whose behaviour, openly admitted by its author, is exposed as deeply dishonourable. We are to understand that Rousseau acted very badly, and that his bad example is intended to illustrate O'Neill's claim that individuals do not have an unrestricted right to procreate; rather they have a right to procreate that is constrained by a duty to ensure that those they bring into existence can be expected to enjoy at least a minimally adequate standard of upbringing.

It is this claim that I will spend time evaluating. However, it helps in the first instance to say something more, albeit briefly, about Rousseau's bad behaviour in order to be absolutely clear why it was so bad, something I have explored further elsewhere (Archard 2010). Rousseau himself insisted in his *Confessions* that he acted entirely properly. He cited in his own defence his chronic and irremediable inability to be a good father: 'Never in his whole life could J.J. be a man without sentiment or an unnatural father. ... in abandoning my children to public education for want of the means of bringing them up myself; in destining them to become workmen and peasants, rather than adventurers and fortune-hunters, I thought I acted like an honest citizen, and a good father' (Rousseau 1749, Book VIII). Of course, Rousseau's honest confession could well have been a rationalisation masking a selfish concern to avoid his parental responsibilities. However, if Rousseau would have made an incontinent and impoverished father – and from what we know of his personality and lifestyle this is not improbable – then his children might well have been destined to become 'adventurers' rather than the honest workers they could develop into at the hands of a public educator.

O'Neill also accuses Rousseau of hypocrisy in abandoning his children since he can be found elsewhere insisting that a parent's duties cannot be delegated or divided (O'Neill 1979: 28). Indeed, in *Émile* he insisted that a man 'has no right to be a father if he cannot fulfil a father's duties' (O'Neill and Ruddick 1979: 225). Yet Rousseau was far from consistent in everything he claimed. Moreover, O'Neill herself would not insist that only the biological parent should act as a custodial guardian of the child. She is careful to specify that the duty that is owed to one's offspring is the provision of 'some feasible plan for their child to be adequately reared by themselves *or by willing others*' (O'Neill 1979: 25; my added emphasis). Imagine then that Rousseau had given over his children to adoptive parents who were only too happy and well-suited to care for them. Presumably he would in doing this have fulfilled his parental duty. O'Neill would not herself endorse Rousseau's claim that somebody has no right to be a parent if he cannot fulfil a parent's duties by his own assumption of the parenting role.

Nevertheless, there is still the issue of Rousseau's procreative recidivism. We might adopt and adapt an Oscar Wilde aphorism to the effect that carelessly producing one unwanted child is unfortunate if understandable; doing so repeatedly to the extent of nearly half a dozen seems culpable. Yet, even here it is not absolutely clear that it is the repetition that is the problem. One can easily imagine that in Rousseau's time there was an unfulfilled demand for adoptable children by fit and loving prospective guardians. Rousseau and his mistress were doing their best to satisfy this demand even if that was not their actual motivation. That being so, all that we would be left with to worry about would be the burdens of pregnancy and childbirth borne by Jean-Jacques' long-suffering mistress.

However, it is clear that the real moral problem lies elsewhere than hypocrisy, unchecked fecundity, and an unwillingness to take on parental duties. As O'Neill notes, we have reason to suspect, as surely did Jean-Jacques and Thérèse, 'that foundling homes do not rear children at even a minimally adequate standard' (O'Neill 1979: 28). The problem is not simply that Rousseau abandoned his offspring to the care of others but that he left them at the gates of awful institutions. The provision made for unwanted children by the foundling homes was simply dreadful. Rousseau knew this, or was certainly culpably inadvertent to the facts if he did not suspect as much. Moreover, it would not have taken much on his part to reassure himself that the foundling institutions would indeed care for his offspring, and bring them up, as he later claimed to be the extent of his ambition for them, to be honest workers and peasants.

In his book *The Kindness of Strangers*, the American social historian John Boswell charts the history and outlines the changing form of child abandonment (Boswell 1988). The creation of foundling institutions, funded and managed by strangers, at the beginning of the thirteenth century inaugurated a significant change, and a dramatic decline in the standards of care provided to abandoned children. Children cared for within such institutions suffered dreadful and predominantly short lives, most dying within a few years of admission. Rousseau thus abandoned his children to a terrible fate, not that of merely 'destining them to become workmen and peasants, rather than adventurers and fortune-hunters'. It was a fate far worse than they would have suffered even at the hands of his clumsy and reluctant parenthood. Inasmuch as Rousseau knew this he did not, as he claimed, act 'like an honest citizen, and a good father'.

Nevertheless, it is also true that he lived at the wrong time to abandon children. In this respect Rousseau suffered the circumstantial moral bad luck (Williams 1993; Nagel 1993) of giving away his children at a time and within a society where the outcome of such abandonment was pitiful. Yet if he had lived in a different time or in a different society his abandoned offspring might well have enjoyed a better life than they would have done if he had decided to be their father. Indeed, had this been the case his actions would not have served as such a felicitous example to illustrate irresponsible procreation and thus merit O'Neill's censure. He would have done what she requires of a biological parent, namely made some feasible plan for his children to be adequately reared by willing others. Leaving to one side his hypocrisy, his patent rationalisations, his persistent exploitation of Thérèse, and his own parental inadequacies, he would have discharged his duties as a parent.

It is this duty – to ensure as far as is feasible that one's child has at least a minimally adequate standard of upbringing – that, for O'Neill, constrains one's procreative right. I will leave to one side the question of whether this duty is indeed properly discharged if one leaves others to bring up one's offspring. I thus acknowledge that the abandonment of children to the care even of willing and capable others may be exploitative of their good intentions. I also leave to one side a distinction that is often invoked by defenders of the bioethical orthodoxy (Wilkinson 2010). This is between the bare act of procreation and acts subsequent to the birth of the child. Gregory Kavka imagines that a couple conceive a child intending to sell it into slavery. Inasmuch as the child's future life is nevertheless barely tolerable, they do no wrong according to the orthodox view. They create a child whose life is better than non-existence. Kavka thinks that the judgement that the parents act permissibly is clearly mistaken and that we thus have a reason to doubt the orthodox view (Kavka 1982). However, one line of response to Kavka's use of this kind of example would distinguish between the couple's action in conceiving the child, and their action subsequent to its birth, namely the enslavement of the child. The second is clearly wrong, the first not obviously so. Similarly, it might be argued that Rousseau did not do wrong in having each of the five children. But he did do wrong in abandoning the children once born at the gates of the foundling institution. I think that the distinction invoked is tendentious. The couple would not have conceived a child had they not been able to sell it into slavery.

They procreated in order to enslave. Rousseau, similarly, continued to procreate only in the knowledge of the possibility of, and with the intention of, the abandonment of the children thus created.

O'Neill can, plausibly I think, say that Rousseau did wrong in abandoning his children, and that he did wrong insofar as he failed to discharge the duty that fell to him *because* he created a child. It needlessly invokes a distinction without moral weight to say that he did no wrong in procreating and then did wrong in failing to provide adequate care for the outcome of his procreation. I shall thus set to one side the invoked distinction. In what follows, I am interested in the justification that might be offered for the central claim O'Neill defends, namely that the right to procreate is contingent upon the making of a plan for the adequate care of the offspring.

O'Neill is careful in her 1979 chapter to make it clear that a person who does not make adequate provision for the child he creates does not have a right to procreate. The restriction in question is *built into* the right. Consider, she says, a liberty right such as that of free speech. 'It is not part of anyone's right of free speech ... to slander maliciously'. In exactly similar terms, she continues, it 'is not part of anyone's right to procreate ... to cause grave harm by their procreation' (O'Neill 1979: 30).

However, there is some considerable distance between 'causing grave harm' to a future child and failing to ensure that the future child will enjoy a 'minimally adequate quality of life'. This is recognised in a much later piece of writing by O'Neill – the chapter on '"Reproductive autonomy" and new technologies' in her Gifford Lectures published as *Autonomy and Trust in Bioethics* (O'Neill 2008) to which I now turn. There she is responding to advocates of 'reproductive autonomy' such as John Harris and John Robertson who press the case for substantial state assistance for the infertile that they might have children. I shall say more about this context in due course.

The immediate point of disagreement is this. O'Neill wishes to resist the idea to which Harris and Robertson, following Ronald Dworkin (Dworkin 1996: 104–5; 237–38), subscribe, namely that the right to procreative autonomy can be seen as simply and straightforwardly deriving from a more general right to autonomous personal choice. Her reason for resisting this view is that procreation is the creation of another human being: 'Reproduction aims to create a dependent being, and reproductive decisions are irresponsible unless those who make them can reasonably offer adequate and lasting care and support to the hoped-for child' (O'Neill 2008: 62). So far her line of argument is consistent – roughly – with the claims of the earlier piece. Responsible procreation ought to be constrained by the requirement that those who are created may reasonably expect to enjoy a minimally decent life.

However, she acknowledges that the advocates of procreative autonomy, such as Harris and Robertson, also and for their own part readily concede that all exercises of autonomy – including procreative autonomy – are properly constrained by the harm principle. Thus they – like O'Neill in her earlier piece – will acknowledge that reproductive autonomy 'may be constrained to prevent harm to others, including preventing harms to future children'. Yet she adds:

> Avoidance of harm is not a sufficiently robust constraint on individual autonomy in procreative decisions. The question to be asked is not just whether reproducing in certain situations ... can sometimes be done without harming. It is whether there are reasonable grounds to think that any child brought into existence can expect to have at least an adequate future.
> (O'Neill 2008: 66–67)

In sum, she believes and argues in both of the pieces cited that the right to procreate is constrained by a duty to ensure that the child created will enjoy a minimally decent or adequate life. This constraint is different from and indeed is considerably more demanding or robust than the requirement merely to avoid harming the future child.

In order to see how much more demanding, we should consider again the parallel with the right to free speech. Remember that in the 1979 piece O'Neill appeared to argue that just as the requirement not to harm – such as to maliciously slander – properly constrains the right to speak freely, so the requirement not to harm the future child properly constrains the right to procreate. Imagine then that the right to free speech must be as robustly constrained as is the right to procreative autonomy. We could then employ analogous reasoning to argue for such constraints, paraphrasing the corresponding parallel view as to the proper limits upon free speech in the following manner: 'The question to be asked would not be whether speaking in certain situations can be done without harming others (by slander or incitement to harmful acts). It would be whether there are reasonable grounds to judge that any speech meets some criterion of adequacy or minimal decency.'

I am sure that this would not be her view. Yet the dilemma that faces her account is a simple one. Either procreative autonomy, like any other exercise of personal autonomy, is limited only by a harm principle. If this is the case then the more robust requirement that future children be guaranteed a minimally decent life is not justified. On the other hand the suggested parallel between the freedoms of speech and to procreate may not be exact. If that is the case then the more robust constraint that operates in the latter case needs to be justified. This justification cannot simply appeal to the familiar harm principle as the standard limit upon all other instances of the exercise of personal autonomy.

There is another way in which it is possible to see how much more robust is the requirement to ensure that the child has a minimally decent life than that the child is not harmed. We can follow this way by spelling out what it would mean to harm the child. On a familiar and somewhat simplified account of harm, A harms B if A's action worsens B's situation from what it would have been in the absence of A's action. So procreation harms the future child only if the child's situation is worsened by being brought into existence. Note that we are contemplating a comparison between the child's existence and non-existence. We are not comparing the creation of two possible children one of whom faces the prospect of a terrible life and the other who does not. The latter kinds of case involve three alternatives, the former only two (Roberts 1998). Furthermore, there are interesting difficulties – first illuminatingly discussed by Derek Parfit (Parfit 1984: 357–66) – that arise because of the 'non-identity' of children conceived by the same people but at different times. When it is a matter of comparing this child's existence with its non-existence the issue is a different one. Here the problem of non-identity does not threaten. Rather, the issue is that one term of the comparison is impossible to grasp, or is such that the comparison is all too simple to evaluate. Either a comparison between existence and non-existence is beyond us, or it can be made. As to the first alternative, in the words of a celebrated English wrongful life case:

> But how can a court begin to evaluate non-existence ... No comparison is possible ... The court ... has to compare the state of the plaintiff with non-existence, of which the court can know nothing; this I regard as an impossible task.
> (McKay v. Essex Health Authority [1982]: 787 and 790)

In regard to the second alternative, if a comparison between existence and non-existence can be made, it might seem obvious – and does so to many – that non-existence is clearly so very bad that even a barely worthwhile life is better than none at all. So either the comparison that motivates an attribution of harm is 'thoroughly obscure' (O'Neill 1979: 29); or it is such that a child is only likely to be harmed by being brought into existence if its life is an extremely miserable one. The life in question would be one that falls well below the threshold O'Neill clearly has in mind when she speaks of an 'adequate' life.

Indeed, those she is criticising, the defenders of procreative autonomy, are pretty clear that they see few if any constraints upon the exercise of this kind of autonomy that could be attributed to the operation of a harm principle. John Robertson, by way of one notorious example, thinks that even if we knew that a prospective parent would seriously abuse her child 'it is not clear that they will enjoy such a horrible life that they never should have been born at all, and thus are harmed by being born to an abusing mother' (Robertson 1994: 82). The view here being baldly summarised – that one can permissibly bring into existence any child so long as its life is better on the whole, even if only barely so, than non-existence – currently represents something of an orthodoxy within contemporary bioethics. It shapes the evaluation made by many bioethicists of the choices that parents and doctors can make about possible future children (Wilkinson 2010).

Let me then offer an outline summary of the contrast between this orthodoxy within bioethics and O'Neill's view. She defends an account of what is owed to the future child by the 'responsible' prospective procreator. Such responsibility is considerably more demanding than what would be required from someone constrained only by the harm principle. Indeed, the avoidance of harm to the future child seems to impose few if any constraints on the exercise of one's right to procreate. Return then to the case of Rousseau and his mistress, and imagine that they were permitted the statement of the following, philosophically informed, exculpation: 'Of course the lives of those that I and Thérèse created were awful and we knew them likely to be such. But those children could, ultimately and in the final analysis, have no complaint against us for we did them no harm. Had we not procreated they would not have come into existence, and their lives, bad as they turned out, were nevertheless better on the whole than the long dark night of non-existence. Indeed were they to have insisted upon our duty of procreative care they would in effect have been demanding that they had not been born. None sought to exercise the right that would have been correlate with this putative duty; to do so would have been to condemn themselves to death'.

Common-sense morality will, I think, judge this type of plea as egregiously tendentious; it will find congenial O'Neill's basic claim that any child we bring into being should at least be guaranteed a minimally decent existence. Some other philosophers reject the orthodox view (Archard 2004; Steinbock 1986). Nevertheless, it is philosophically difficult to motivate her demand for 'procreative responsibility'. To start to see why, let me make two points. The first concerns the nature of the act, which it is proposed should be constrained by a requirement of 'responsibility'. O'Neill is right to chide Ronald Dworkin and John Harris for drawing an analogy between procreative freedom and a right to self-expression, such as a right to the exercise of one's own religion. Reproduction is indeed different from self-expression; and that difference does, in important part, lie in the fact that a child is brought into existence (O'Neill 2008: 61). Nevertheless, that difference can also serve to explain the fundamental significance of the procreative act to the procreator. The possibility of bringing into being another human being engages some of our most important interests – in seeing concrete fulfilment of a loving relationship, in being thereby able to devote ourselves to the care of a child that is ours, in simply creating a new life. Harris thinks that having children is what 'gives point and meaning to existence' (Harris 1989: 149). For these kinds of reason Robertson (chapter 2) concludes that procreative liberty has 'presumptive priority'. Our procreative acts matter greatly to us, and in consequence we need very good reasons to interfere with the exercise of these choices. Similarly, it is because the exercise of a freedom to speak or to express ourselves engages fundamental if different interests that we demand of those who would limit its exercise good reasons for their doing so.

Second, it is not sufficient in defence of procreative responsibility simply to say that 'reproduction aims to create a dependent being'. Harris and Robertson, and those who follow them, acknowledge as much. On their account we should both recognise the fact that our contemplated acts – such as procreative ones – may harm others, and endorse the normative principle that the occasioning of harm would be a good and proper reason not to act. However, they maintain, in accordance with the terms of the standard liberal principle, that the occasioning of harm is the *only* good reason to desist from acting. Furthermore, we can harm future persons – those we might create by our procreative acts – only if their lives are likely to be so poor as to be worse than not existing in the first place.

The problem is not, it should be quickly noted, that the requirement insisted upon by O'Neill is an impossibly imprecise one. It is, of course, hard to know exactly when a life is an adequate or a minimally decent one. But it may be just as hard if not more so to know when a life is better than non-existence. The judgement that it would have been better not to have been brought into existence is not equivalent to the judgement that it is better not to continue existing, nor to the judgement made by someone that his life is not worth continuing. We can surely make a fairly good fist of estimating when a future life will be more than just bearable and thus meet a threshold of adequacy. The real problem is, of course, why one should set the threshold for permission to procreate higher than the orthodoxy insists upon – the distance in thresholds being that between a minimally decent life and a life that is merely better than non-existence.

One problematic aspect of setting the higher threshold is that the scope of irresponsible procreation is thereby greater. For it can seem counterintuitive to judge as impermissible some instances that fall within the expanded scope of irresponsibility. Consider the case of procreating in a situation of extreme poverty. In her 1979 chapter, O'Neill identifies 'abysmal poverty' as one of a range of situations which, 'if there were no available alternative arrangements for the child's rearing, would make a decision to procreate unreasonable' (O'Neill 1979: 29). Imagine that such poverty is blameless – on the part of both the prospective procreators or of others – either because it is the outcome of the couple's brute bad luck, or because the distribution of resources that so disfavours them can be attributed to the exercise by all of legitimate property rights. Imagine further that the abysmal poverty is such as to make the child's life less than minimally adequate but still better than non-existence.

I think that many would judge that the desperately poor couple have a right to procreate; and, further, would also think that the fact that the child is not harmed by being brought into existence (in the sense already explained) is sufficient reason to allow them to exercise this right. Even those who do not share this judgement will most probably acknowledge that there is nevertheless a strong presumption in favour of allowing a desperately poor couple to have a child, one that demands of those who would deny them such an opportunity that they adduce very good reasons for doing so. Arguably, the fact that the child's life is not an 'adequate' one even if it is at least better than non-existence is not a good enough reason to limit their procreative choices.

O'Neill's treatment of the problem of procreative responsibility is in a piece much preoccupied with then contemporary discussions of the justifiability of coercive population polices. Such policies impose limits on the number of children a couple may have. No-one, I think, believes that the right to procreate is the right to have as many children as one chooses (Statman 2003; Conly 2005). It is, minimally, the right to have at least one child. Thus, coercive population policies need not always infringe the right to procreate. Yet, at some point there will be a problem. The right of some couple to have at least one child may be denied on the grounds that the social circumstances do not allow them to make feasible rearing plans for any such child.

In such a situation there is a conflict between a putative right to procreate and those moral considerations that determine the justice or injustice of the social circumstances that would constrain its exercise. Indeed, O'Neill acknowledges that any resolution of such a conflict may come down to a question of the relative standing of property rights and rights to procreate. The former rights justify both the good fortune of those enjoying circumstances favourable to responsible procreation and the ill fortune of others not so favoured. She defers discussion of this question of their relative standing (O'Neill 1979: 36–37).

This is indeed a difficult matter, which does not admit of easy resolution. The following questions immediately press: if the social circumstances that prevent a couple from responsibly procreating are the result of injustice (either generally or in particular against them), then would they have a right to procreate, even though they could not satisfy the requirement that their child would enjoy a minimally decent life? They might have a claim against those responsible for the injustice that the means to ensure their child enjoy a decent life should be guaranteed. However, if they could not reasonably hope to secure such means, would it follow that they should not procreate? If the social circumstances in which a couple cannot responsibly procreate are *not* the result of injustice, does it seem fair that a couple be denied the opportunity to have a child? The right to procreate protects interests of considerable value and weight. Why then should a couple not be permitted to have the one child their heart so greatly desires? The child will at least enjoy a life just worth living even if not minimally decent.

Setting to one side these questions, I want, in the concluding parts of this chapter, to examine some of the ways in which the problem – of how to make sense of and justify a charge of procreative responsibility – might be addressed. One unsatisfactory move is to think of procreative irresponsibility as a form of harmless wrongdoing. Thus we can imagine cases in which we hold both that someone has acted wrongly and yet that no-one's situation has been worsened as the result of that action. For instance, an airline refuses to sell a plane ticket for morally indefensible reasons (that the purchaser is black or a woman) but for a plane that, it transpires, crashes killing all on board. The victim of the refusal is clearly wronged but is nevertheless made better off (Woodward 1986: 810–11). Procreative irresponsibility does not fit within the category of harmless wrongdoing for the obvious reason that if it is wrong to bring into being a child whose life is very poor it is wrong precisely because of what is done to *that* child by virtue of bringing him or her into existence.

Does it make a difference that the act of creating a child whose life is less than minimally decent is deliberate? O'Neill is explicit in her 1979 chapter that her 'interest is mainly with the obligations and rights of persons who *decide* to procreate' (O'Neill 1979: 29). It is not entirely clear to me how much significance we should attach, and why, to the making of a decision to procreate. Obviously those who decide to procreate may also – and perhaps in the very same act – explicitly undertake to provide a certain level of care for the subsequent child. Conscientious parents set out to have a child that they will provide for. The failure to ensure that the child receives a decent upbringing is a straightforward violation of that undertaking.

However, people can deliberately decide to have but not to rear or to make provision for the rearing of the child. Their actions are, I agree, culpable. But I am not sure that we should see them as the only culpable procreators. We would surely not wish to exempt from moral blame those whose procreative acts are not deliberate but are nevertheless careless or negligent. The feckless procreator – and perhaps Rousseau best fits this description – may not make a deliberate decision to bring into existence children whom he disdains to care for. But he surely acts irresponsibly.

In her 2008 chapter, officially regulated fertility treatment is the immediate context for O'Neill's criticism of the ideal of 'reproductive autonomy' defended by Harris and others. Does this make a difference? Clearly those who come to fertility clinics and who undergo treatment declare – either explicitly or implicitly by their actions in seeking treatment – that they want to have a child whom they will care for. They may be taken as making the undertaking to provide a decent upbringing for the child the clinic will help them to have. But there is this important difference between fertility treatment and 'natural' procreation.[1] This is that it is possible to regulate the former. Or, more particularly, that it is possible to regulate the creation of children by means of fertility treatment without the moral costs that would attach to the regulation of 'natural' procreation.

Consider, then, that licensed fertility clinics in the United Kingdom are required to consider the 'welfare of the child' in each and every case of treatment. Leaving to one side the question of how this is to be understood the fact is that clinics are in a position effectively to 'license' prospective parents along just the lines – a consideration of the likely harms that might befall any child born to these individuals – specified by defenders of parental licensing (LaFollette 1980).

Those who criticise such practices may point to the injustice in demanding of those who procreate in one fashion what we do not demand of those who procreate in another. John Harris, for instance, says that 'it seems invidious to require that people who need assistance with procreation meet tests to which those who need no such assistance are not subjected' (Harris 1998: 7). The reply to Harris is obvious. First, one person's *modus tollens* is another's *modus ponens*. If procreation ought to be regulated out of regard for the welfare of any future child then it ought, *ceteris paribus*, to be regulated howsoever the child is created. Thus, if there are good reasons to do so in the case of fertility treatment, then there are good reasons also to do so in the case of 'natural' procreation. However, it seems clear, second, that we do have good reasons for making the 'invidious' distinction between the forms of reproduction; and that these have precisely to do with the moral costs of regulating 'natural' reproduction. We could regulate such reproduction but only at the expense of considerably more official intrusion into the lives of individuals than is conscionable and than is required in the case of regulated fertility treatment.

This brings us back to the basic question raised by O'Neill's demand in her 1979 chapter that the right to beget should be restricted by the requirement that the begetter make a feasible plan for the child to be adequately reared, and repeated in her insistence that procreative autonomy be exercised 'responsibly'. The question is: what justifies this demand?

Derek Parfit introduces the case of the 14-year-old whose failure to defer pregnancy results in her child having a poor life to illustrate the 'non-identity' problem. He asks himself whether our objection to her behaviour could not be captured by the thought that she thereby violated the child's right to 'a good start in life'. He supplies a two-stage answer (Parfit 1984: 364–65). In the first stage he simply invokes the terms of the non-identity problem to show that the child she did have at 14 could not have had that right fulfilled. Had the 14-year-old deferred conception then the child she would have had would have enjoyed a good start in its life. But, of course, *that* child would have been a different child to the one she had at 14.

In the second stage Parfit re-phrases the objection in the following terms: 'It is wrong to cause someone to exist if we know that this person will have a right that cannot be fulfilled.' Put in these terms the non-identity problem does not apply. The suggestion is that it was wrong of the 14-year-old to have a child whose right to a good start in life could not be fulfilled. Parfit's response is that inasmuch as somebody can subsequently declare himself to be glad to be born he thereby waives the right in question. We imagine that the child born to the 14-year-old does not in later life complain to her mother, 'You did me wrong in bringing me into existence when my right to a good start in life could not be fulfilled'. She does not make this complaint because she is, on balance, happy to be in existence. That she is, on balance, happy to be alive can be taken as equivalent to her waiving the right. For insisting upon the fulfilment of the right would require that she not have been born; and she is happy to have been born.

I leave to one side questions relating to the distinction between wishing, once born, to stay alive and wishing that one had not been born. The important point is that, according to this reply from Parfit, a right to a certain kind of life that might be claimed against the procreator has no force (it would be waived) for the person for whom her life is worth continuing. And note that a life worth continuing might be only marginally better than non-existence and thus fail to meet the standard of adequacy or minimal decency insisted upon by those who demand procreative responsibility.

The argument at play seems to be of the following kind. I have a right to a decent life, and I am wronged by those who procreated me if they brought me into existence knowing (or being reasonably sure) that I would not have a decent life. Since, however, I wish to continue living a less than decent life I thereby waive that right. I do so inasmuch as I could only claim the right against my procreators by insisting that I should not have been born. And this I do not insist upon.

However, this argument seems badly misguided. For I can consistently claim both that I do not want to give up the life that I have and that I was wronged by being given the life that I have. Imagine that I have a right to medical treatment, which both saves my life and ensures a certain quality of life, but that I am given a treatment which saves my life at serious cost to the quality of my life. I do not waive my right to the better treatment on the grounds that absent the treatment I did get I would no longer be alive. I am still wronged by having been given the poorer treatment even if I could not now receive the better treatment, and even though the treatment I did receive ensures I am still alive.

I thus have great sympathy for an approach of the kind favoured by Joel Feinberg who claims that every person has a 'birthright' to the fulfilment of certain interests. Further, 'if you cannot have that to which you have a birthright then you are wronged if you are brought to birth' (Feinberg 1984: 99). Denying someone the opportunity to enjoy that to which they have a right is a violation of that right; as is bringing into existence a person knowing (or being reasonably sure) that she will not have an opportunity to enjoy that to which she has a right.

Now of course there is much more that needs to be said in explication and defence of this account. However, it does by and large fit with O'Neill's basic view. In the first place, the 'birthright' approach makes sense of her thought that the requirement to ensure that those one creates enjoy a decent life is a restriction built into the right to procreative autonomy. She insists that this restriction is not an external constraint upon the proper exercise of the right, as is the harm principle, but part of what the right to procreate is. That one can exercise a right only inasmuch as another's right is respected is consistent with this view.

Second, the birthright claim spells out why it matters that the right to procreate is not just an extension of the general right of personal autonomy, and is not such an extension inasmuch as it involves the creation of another human being. For what one creates is someone with a right to be born to a certain kind of life. This approach derives its plausibility from the thought that the exercise of one person's rights must at least be consistent with the possession by others of *their* rights. Grant that the right to procreative autonomy is one of the rights that adults possess. Then it follows that the exercise of any of those rights cannot be such that it subverts or vitiates the enjoyment by others of *their* rights. It would thus be wrong for someone to exercise her right to procreate in such a fashion that the human being she brought into being could not enjoy his 'birthright'. Third, the birthright claim gives expression to the idea that a newly born person is entitled to more than just a life that is better than non-existence. It has a right to a minimally decent life. Fourth, it captures the thought that when someone is brought into existence to endure a barely tolerable but inadequate life a wrong is done to them. The wrong that is done is the violation of their birthright.

O'Neill may not like the talk of 'birthrights'. However, she is, in my view, entirely correct to believe that there is no unrestricted right to procreate. That alone makes her work in this area exemplary and rightly influential. Justifying the restrictions that ought to be built into that right is the important task for those who remain unpersuaded by and unsympathetic to the orthodox view of procreative liberty.

Note

1 The scare quotes around 'natural' are deliberate and intended to warn the reader against any assumption that one form of procreation is normal in either a descriptive or normative sense. Note too that the UK is akin to many other jurisdictions in only regulating forms of artificial reproduction where the foetus is created *ex utero* (self-insemination, for instance, would not be regulated).

Bibliography

Aiken, W. & LaFollette, H. (1980) *Whose Child? Children's Rights, Parental Authority and State Power* (Totowa, NJ: Rowman and Littlefield).

Archard, D. (2004) 'Wrongful Life,' *Philosophy* 79: 403–20.
——(2010) 'The Obligations and Responsibilities of Parenthood,' in Archard, D. and Benatar, D. (eds.) *Procreation and Parenthood: The Ethics of Bearing and Rearing Children* (Oxford: Oxford University Press): 103–27.
Boswell, J. (1988) *The Kindness of Strangers: The Abandonment in Western Europe from Late Antiquity to the Renaissance* (London: Allen Lane).
Conly, S. (2005) 'The Right to Procreation: Merits and Limits,' *American Philosophical Quarterly* 42(2): 105–15.
Dworkin, R. (1996) *Freedom's Law* (Oxford: Oxford University Press).
Feinberg, J. (1984) *Harm to Others* (Oxford: Oxford University Press).
Harris, J. (1989) 'The Right to Found a Family,' in G. Scarre (ed.) *Children, Parents and Politics* (Cambridge: Cambridge University Press): 133–56.
——(1998) 'Rights and Reproductive Choice,' in Harris, J. and Holm, S. (eds.) *The Future of Human Reproduction: Ethics, Choice and Regulation* (Oxford: Clarendon Press): 5–37.
Kavka, Gregory S. (1982) 'The Paradox of Future Individuals,' *Philosophy and Public Affairs* 11(2): 93–112.
LaFollette, H. (1980) 'Licensing Parents,' *Philosophy and Public Affairs* 9(2): 182–97.
McKay v. Essex Health Authority [1982] ALR 2 771.
Nagel, T. (1993) 'Moral Luck,' in Daniel Statman (ed.) *Moral Luck* (Albany NY: SUNY Press): 57–71.
O'Neill, O. & Ruddick, W. (eds.) (1979) *Having Children: Philosophical and Legal Reflections on Parenthood* (New York: Oxford University Press).
O'Neill, O. (1979) 'Begetting, Bearing, and Rearing,' in O'Neill and Ruddick (eds.) (1979): 25–38.
——(1988) 'Children's Rights and Children's Lives,' *Ethics* 98 (3): 445–63.
——(2008) *Autonomy and Trust in Bioethics (Gifford Lectures)* (Cambridge: Cambridge University Press).
——(2009) 'Applied Ethics: Naturalism, Normativity, and Public Policy,' *Journal of Applied Philosophy*, 26:3 (Autumn): 219–30.
Parfit, D. (1984) *Reasons and Persons* (Oxford: Oxford University Press).
Roberts, M. (1998) *Child Versus Childmaker: Future Persons and Present Duties in Ethics and the Law* (Boulder: Rowman and Littlefield).
Robertson, J. (1994) *Children of Choice: Freedom and the New Reproductive Technologies* (Princeton: Princeton University Press).
Rousseau, J.-J. (1749) *Confessions*. Translated and with an Introduction by J.M. Cohen (Harmondsworth: Penguin Classics, 1952).
Statman, D. (2003) 'The Right to Parenthood: An Argument for a Narrow Interpretation,' *Ethical Perspectives* 10(3–4): 224–35.
Steinbock, B. (1986) 'The Logical Case for "Wrongful Life",' *Hastings Center Report* 16 (April): 15–20.
Wilkinson, Stephen (2010) *Choosing Tomorrow's Children: The Ethics of Selective Reproduction* (Oxford: Oxford University Press).
Williams, B. (1993) 'Moral Luck,' in Daniel Statman (ed.) *Moral Luck* (Albany NY: SUNY Press, 1993): 35–55.
Woodward, J. (1986) 'The Non-Identity Problem,' *Ethics* 96, 4: 804–31.

Part 4

TRUSTWORTHINESS AND TRUST

10

WHAT IS TRUST?

Annette Baier

One of the paradoxes explored by Onora O'Neill, especially in her Gifford Lectures, is that some measures taken to increase trustworthiness in professionals, such as increased auditing and increased openness, may fail to increase trust, and may even worsen mistrust. But is it really trustworthiness which could be thought to be encouraged by demanding more audits, and making known what they showed? As I understand trust, it itself involves economizing on monitoring, supervision, and audits, and leaving the trusted to get on with their work with minimal audits and minimal supervision. So increasing these is of course displaying decreasing trust – simply replacing it with audits, supervision, threats, sanctions and coercion. To be worthy of trust, as I understand it, is to be worthy of being left fairly unmonitored and unsupervised, needing to be only minimally checked-up on, given discretionary powers in looking after whatever is entrusted to one. Even if the audits did show good performance, that would be performance when subject to audit, so not yet when really trusted.

But of course O'Neill does not agree with me about what trust is. She rejects my definition of it as willingness to be vulnerable to the trusted, to rely on their competence and goodwill, when we entrust something we care about to their care.[1] As she rightly says, this requirement of the assumed goodwill of the trusted makes most sense of personal trust relations, not of trust in professionals and organizations (let alone, I might add, of trust, if that is the right word for it, in machines or computer programs, in things like Wikipedia). I may know my doctor finds me foolish and irritating, and has little goodwill towards me, but trust her professional standards enough to believe she will not deliberately let me be harmed by her. But goodwill does not require liking, and the minimal goodwill I spoke of is merely absence of ill will, of willingness to harm, so I would still say that it is the goodwill of my doctor, as well as her competence, that I rely on when I trust her. O'Neill does not say if she accepts my claims, taken from Niklas Luhmann,[2] that, by accepted vulnerability, I meant letting the trusted take care of something one cares about, giving that one discretionary powers, so not insisting on frequent audits or any supervision. (O'Neill does not refer to Luhmann in her Gifford Lectures, but does mention him in her Reith Lectures.)

The trust I analyzed was between individual persons, whereas what O'Neill was concerned with was trust or mistrust between the general public and some powerful profession, or organization, and that difference in context may explain, to some degree, the differing emphases in our accounts. Rightly do we take professionals to be accountable to those they serve, as any trusted person is to the one who trusts, but accountability may take a different form when it is whole professions that are accountable, than when it is a private individual, trusted on a specific matter. And when it is an organization such as a hospital that is trusted, or mistrusted, it is procedures as well as individuals that may be at fault when one is let down. If one is discharged from hospital without the prescriptions one needs for continued healing, this may be the fault of the doctor in whose care one was, in hospital, but if more than one specialist was involved, each may have assumed the other wrote the needed prescriptions, while the hospital had no procedure in place to allocate this responsibility clearly. Of course, procedures have human designers, so perhaps the superintendant of the hospital bears the main blame, in such a case, but it often takes some particular "medical misadventure" for the inadequacy of procedures to become evident. When such failure becomes evident, one does not trust the inadequate procedures again: one expects them to be revised. But when it is an individual who lets one down, one may well trust that same one to do better, next time. We forgive some delinquent individuals, who have let us down, but we replace faulty procedures.

If I trust you to feed my cat, no procedures need be involved. I will not come to check whether you do or do not do the feeding, but will expect some report from you on my return. Should I *hire* you as cat feeder, I may not at first trust you, and so may well supervise you for a while, as well as demand an account from you of what exactly you did, once I leave the task to you. I may even insist that certain procedures, such as washing the food dishes, be carried out, and supervise at first to see that they are. But supervised reliance is not trust, as I understand it. To increase monitoring will be to leave less scope for real trustworthiness, if that means lack of need for external monitoring (though not lack of need for some sort of account, given by the trusted, of what they did). O'Neill, I think, confuses placing trust with deciding to rely on someone or something. Hiring someone whom I then supervise involves reliance on the hireling to get the job done, as well as reliance on oneself as supervisor, but not trust in the one who is hired. (One's reliance on oneself as supervisor does count as self-trust.) Trust is a special subspecies of confident reliance, and deciding to trust is just one way in which a trust relationship may be begun. Sometimes one just finds oneself trusting. I may have come to rely completely confidently on my fellow drivers not to break the rules of the road when, for all they know, a traffic cop is there watching them, ready to penalize. But this is not to trust them, it is only to rely on them, and on the cop to do his job. When it is evident that no cops are watching, one does rely on the assumed goodwill of other drivers, their wish not to harm us, any more than they want to harm themselves, as well as their competence. So then we can be said to trust them. If we take courses in defensive driving, this shows some lack of trust in other drivers. And do we *decide* to rely on or to trust the traffic cop, or other drivers? Do little children *decide* to trust the adults whom they do trust? Decisions come in more when we decide to cease trusting, or decide whom not to trust, and such decisions are guided by involuntary feelings of suspicion, just as trusting itself has an affective dimension, well explored by Karen Jones.[3] As I said, in my Tanner Lectures, trust is one of those phenomena that challenges the usual division of mental phenomena into cognitive, affective, and volitional.[4] Trust is all of these: it is based on what we believe about another person or agency, it requires that we feel safe in their hands, and it usually involves a voluntary act of entrusting, or placing trust.

A recent analysis of trust, by Cristiano Castelfranchi and Rino Falcone,[5] brings in all these elements. They take trust to be a five-place relation, where x, believing y, in circumstances C, to be competent and willing, delegates some task, t, to y, in order that x's goal G be attained. By "delegate" they do not mean to imply that x might have done t herself, since in many cases, such as trust in experts, she is not capable of so doing. The circumstances C in which x believes y to be trustworthy, if given this task, may include reference to some authority keeping check, so some monitoring is not ruled out by their definition, nor some audits by x of how y is doing. But to delegate is to hand over control, to step back and let y do the job, to leave her to Beaver. The problem in incorporating this element of delegation into the concept of trust is that it makes little sense when the trust is self-trust (a concept Castelfranchi and Falcone, rightly, want to allow for). I may indeed decide that I am competent to do task t myself, so allocate it to myself, rather than to some other, but I can scarcely be said to "delegate" it to myself. Castelfranchi and Falcone allow (p. 15, note) that they have given a special weakened sense to "delegation." The trouble with O'Neill's concept, in as far as she has spelled it out, is that, if it allows monitoring and supervision, it does not seem to allow for any sort of handing over something to the trusted, leaving it to her. But if I trust my babysitter, although I may well phone in to make sure there are no problems, I certainly do not supervise her. Trust does not rule out some monitoring, either by the truster or by others, to correct for faults, but does require that it be less than when an untrusted agent is given the task. The conditions in which one entrusts anything to anybody usually include the background presence of police, and the courts, should one have to call them in.

It is true, as Castelfranchi and Falcone recognize, and as I had not, when I wrote about trust, that it is only within some conditions, often very hard to specify, that one has the confidence in the trusted's competence and willingness which leads one to entrust some matter to her. I do not expect my babysitter to be able to look after my children if faced with an armed intruder and abductor. Normal conditions are the default version of the value for C, and they exclude armed attack.

It is also true, as O'Neill, and Castelfranchi and Falcone recognize, and as I had not, that the trusted need not be a private individual, but may be a firm or agency. It is always a person, an agent with a mind, who does the trusting, but it may be something more impersonal which is trusted.

(Castelfranchi and Falcone restrict trusting to "cognitive agents," which may include more than human persons. Indeed their "socio-cognitive computational model" is geared to include artificial cognitive agents as trusters, while the trusted for them may include things like procedures, which have no cognition (*Trust Theory*, p. 14). I would prefer to say that we confidently rely on procedures, and restrict talk of trust to reliance on agents who have a will, whose goodness is relied on when we trust.) My own account supposed that the trusted is always something capable of good or ill will, and it is unclear that computers or their programs, as distinct from those who designed them, have any sort of will. But my account is easily extended to firms and professional bodies, whose human office-holders are capable of minimal goodwill, as well as of disregard and lack of concern for the human persons who trust them. It could also be extended to artificial minds, and to any human products, though there I would prefer to say that talk of trusting products like chairs (*Trust Theory*, p. 50) is either metaphorical, or is shorthand for talk of trusting those who produced them.

To trust another is to feel safe with her, and we often speak of trust when there is no specific "task" we expect the other to do, nor any very definite "goal" we have in mind in associating with those we trust. To trust someone is to expect no harm from that one. Mistrust can be quite diffuse and general, not confined to the fear that some task not be properly performed, some goal of one's own thwarted by the mistrusted one. When I first visited Vienna, when it was a city still occupied by the troops of the allies who had conquered it, people on the street looked suspicious of all their fellows, as if reluctant to emerge from behind closed, locked doors, to have any dealings with others. One could almost smell the fear. A bad climate of trust is not restricted to the times when one cannot safely delegate some task, nor get someone else's cooperation in attaining some goal, without intense supervision and monitoring. It is at its worst when one fears having anything whatever to do with others, when one shrinks into oneself, unwilling to allow oneself to be at all vulnerable to others, in any capacity. To increase trust, it is not enough to try to make people trustworthy; one also has to make them willing to give trust. This means that to increase trust, one must work on the mistrustful as well as the mistrusted.

Once trust has broken down it is very difficult to rebuild it. It is a kind of miracle it is ever there in the first place. Children instinctively trust their parents, but if they are neglected or abused, may become barely capable of trusting anyone. David Hume, like John Locke, saw that, as Locke said, we "live upon trust," and looked in his social philosophy at ways in which we can extend it from friends and family to strangers.[6] Locke was not referring only to trust in governments when he said that we live on trust. Magistrates are a social invention, so extending trust, is for Hume a latecomer, presupposing more basic inventions to extend trust. Hume's account of a social convention is of cases where we all perceive a common interest in adopting some rule, and express this perception so that all know that all see and recognize it. Common customs of greeting are cases of this: if I am willing to bare my head to you, by raising my hat, I am trusting you not to attack my bare head. Such "I come in peace" signals include the outstretched hand, displaying that it holds no weapon, and that I am willing for it to be temporarily put out of other action by being clasped by the other. Hume saw us as using this device of convention, when there is perceived and expressed common interest, to create ways in which trust on particular matters could be extended to strangers, as when we invented promise and contract. These conventions, at least in small groups, are self-reinforcing: no-one wants to be known as untrustworthy, so we have a strong motive to keep our agreements. But of course the conformers to the convention are vulnerable to any "sensible knaves" who free-ride on the conformity of others. We deplore such knaves, but we have to be willing to be vulnerable to them, as well as to all the others who do not in fact wound us. Contract is a device for ensuring some reliability, since defaulters can be sued for breach of contract. Professionals such as physicians do sign employment contracts with hospitals, but not with private patients, where the patients' trust rests mainly on the certificates on the physician's office walls, and on hearsay from other patients, as well as on their instinctive reaction to the presence of the physician. It is a vital life skill we all use, this quick summing up of another person, from experience of her face and gaze. Someone who will not look us in the eye we instinctively mistrust.

Any adequate account of trust must cover those cases where there is no particular task we allocate to the trusted, but merely feel safe when moving among them, as well as cases where a definite task is allocated. If unsavory neighbors move in beside where I live, I may not trust them enough to have any dealings with them, and may fear for my cats. I suppose it is always at least one's safety, and that of those one loves, that one entrusts to those one trusts. So fear and suspicion are the opposite of trust. The fear need not be for any definite strike. If I knew exactly what to fear from my new neighbors, for example burglary, then I would be able to take some measures to protect against it. But if all I fear is some strike against me, perhaps laying out poison for my cats, or arson, or who knows what, then my lack of trust is general, not relativized to some goal, and some risk to it. The worst mistrust is when we cannot say exactly what it is we fear that the mistrusted will do. Most of us do trust our neighbors not to harm us or ours, and life would be intolerable if this were not the case. Default trust has to be the norm.

In the sorts of cases O'Neill is concerned with, when it is health services and hospitals that are either trusted or mistrusted, then there is a specific goal, namely improved health, which is involved. When we have reason to fear that our hospitals are neglecting simple cleanliness measures, or that they are out to profit from their patients, then our mistrust can be directed at the danger of specific harms, such as infection and overcharging. Then inspection and audits may indeed be the right response, to correct these ills. But not all cases of mistrust are as focused as this. My mistrust of my hypothetical new neighbors is diffuse, rather than precisely focused, but surely counts as mistrust. Any adequate analysis of trust must cover both localized and goal-relative trust – such as that which we have, if we are lucky, in our physicians and hospitals, and which the Castelfranchi and Falcone account covers beautifully – and the vaguer sorts of trust, such as trust of neighbors and those we pass on the street, or sit beside on a train. It seems to me that acceptance of vulnerability covers all the cases of trust: it is the willingness to let the trusted be in a position to harm us, since that is the position they have to be in to do what we expect them to do for us, while being fairly confident that they will not in fact harm us. O'Neill (in private correspondence) tells me that she rejects an "attitudinal" account of trust, since she takes trust to be something that is intentionally "placed" in the trusted, where the placing may or may not be intelligently done. But my account of trust as entrusting surely allowed, even overemphasized, that trust can be deliberate. But it also took the placing or entrusting to be done with the confidence that the trusted, although the position we let him have gives him the means to harm us, would not in fact do so – that is, would not use the power we give him to harm rather than help us. Of course, this vulnerability is not something we tend to dwell on, when we trust, just something we become aware of, when we reflect on it. And vulnerability does not entail *danger* of wounds, merely being unprotected against them. I remain unsure why O'Neill rejects this analysis, which allows for deliberate decisions to entrust, as well as for attitudes of confidence, despite our possibly acknowledged vulnerability. Of course, it remains a sort of miracle that we do have this default trust in each other. But usually we do. Mistrust has to be the exception, not the rule.

There are various ways in which we are knowingly vulnerable to our fellow-persons, not all of them counting as trust. I may contract a disease from another, through voluntary contact, but through no fault of hers, if she did not know she had a communicable disease. And of course I know there are such diseases, so when I saw her, and caught the disease, I had voluntarily assumed the risk, always there to some degree, of catching something nasty. I may be pressed to death by a person's weight, along with that of those behind her, in a crush of crowds, where neither her will nor her ability is at all involved in what happens. And I know there is always some such risk, in large crowds. We are knowingly vulnerable to our fellow persons in many ways, besides having trusted them. What is special to the vulnerability trusting brings seems to me to lie in the fact that the will of the trusted, as well as the one who trusts, is involved.

Why do we ever trust another person? I think that there is room, in the analysis of trust, for a sixth place, in addition to the five which Castelfranchi and Falcone recognize. This sixth place is for the reason, r, that x trusts y to carry out the task t, or to do vaguer things like not intentionally harm x. To some extent their concept of x's evaluation of y, the trusted, does include this, but that evaluation can be based on many different things, so an extra variable is needed. Truster x must believe something positive about y, to place her trust in him. It can be as weak as liking the look of him and knowing nothing against him, or it may be as strong as prior experience of y's competence and reliability, or it could be having references from others whom one trusts, telling one that y is trustworthy. Little children who trust their parents have their experience of the parents' past care of them as their reason. Why do I feel safe walking the streets of my town, why do I trust my fellow residents to share those streets with me? Partly because of the police presence, but mainly because I cannot see that they have reason to attack me. In allowing a place, r, for the reasons one trusts, I do not want to deny that, in normal conditions, the value for r is simply "no reason not to."

In the cases O'Neill is concerned with, there is some reason not to trust the professionals in question. Then the job of rebuilding trust must involve not merely getting the professionals to perform better, but also getting ordinary people to believe that their lives and health can safely be left in their hands, first without much trust, when those professionals are closely monitored, then slowly relaxing the monitoring, so showing real trust. To do that we must have reason to think that such professionals are self-monitoring, do not need any external monitor. Judging when to reduce the monitoring, and how far, is a delicate matter, and who should be trusted with it is one of the hardest decisions. The attitude of patients may indicate that they feel safe, without special safeguards, and, even if their trust is occasionally misplaced, that is better than constant mistrust, and perpetual monitoring. Public servants have to be trusted to judge how many safeguards are needed, for other professionals, and ordinary voters have to be trusted to evict governments who appoint untrustworthy or corrupt public servants. Climates of trust come as webs, where one form of trust depends on others, including trust in those like the police who pose a threat to wrongdoers. It takes social genius to redesign such webs, so that the climate improves, and trust becomes the default attitude, as it must be, if life is to be tolerable.

When I said that trust is the default attitude, it was trust of individual persons I had in mind, but many of the cases of mistrust O'Neill is concerned with are mistrust of powerful institutions, such as the press, the BBC, or the medical establishment. Power corrupts, and so perhaps mistrust is the appropriate default attitude to any powerful group. Rightly did Luhmann devote his book to "Trust and Power," since the powerful are those most likely to be mistrusted, and trusting gives new power to the trusted. But of course, if I mistrust the medical establishment, I will mistrust my own family doctor, of which she is a lowly member. If such mistrust is often proper, then such professionals face the daunting task of replacing mistrust in them with trust. As O'Neill has emphasized, increased monitoring is not the same as quality control. It may instead lead professionals to fixate on passing the tests the monitors set, rather than improving their ability to do their job well, to heal if they are physicians, to report facts responsibly, if they are journalists. For to be trustworthy, it is not enough that their audits and paperwork be fine, it is necessary that they can be left to do their job well without too many audits and without constant monitoring. To achieve this, quality control must go on in their training and certification, and in periodic retraining. The monitoring should be internal to the profession, if professionals are to be trustworthy. To institute external monitoring may be necessary when mistrust grows, but that is a display of mistrust, not an effective way to restore trust. To display mistrust is never a good way to make a person trustworthy. Trust can be self-fulfilling, and so can mistrust. As the knowledge that others trust us can spur us on to be worthy of their trust, so the knowledge that they mistrust us can bring out the worst in us. So if there is a crisis of trust in our society, the last way to solve it is by displaying our refusal to trust by increased external monitoring. We need to go to the heart of the problem, the quality of service the professionals provide, the quality of their training and retraining. Some[7] have spoken of the cunning of trust, that it can evoke trustworthiness. There is no cunning in responding to untrustworthiness with manifest mistrust – that is natural but scarcely clever, or likely to reform the mistrusted. It will offend them, and if the form our mistrust takes is increased monitoring, it may make them concentrate on passing the tests we set, rather than doing their main job better. So what should we do, when faced with a profession that has lost our trust? Much the same as we would if faced with a spouse who has betrayed our trust: let them know that we are aware of the betrayal, let them know what we expect of them, and give them a chance to show that they can do better, by risking trusting them again. So if the medical profession has lost our trust, we should let it know what is expected of it, appeal to it to reform itself, possibly by revising its procedures, give it a chance to do better, and so risk trusting it again. Trust is a response to risk, and is always risky. But when it works it is worth the risk. The division of labor means that there will be many people we have to trust to do what we cannot do for ourselves, and we need assurance, not just trust, that they are being properly trained for the work we entrust to them. It is to their training we should look, when professionals prove untrustworthy. And to overcome any crisis of trust, we must remember what trust is, and not try to replace it with control. If, to get more security, we insist on rigid control, then we should be clear that this is different from trust, and is not the way to make anyone worthy of trust. For anyone to show that she is worthy of trust, there must be someone willing to trust her, to leave her to monitor herself. Before she is trusted, she may indeed exhibit character traits which augur well for her performance if trusted; she may show indicators of trustworthiness, such as skill and carefulness.

I have in the past suggested that trust and trustworthiness are best attained when there is some approximation to equality between the parties, and when the trust is reciprocal. It is very difficult, after infancy, for the powerless to trust the powerful, and easy for the powerful to depend on their power to get away with bad behavior. O'Neill sees trust as a response to perceived trustworthiness, as indeed it is, but it is equally true that trustworthiness is, to some degree, a response to trust. A person who is never trusted cannot show that she is worthy of trust. Whatever she has displayed before, if it has been under conditions when she is monitored and watched, cannot give us full assurance of what she will do when trusted, that is when left minimally monitored. Only good behavior when trusted can show that she is trustworthy.

In her Aronui lecture at Otago University[8] in September 2010, O'Neill allowed Luhmann's point, that trust saves "transaction costs." If we attempted to do without it, we would have to put in place costly methods of constant monitoring, or the legal safeguards of contract. Trust is a response to perceived trustworthiness, but the test of that is not how one performs when monitored, but when trusted, that is, left minimally monitored. To make as sure as we can that someone is trustworthy, we have to make sure she is competent to do the task left to her, and that she has stronger motive to fulfill than to betray our trust. If there is a great power discrepancy between powerless truster and powerful trusted, then the trusted can be fairly confident she can get away with a bad performance or can cut corners. Should it be the powerful who is trusting the relatively powerless, then fear may stop her performing badly, until she sees a chance to alter the power balance by misuse of her discretionary powers, using them to benefit herself rather than to care for what was entrusted to her. Fear may make a person reliable, but scarcely trustworthy, since she cannot be expected to have even minimal goodwill to one who intimidates her. Trustworthiness can only be displayed by those who are really trusted – those that are left fairly unsupervised. Competence can be measured beforehand, and character displayed, before trust is given. It is usually given as a response to proven competence, and presumed good character. Then it is a response to *expected* trustworthiness; but until it is given, such trustworthiness has to be taken on trust, since it is only by trusting that we discover if the one we trust really is trustworthy. I agree with O'Neill that we need to focus on trustworthiness, but it is not audits that will measure it, since they measure how the audited perform when trust is withdrawn and replaced by monitoring and audits.

Jonathan Dancy, reviewing my writings on trust, asked "Can we trust Annette Baier?"[9] Philosophers are expected to probe for good reasons, and to expose bad reasons. Their attitude to one another is unrelenting suspicion of non sequiturs, and hidden assumptions, taking as little as possible on trust. What did the BBC trust O'Neill to do when they appointed her Reith lecturer? Did they expect her to ask how trustworthy the media are? (She did say "sorry," when reporting how little journalists are trusted.) Presumably the BBC knew what philosophers do, were aware that critical thinking is our professional responsibility. One thing we try to avoid is conceptual confusion. The concepts of trust and trustworthiness are closely connected, but we have to beware of circularity in our explication of them. Trust is more than attribution of trustworthiness, since one can have that without any entrusting of anything to the one believed to be trustworthy. O'Neill says trust is a response to trustworthiness, so it is with the latter we must start. I say that "trustworthiness" is a compound word, and means "being worthy of trust," so it is with trust we must start. Trust is more than belief in the trusted's trustworthiness, or any affective accompaniment of that; it also involves knowingly putting oneself in her power, giving her discretionary powers in looking after something one cares about. Trustworthiness can only be displayed if one is trusted, if someone leaves one in charge of something that matters to her. No measurements of competence or of good character out of that context, the context of trust, can serve as a sure measure of trustworthiness. Only on-the-job performance shows trustworthiness – or the lack of it. So until we trust, we cannot discover trustworthiness. But O'Neill has not told us what it is to trust, only that it is a reasoned response to trustworthiness, and is not the same as having a guarantee of that. Like a good Kantian, she thinks it is our duty to be trustworthy, not our right to be able to trust safely, which we should be considering. But she still owes us an account of what it is that the trustworthy are worthy of, and of what it is to trust. My account may be defective, but she has given us no account, beyond stressing that trust is something that is placed. Until we are clear what trust is, we cannot know what it is of which the trustworthy are worthy.[10]

Notes

1 I defined it this way in "Trust and Antitrust," which, along with other essays on trust, including my Tanner Lectures, can be found in my *Moral Prejudices* (Cambridge, MA: Harvard University Press 1994). For O'Neill's rejection of this view, see her Gifford Lectures, *Autonomy and Trust in Bioethics* (Cambridge: Cambridge University Press, 2002), 13–14.
2 Niklas Luhmann, *Trust and Power* (Chichester: Wiley, 1979).
3 Karen Jones, "Trust as an affective attitude," *Ethics*, 107 (1996), 4–25.
4 See my *Moral Prejudices* (1994), 132.
5 Cristiano Castelfranchi and Rino Falcone, *Trust Theory: A Socio-Cognitive and Computational Model* (Chichester: John Wiley and Sons, 2010).
6 John Locke, *The Correspondence of John Locke*, ed. E. S. de Beer. Vol. 1. (Oxford: Clarendon Press, 1976), p. 122; David Hume, *A Treatise of Human Nature*. Edited by L. A. Selby-Bigge and P. H. Nidditch (Oxford: Clarendon Press, 1975 [1737]).
7 Philip Pettit, "The Cunning of Trust," *Philosophy and Public Affairs*, 24 (1995), 202–25.
8 The Royal Society of New Zealand, Aronui Lecture Series, 2010, available at http://www.royalsociety.org.nz/events/annual/aronui-lecture/2010-series/
9 Jonathan Dancy, "Can We Trust Annette Baier?" *Philosophical Books* 36: 4 (1995), 237–45.
10 I am grateful to the editors of this volume for good suggestions on how to improve my first draft. Onora O'Neill also gave me helpful reactions to my first draft, and Rino Falcone and Karen Jones also gave me valuable feedback.

11

DISTRUSTING THE TRUSTWORTHY

Karen Jones

Onora O'Neill has done more than anyone to bring into theoretical focus the practical problem that would-be trusters face: how to align their trust with trustworthiness (O'Neill 2002a, 2002b, especially chapter 2, 2005). Trust and trustworthiness fail to be in alignment when the untrustworthy are trusted and the trustworthy are distrusted. It is easy to think that only the first misalignment is of significant practical concern, for when we trust the untrustworthy the result can be catastrophic. However, as O'Neill persuasively argues, failure to trust the trustworthy is also costly; indeed, depending on context, it can be more costly than failed trust. The costs include undue anxiety on the part of the distrusting, forgone opportunities for cooperation and dependency, and costly replacements for trust including auditing and accountability regimes, which at best displace trust from one group onto another and at worst create perverse incentives that make those they monitor less trustworthy (O'Neill 2002a, 2005). Trust-responsiveness, which motivates people to respond to trust with trustworthiness, has as its opposite distrust-responsiveness, which undermines the internal motivations towards trustworthiness of those who find themselves unjustly distrusted (Kramer 1999).

In this chapter, I focus on the problem of misplaced distrust where I include in this category distrust of the trustworthy as well as distrust of those who are not yet, but perhaps could become, trustworthy were it not for the ill effects of those regimes designed to bolster trust that are the target of O'Neill's critique of unintelligent accountability. O'Neill identifies "unintelligent" accounts of trust – by which she means accounts of trust that emphasize attitude and affect over judgment and choice – as part of the problem. An intelligent account of trust – by which she means one that emphasizes judgment and choice – supports intelligent approaches to accountability (2005: 33).

I propose to defend affective attitude accounts of trust against this charge. It is possible to acknowledge that trust contains an affective component without thereby seeing it as impervious to reasons or unable to be discriminating. What trust is and when it is justified are two separate, though connected, questions. Further, unless we recognize the affective component of trust we will not be able to fully appreciate trust's pathologies, including its susceptibility to being undermined by isolated but dramatic breaches of trust and its vulnerability to prejudice and stereotype. These give rise to the problem of unwarranted suspicion, where the fault lies on the trust side of the trust/trustworthiness pairing. Sometimes, however, the fault lies on the trustworthiness side: there can be something missing from the trustworthy person or institution that is unable or unwilling reliably to signal to would-be trusters that they can be counted on. Understanding the conceptual complexity of the failings from both sides requires first that we get clearer about what trustworthiness is and make a distinction that has not been clearly made in the literature between basic and rich trustworthiness (Jones 2012).[1] It turns out that the problem of intelligent accountability is a special instance of a more general problem: the problem of how to scaffold rich trustworthiness.

Basic and rich trustworthiness

Just as there is no agreement about what trust is, there is no agreement about what trustworthiness is. Nor is this surprising: accounts of trust have companion partner accounts of trustworthiness and not just any account of trustworthiness will fit with any account of trust. Thus, disagreement over the nature of trust carries over to disagreement about the nature of trustworthiness. For example, trust-as-confidence accounts, which equate trust with the confident expectation that the other will behave as anticipated, build in no presuppositions about the motivational structure of the trustworthy (Gambetta 1988). Any motive will suffice, be it habit, fear, sense of obligation, or mere behavioral regularity that occurs in ignorance of, or without regard to, the expectations others have about what you will do. All that matters is that the trustworthy have psychological structures sufficient to get the job done. Trust-as-confidence partners naturally with trustworthiness-as-reliability. Goodwill-based accounts (Baier 1986, Jones 1996), which analyze trust as presupposing goodwill on the part of the one trusted, are at the opposite end of the spectrum and fit only with highly restricted accounts of trustworthiness that require motivation from goodwill. In between lie many mid-ground options.

Though she does not offer an explicit account of trustworthiness, it is clear enough that O'Neill favors a relatively open account that lies somewhere in this middle terrain: "Trust in others' truth claims is well-placed if their words are, or turn out to be, true of the world. Trust in others' commitments is well placed if they duly act to shape the world, making it true to their word or to their implied commitments" (2005: 42). The trustworthy can have a variety of motives for living up to those commitments, from recognized obligations, to desires to "play by the rules" (O'Neill 2002b: 14).

In what follows, I will work with a relatively open account of trustworthiness so that it begs no important questions: the trustworthy act in the ways that they are being counted on to act, in full or in part out of recognition that so doing may be expected of them. Call this "trustworthiness as responsive reliability."[2] I take this account of trustworthiness to be congenial to O'Neill insofar as it fits with Richard Holton's (1994) account of trust, which she endorses (2002b: 13–14) and maintains her emphasis on judgment and choice (2002a, 2002b, 2005). Drawing on Strawson's (1974) notion of reactive attitudes – those attitudes that we take towards people when we view them from the participant stance, as fellow agents who can be held accountable for what they do – Holton argues that trust is reliance invested with reactive attitudes: "When you trust someone to do something you rely on them to do it and you regard that reliance in a certain way: you have a readiness to feel betrayal should it be disappointed, and gratitude should it be upheld" (Holton 1994: 67). Trust is thus an attitude that can only be had towards beings who are capable of recognizing the normative expectations – or expectations of, as opposed to expectations that (Hollis, 1998) – that others may have of them. The account occupies a mid-ground position in that it is more restrictive than trustworthiness-as-reliability accounts since it applies only to agents towards whom one can take the participant stance. Moreover, it does not include reliance on others where we lack the relevant dispositions to reactive attitudes, as when Kant's neighbors, say, relied on his regular habits to learn the time. It is, however, far less restrictive than accounts that link trustworthiness with goodwill. The responsiveness to expectations that the trustworthy show could be grounded in any number of commitments; nor need these commitments contain any direct reference to the truster. For example, on this account, a trustworthy doctor is one who is reliable in her medical care in part or in full because she recognizes the expectations of good professional practice that apply to her as a doctor. A trustworthy friend will meet the expectations negotiated as part of that particular friendship out of care and concern for the friend.

Like all other accounts of trustworthiness available in the literature, trustworthiness as responsive reliability has tacit three-place structure because, like them, it is designed to fit an account of trust that itself has three-place structure. It is universally agreed that trust must be analyzed as a three-place relation: A trusts B to do Z.[3] Since trust and trustworthiness are paired concepts, it follows from this that trustworthiness also has three-place structure: B is trustworthy with respect to A regarding the performance of Z. It is possible for an agent to be trustworthy with respect to some people regarding a type of action, but not trustworthy towards those same people regarding a different type of action (think of a generous friend who cannot be relied on in a medical crisis), and it is possible to be trustworthy towards some but not others regarding a type of action. This is just as well, for, as O'Neill argues, our trust must become discriminating if it is to become wise. What we need to know is not whether people in general, or people who hold a particular office, are trustworthy in general, but who we ourselves can trust to do what under what circumstances: "Well-placed trust requires discrimination: it is directed selectively at specific claims and at specific undertakings" (O'Neill 2005: 42).

It might be objected, however, that any three-place account of trustworthiness is missing something, for we often apply the word "trustworthy" to people without qualification and we would certainly withhold it from someone who could only be relied on by a few select individuals across a meager range of domains, even though a three-place analysis yields the verdict that they are trustworthy with respect to those people in those domains. We can get clearer about what is missing by backing up and asking what we, as potential trusters, are looking for: we want to find someone who will enable us to extend the efficacy of our agency by doing on our behalf something that we cannot do, or do as easily or as well, for ourselves: we want doctors to look after our health, plumbers our pipes, babysitters our children and so on across of wide range of potential dependencies that it would be advantageous for us to enter into on the supposition that our dependency would be met with trustworthiness. As finite agents, we want to be able to draw on the resources of competence that are out there and that could be recruited to advance our ends, including ends that are necessarily shared and so cannot, as a matter of logic, be achieved without others. That's why we care that there be trustworthy others, in the sense that there be people out there who can be counted on to follow through with their commitments and to act in the ways that we are relying on them to do. But we care about more than this. As finite agents we have limited information and limited time to search for more. We want the competent who can be depended on in the ways we need to identify themselves and we want those who are not up for a particular form of dependency, whether because they lack the competence or the inclination, to identify themselves before we embark on a reliance that is apt to be disappointed. We want those we can trust regarding a particular domain to signal their trustworthiness to us, so we can work out where – and where not – to turn.

Call three-place trustworthiness "basic trustworthiness" and call basic trustworthiness that reliably signals its presence "rich trustworthiness." I chose these labels because rich trustworthiness is basic trustworthiness+ rather than because basic trustworthiness is conceptually more basic or more intuitive than rich trustworthiness. I suspect that the reverse is true: basic trustworthiness is a term of art, a notion we need to introduce to talk about a property that matches trust once we recognize trust's three-place structure; rich trustworthiness is a clarification of that ordinary notion of trustworthiness that we use when we describe people as being trustworthy or not and that is evident in our association of trustworthiness with honesty, with eschewing false presentation, and with transparency (though, following O'Neill, I will argue that this last association is incorrect). Rich trustworthiness is two-place in structure: B is richly trustworthy with respect to A just in case (i) B is willing and able to signal to A those domains in which A can rely on B and (ii) there are at least some domains in which A can rely on B. The second clause is needed because it would be odd to claim that someone is richly trustworthy if they always signaled out; that is, always reliably signaled that they could not be relied on. Bringing the notion of rich trustworthiness into focus brings the problem of reliable signaling to the center of our investigation of trustworthiness.

Signaling

Signaling is communicative and takes place against a vast social background including norms and shared understandings of what can be expected of whom. Some of the background norms are moral, others professional; some are localized, others broadly based. Expectations can be based on something as informal as assumptions about style or mode of dress, age, or way of talking: people who look and act like this can be relied on in the following ways. At the other pole of formality are expectations that are the result of purpose-designed signaling mechanisms such as certification boards, whose task it is to both ensure that the people they certify are up to appropriate standards and to communicate that fact to the community at large. Because we live in a world in which how we present ourselves and who we are taken to be carries with it social meanings, we are inevitably signaling, rightly or wrongly, who can rely on us for what. In order to signal we need do nothing at all. Sometimes, signaling correctly requires merely that we do not disrupt these standing social signals. At other times, signaling correctly requires active moves to disrupt them, whether by signaling that we can be counted on for less than might have been reasonably supposed, given who we are taken to be, or by signaling that we are reliable in ways that might not be expected of us. Standing social signals can be exploited by untrustworthy agents, whether actively by signaling they have the properties characteristic of agents who tend to be trustworthy in a given domain when they do not, or passively by allowing signals that they know to be false to stand uncorrected. Signaling can be accomplished in many ways, including but not limited to: appearance, comportment, words, glances, deeds, certificates, titles, institutional roles. Direct verbal reassurance of trustworthiness is apt to be the least effective of communicative tools, for as Baier reminds us:

"Trust me!" is for most of us an invitation which we cannot accept at will – either we do already trust the one who says it, in which case it serves at best as reassurance, or it is properly responded to with, "Why should and how can I, until I have cause to?"

(Baier 1986: 244)

Past track record of acting in the way required is apt to be the most effective mode of signaling to would-be trusters the domains in which one can be trusted. But we do sometimes take up explicit invitations to trust, and it is not irrational to withhold trust from those with good records. Trust looks to the future and is underdetermined by evidence from past action (O'Neill 2002b: 14–15).

Displaying rich trustworthiness takes social competence. One needs to be alert to standing background assumptions and to know what signals a given group of would-be trusters can interpret correctly. What counts as a good signal is highly audience and context dependent. It is possible to mis-signal accidentally and so inadvertently invite trust. Just as some are insensitive to their location within networks of expectations and norms and so fail to notice the ways in which others are apt to rely on them, thereby making reliability improbable, others are insensitive to signals that normally competent would-be trusters can receive. Being deaf to standing social signals or attempts to depart from them, the insensitive might unreasonably assume that someone can be relied on in a given domain when there was no basis for attributing any such commitment to them. If they go ahead and trust and the one-trusted becomes aware of it, that trust will be experienced as presumptuous and perhaps even coercive. Someone who lacked three-place, or basic, trustworthiness with respect to this person in this domain nonetheless had rich trustworthiness and did their best to head off an unwelcome reliance. Through no fault of their own, they are now faced with the choice of letting down the truster or of following through on something to which they had neither expressed nor implied commitment.

When signaling fails

Not all failures of trust to align with trustworthiness stem from failures in signaling. Some misalignments are simple failures of basic trustworthiness, whether due to lack of competence or will. A is trusting B to do Z, but B is unable or unwilling to do Z. Fault for this misalignment typically lies with the one-trusted. In contrast, when trustworthiness is met with distrust, the problem lies in signaling. With the problem firmly located, it becomes clearer what questions need to be addressed if we want to remedy it, namely: When and why does signaling fail? Who is responsible for its failures?

O'Neill has addressed this mismatch in her work on the "culture of suspicion," where she has done much to identify toxic remedies, or would be remedies that undermine the very trustworthiness of which they are supposed to provide reassurance (2002a, 2002b, 2005). In what follows I want to situate that work in the context of other signaling failures and to argue that a full understanding of one side of the failure requires recognizing the role of affect in explaining why we sometimes withhold trust, despite the best signaling effort of the trustworthy. To recognize the role of affect in disrupting signal reception is not to endorse it, but it is to become alert to just how hard the problem can be to fix.

Failures in rich trustworthiness

When trustworthiness is met with distrust, responsibility for the misalignment can lie on either side. Let's first look at the territory O'Neill addresses, namely, failings responsibility for which lies on the side of the trustworthy. Signaling is communicative. It is consummated only when it receives the right kind of uptake by the intended audience. Full uptake is achieved when the would-be truster becomes willing to trust, whether or not they actually go on to trust; partial uptake is achieved when the intended audience judges that the other is trustworthy. Having rich trustworthiness requires at least the following communicative skills: understanding what kind of information the intended audience needs in order to reach a decision that their trust would likely be met with trustworthiness; understanding how to communicate that information to that audience; understanding impediments to effective communication and how they might be removed. I address each in turn.

By hypothesis, our would-be trustee is trustworthy with respect to the potential truster regarding the matter in question and they are trying to communicate that fact. What the would-be truster needs to know before placing trust is circumscribed. They do not need to know about the trustworthiness of the would-be trustee in other domains except insofar as trustworthiness there might be indicative of trustworthiness regarding the matter at hand. Nor do they need to know that the would-be trustee is trustworthy towards other people who belong, or are perceived to belong, to different categories – again, except insofar as trustworthiness towards people like that is indicative of trustworthiness towards them. The information about competence must also be information about the relevant competencies. Of importance here is O'Neill's work on the ill-effects of proxy measures for performance that are inadequate as markers of what we want to measure but are chosen because they are quantifiable and can be checked off by non-experts (O'Neill 2002a, 2002b, 2005). In deciding whether or not to send our child to the local public high school we need to know whether that school can be trusted to provide an environment free from bullying that will enable that child to flourish academically, creatively, and socially. Instead we may be provided with information about student performance on standardized tests, information that simply doesn't address what we, as concerned parents, need to know. (And, worse, the demand to provide such information takes attention away from the goals of a good education as teachers teach to the test.)

The second skill the richly trustworthy need is the ability to *communicate* the right sort of information to those who would trust them if only they knew they could. As O'Neill notes, simply making that information available is not enough. Ideals of transparency can give rise to "information dumping" – all you need to know is out there, but good luck finding it and good luck being able to interpret it (O'Neill 2002a: 61–81). Different audiences require different communicative strategies. Recall that rich trustworthiness is two-place: one may be willing and able to signal one's basic trustworthiness to some but not others. We want people and institutions to be richly trustworthy towards *us*. Sometimes, rich trustworthiness is an *obligation*: moral or social norms assign to a particular person, groups of people, or institutions the job of signaling their trustworthiness to a given audience. When this is so, proper communication is itself an obligation. Sometimes, rich trustworthiness is a gift, something we routinely, freely give to each other when we invite trust we mean to honor.

The third skill the richly trustworthy need is the ability to anticipate impediments to the reception of their message and the practical wisdom to know how they might be removed. Often it is our own past behavior that is the largest impediment to communicating that we can now, at last, be trusted. If our betrayal was spectacular or if those we let down confront us about it, we cannot but be aware of the problem. Unfortunately, it is not always as straightforward as this: we may be unaware of the trust we betray and we may interpret our own track record differently from those to whom we would signal our trustworthiness. What they see as evidence of failure in a relevant domain we see as showing incapacity in a non-related area; they see similarity between themselves and those we have let down in the past, we see difference. It would be too much to demand of the richly trustworthy that they be able to anticipate all signaling problems arising from divergent interpretations of track record, because some interpretations are idiosyncratic or irrational. To earn the title "richly trustworthy," one needs the lesser but still hard-to-acquire skill of anticipating alternative readings of that record that are plausible for reasonable members of the intended audience. In societies divided along class and race lines, so that members of different social groups have different life experiences and bring different presuppositions to bear in interpreting their social world, it can take hard imaginative work to be richly trustworthy across social divisions (Jones 2002).

Apologies, offers of compensation and other work of "moral repair" (Walker 2006) can also be important ways of communicating that one's past behavior is just that and no longer predictive of the future. When past track record has been poor, or when it is entirely unknown, the best signaling method is "walking the walk" – actually doing something that shows your reliability. If the level of distrust is high enough, however, it might be impossible for a person or institution to get uptake for their attempts to signal that they can be trusted in a domain. The richly trustworthy will know when they need to call on the help of others and will be wise in who they choose. The solution might require using mutually trusted third parties to assist in signaling trustworthiness. Often this job is informal and personal, but when the problem is lack of trust in institutions, the solution needs to be at the level of institutional design. Some of the signaling work will need to be taken over by independent institutional bodies, which is where intelligently designed accountability regimes become indispensable. Responsibility for rich trustworthiness can be distributed.

It is clear even from this brief examination of the skills needed to convey three-place trustworthiness to an intended audience that rich trustworthiness is no easy thing. Moreover, by restricting the discussion to cases where the would-be trustee has basic trustworthiness and is encountering problems signaling it, I've left out a good part of the problem of being richly trustworthy, which is the problem of having accurate self-perception of the zones and limits of one's own basic trustworthiness.[4] So as to keep focus on the problem of mistrusting the trustworthy, rather than enter that territory let's turn instead to looking at the problem from the side of the would-be truster.

Affect and uptake

When rich trustworthiness fails to receive uptake in trust the problem lies with the truster. Something is stopping them from either receiving or acting on a well-sent signal. In what follows I argue that often – I have no investment in the claim that no other mechanisms are present – the problem lies in affective distortions on the part of would-be truster. Trust displays three recognized hallmarks of emotions: evidence tampering, recalcitrance, and spillover. The best explanation of why trust behaves like this is that it has an affective or emotional component.[5]

Trust and distrust have a tendency to be self-confirming. On an affective attitude account of trust, trust functions as a *biasing* device (de Sousa 1987, Damasio 1994). It shapes how we interpret the words and deeds of others. Where possible, and even if it takes some ingenuity, we will interpret the words and actions of those we trust in ways compatible with their trustworthiness (Jones 1996). Conmen of all stripes rely on trust's tendency to evidence tamper. Distrust evidence tampers in the reverse direction and it can make us deaf to perfectly decent signaling. There can be enough evidence available for us to believe that someone is trustworthy in a domain and yet we do not because our capacity to interpret that evidence is undermined by our distrust. Prejudice and stereotype often work in this way. Despite some progress in challenging racist belief, fast pre-judgment assessment of black men in the USA continues to reveal entrenched racism. A young black man is more readily interpreted as threatening or suspicious than a young white man engaged in the same kind of behavior and this in turn contributes to explaining why they are more likely to be stopped by the police. By doing nothing at all they are taken to be signaling untrustworthiness. When a trustworthy member of a group that experiences identity-based prejudice tries to signal that they are trustworthy in a domain in which, according to the stereotype, they are not expected to be, the signal risks misfiring. The problem here is not in the signaler but in the distrusting recipient, who interprets the signal through the lens of their distrust.

Trust shows another phenomenon familiar from work on the emotions: recalcitrance (Greenspan 1988, D'Arms and Jacobson 2003). Recalcitrance occurs when judgment and affect part company. It is most visible when at its irrational extreme in phobias. Fear of flying is compatible with full knowledge of the general safety of aviation and is not dispelled by rehearsing those facts however carefully. Our trusting can, and often does, part company from our believing: trust operates at a different level from mere belief. It is the largely unreflective result of our social experiences and reflects our prejudices and cognitive habits at least as much, if not more than, our judgments about trustworthiness. To think of trust as simply a matter of judgment and choice is to locate trust and distrust too shallowly within the agent's psyche and so not to see the kinds of pathologies to which it is vulnerable. While it is relatively easy for our reflection and judgment to bring about a change in our beliefs about trustworthiness, it is much harder for them to bring about a shift in our trust and distrust. We can believe that someone is trustworthy and so be willing to assert their trustworthiness and reason on its basis. Yet this belief may or may not be reflected in the cognitive and affective habits with which we approach the prospect of being dependent on them. We can believe that they are trustworthy and yet be anxiously unwilling to rely. The problem of trust parting company from belief manifests itself also in the move from the general to the particular: we can judge that members of a group, overseas trained non-white doctors, for example, are neither more nor less trustworthy than the generality of doctors and yet not be equivalently disposed to trust them. A richly trustworthy person trying to signal their trustworthiness in a domain in the face of prejudice may get only partial uptake: recognition at the level of judgment that, yes, trust can be placed there, but still no reliance.

Distrust and trust are vulnerable to spillover. Spillover happens when an attitude loses focus on its original target and spreads to neighboring targets. It is easiest seen in anger: when we are angry at someone for something, it is all too easy to become angry at them for something else; when angry at our partner, it is all too easy to become angry at our co-worker. Anger readily over generalizes and seeks out other related (and not so related) targets. Distrust behaves the same way. Consider the case of Jayant Patel, known as Dr Death, a surgeon trained in India and the USA, who worked at a regional hospital in Queensland Australia from 2003–5. Prior to working in Australia he had been found medically negligent and placed on restricted practice in both New York and Oregon. In 2010, his incompetent surgical practice led to convictions for manslaughter and grievous bodily harm. An inquiry into the affair determined it probable that he was responsible for at least 13 deaths while working in Queensland.[6] The case revealed problems in regulation, implementation, accountability structures, and workplace environment, where whistle-blowers were ignored or bullied. It also amplified an existing ambient racism in Australian society, which has had a corrosive effect on trust in non-white foreign trained doctors.[7] Spillover unquestionably followed the 9/11 attacks and its effects still continue. Distrust readily falsely generalizes, even among those who, at the level of calm judgment, recognize their generalizations are not warranted. Spillover distrust prevents the trustworthy from being able effectively to communicate their trustworthiness.

Remedy

It might well be better if trust were a matter of judgment and of choice; if only trust could be as fine-grained and responsive to evidence as judgment, as flexible and controllable as action. But it isn't and if we overlook the gap between judgment and choice and trust then we will locate the problem of distrusting the trustworthy too shallowly. We will be alert to the problems of signaling from the trustworthiness end and so focus there in our search for remedy, where O'Neill has proposed some excellent remedies and exposed some stupid ones. This is fine, as far as it goes and sometimes it goes far enough – sometimes, the problem is at the trustworthiness end – but sometimes it is at the trust end and sometimes at both ends at once.

It might be thought that the only remedies we can try, as a matter of social policy, are those that aim to improve signaling, especially in institutional contexts where the work of signaling can be distributed. We can devise new and better ways of doing it and reject inefficient and destructive approaches, replacing unintelligent with intelligent accountability. When it comes to affective distortions, especially those that result from identity-based prejudice, however, we must each of us do the hard work of disrupting the schemas that promote bias, including bias in who we trust. We each of us have to work on our own pathologies of distrust, whether they be pathologies that arise from individual history, or broadly shared pathologies that arise from social inequality. Nothing much here for a policy-maker to get purchase on, or so you might think. However, if we reflect on the role of the media and politicians in encouraging recalcitrance and spillover, we can see that there are steps that can be taken to improve public trust that work from the trust end. Sensationalist reporting of dramatic but isolated instances of untrustworthiness fill the newspapers and the television. Spillover is fostered when the race or ethnicity of minority offenders is mentioned even though it has no bearing on the crime. The media is not the only guilty party; politicians regularly fan fear of asylum seekers to use for their own political ends. There are ways of approaching the problem of misplaced distrust from the trust end and a humane and just approach to many policy issues including those surrounding refugees, immigration, and multiculturalism depends on it.

Notes

1 A distinction in this neighborhood is noted by Nancy Potter in her work on trustworthiness as a virtue. She identifies the core dispositions of those who possess trustworthiness as a virtue to be "They give signs and assurances of their trustworthiness" and "They take their epistemic responsibilities seriously" (Potter 2002: 174–75). However, she embeds in her account of trustworthiness commitment to egalitarian politics and to recognizing difference. I think this makes her account of trustworthiness an account of how to be trustworthy towards those who share a similar moral and political orientation.
2 A related account is implicit in Walker's discussion of trust, which also draws on Holton (1994). See Walker 2006: 80.
3 Or related alternatives, such as Baier's (1986) "to look after valued item C," or Jones' (1996) "in domain of interaction, D."
4 That problem is the focus of my discussion of rich trustworthiness in Jones 2012.
5 In my earlier work, I analyzed this component as an attitude of optimism that the goodwill and competence of the other will extend to cover the domain of interaction. I now think that, while it is correct to suppose that trust is an attitude of optimism, it is incorrect to think it must be targeted at goodwill: "goodwill" is either a meaningless catchall or too narrow (Jones 2010). However, for my purposes here it doesn't matter how the affective component of trust is analyzed, only that it is acknowledged.
6 The *Queensland Public Hospitals Commission of Inquiry Report*, also known as the *Davies Report*, is available at: http://www.qphci.qld.gov.au/
7 As reported on ABC radio, 6 July 2005. http://www.abc.net.au/pm/content/2005/s1408475.htm

Bibliography

Baier, Annette 1986. "Trust and Antitrust," *Ethics*, vol. 96, pp. 231–60.
Damasio, Antonio 1994. *Descartes' Error*. New York: Putnam.
D'Arms, Justin and Daniel Jacobson 2003. "The Significance of Recalcitrant Emotion (or, Anti-Quasijudgmentalism)." In Anthony Hatzimoysis (ed.), *Philosophy and the Emotions*. Cambridge: Cambridge University Press.
de Sousa, Ronald 1987. *The Rationality of Emotion*. Cambridge: MIT Press.
Gambetta, Diego 1988. "Can We Trust Trust?" In Diego Gambetta (ed.), *Trust: Making and Breaking Cooperative Relations*. New York: Basil Blackwell.

Greenspan, Patricia 1988. *Emotions and Reasons: An Inquiry into Emotional Justification.* New York: Routledge.
Hollis, Martin 1998. *Trust Within Reason.* Cambridge: Cambridge University Press.
Holton, Richard 1994. "Deciding to Trust, Coming to Believe," *Australasian Journal of Philosophy,* vol. 72, pp. 63–76.
Jones, Karen 1996. "Trust as an Affective Attitude," *Ethics,* vol. 107, pp. 4–25.
——2002. "The Politics of Credibility." In Louise Antony and Charlotte Witt (eds), *A Mind of One's Own: Feminist Essays on Reason and Objectivity,* 2nd edn. Boulder, Colo.: Westview Press.
——2010. "Counting On One Another" In Arne Gron and Claudia Welz (eds), *Trust, Sociality, Selfhood:* 67–82. Tubingen: Mohr Siebeck.
——2012. "Trustworthiness." *Ethics,* vol 123, pp. 61–85.
Kramer, Roderick 1999. "Trust and Distrust in Organizations," *Annual Review of Psychology,* vol. 50, pp. 569–98.
O'Neill, Onora 2002a. *A Question of Trust: The BBC Reith Lectures 2002.* Cambridge: Cambridge University Press.
——2002b. *Autonomy and Trust in Bioethics.* Cambridge: Cambridge University Press.
——2005. "Justice, Trust and Accountability." Published as "Gerechtigkeit, Vertrauen und Zurechenbarkeit" in Otto Neumaier, Clemens Sedmak, Michael Zichy (eds), *Gerechtigkeit: Auf der Suche nach einem Gleichgewicht.* Frankfurt: Ontos Verlag: 33–55.
Potter, Nancy 2002. *How Can I be Trusted? A Virtue Theory of Trustworthiness.* Lanham, Maryland: Rowman & Littlefield.
Strawson, Peter 1974. "Freedom and Resentment." In his *Freedom and Resentment.* London: Methuen.
Walker, Margaret 2006. *Moral Repair: Reconstructing Moral Relations After Wrongdoing.* Cambridge: Cambridge University Press.

12

TRUST IN INSTITUTIONS

Daniel Weinstock

Introduction

Trust has reemerged in the last couple of decades as a major theme in moral and political philosophy, as well as in empirical disciplines such as political science and sociology. A number of reasons have fuelled this trend. Among moral philosophers, it is probably fair to say that interest in trust reflects an impatience with the emphasis that has been placed by mainstream Anglo-American analytic philosophers on concepts such as rights and obligations, that is, on concepts that purport to denote the ways in which agents should act toward one another, without attending to the moral psychological conditions of ethically sound human relations.[1] Among political philosophers and sociologists, much recent work has reflected the importance of Robert Putnam's seminal work on social capital. In a series of books and articles, Putnam has argued forcefully that relations of trust that emerge among citizens in informal institutions in civil society (including, notoriously, bowling clubs!) play an important role in the civic education of citizens, and in their acceptance of norms of fair-play and collaboration.[2] Among the many virtues generated according to this account by cultures of trust, the avoidance of wasteful expenditure by the state and by citizens in the surveillance of citizens with whom one collaborates has been emphasized and extolled by scholars such as Francis Fukayama.[3] In earlier work, I have argued that trust among citizens provides us with a more theoretically plausible way to account for social unity than do concepts such as "identity" and "shared values."[4]

While they differ in tone and emphasis, the scholarship that has generated this renewal of interest has had to do with "horizontal" trust, that is, with trust that obtains among agents in (largely) face-to-face contexts, outside of formal structures of authority. Moral philosophers are, for example, interested in the kinds of traits of individual character and patterns of behavior that qualify an agent as trustworthy, and with the kinds of affect that go into both signaling one's trustworthiness to others, and into trusting others appropriately.[5] Some political philosophers have taken up the call that Putnam's work can be taken to have issued and have investigated the conditions of healthy associational life.[6]

But the question of trust also poses itself, quite crucially, in a range of "vertical" contexts, that is in contexts in which agents must decide whether or not to trust agents who hold positions of institutional authority over them, or to trust "faceless" institutions with which they have relations that are largely unmediated by sustained human contact. Figuring out the conditions under which we should trust such powerful agents and institutions (indeed, figuring out whether "trust" is the kind of attitude we should be aiming to cultivate), and articulating the ways in which these institutions can show themselves to be worthy of the trust of citizens should loom more largely in the agenda of political philosophers than it does, given how deeply we interact with these powerful institutions on an almost daily basis (the state, the market, the law, medicine, the media, to name just a few).[7] Empirical work, both survey-based[8] and historical[9] has begun to emerge, but properly normative work lags sorely behind.

The recent work of Onora O'Neill constitutes an important exception. She has focused our attention on the fact that in complex modern societies, the question of trust arises in myriad complex institutional settings, so that "we need social and political institutions that allow us to judge where to place our trust."[10] Though her most sustained work has been devoted to the issue of the conditions that underlie trust in medical institutions,[11] she has also made important contributions to our understanding of the conditions that underlie trust in government and in media.

My intention in this essay is to take up three challenges posed by O'Neill in her (in my view quite justified) complaint that core social institutions in modern liberal democracies do not at present function so as to warrant the conferral by citizens of trust. A first, preliminary challenge has to do with the analysis of the commonly held perception that we are currently living through a "crisis of trust." O'Neill has expressed puzzlement at this perception, noting that the opinions about the trustworthiness of institutions that people profess are rarely matched by action. By distinguishing between cognitive and volitional dimensions of trust, I provide an interpretation that makes sense of this apparent gulf.

An analysis of the obstacles that face citizens in deciding whether or not to trust powerful social institutions provides me with tools with which to elaborate on two further complaints voiced by O'Neill. They have to do, first, with the constructive role that media can perform in enhancing the capacities that citizens have to place trust (and distrust) wisely, and second, with the nature of the institutional mechanisms that must be put in place in order to alert citizens to the presence of problems with these institutions justifying the withholding of trust, and to suggest appropriate remedies that make these institutions resilient against the factors that are most likely to adversely effect an institution's trustworthiness.

Complexities of trust

We form judgments as to the trustworthiness of the other agents with whom we come into contact on a daily basis. The ability to do so in a fairly reliable way is key to our survival, and various mechanisms upon which we habitually rely in order to confer or withhold trust have most likely been fine-tuned over millennia by evolutionary processes. The neurochemical substrate of attitudes such as trust is just beginning to be understood,[12] but work in the area of neurobiology provides us with fairly decisive evidence to sustain the thought that in determining whether or not to trust another individual, we routinely fall back on what experimental psychologists have termed "system 1" processes,[13] that is processes that call on intuitive judgment rather than reasoning.

Now, clearly, our intuitive heuristics sometimes get it wrong, either because we fail to pick up on cues that should have alerted us to the trustworthiness or untrustworthiness of an individual, because the correlation between these cues and trustworthiness is not perfect, or because some unscrupulous agents are able to mimic the cues alerting us to trustworthiness sufficiently well to open us to the risk of exploitation. In this, as in many other matters, we need to back up our intuitions with reasoning. We need to be alive to the possibility that intuition is leading us astray for one or another of the aforementioned reasons, and develop more explicit tests allowing us to determine whether or not to trust the agents we come into contact with. In other words, we need to be vigilant. But what does this mean, exactly?

To begin this inquiry, we need a working definition of what we mean by "trust." Russell Hardin has argued for what he calls the "encapsulated interest account" of trust. According to this view, "my trust turns [...] on whether the Trusted counts my interests as his or her own *just because they are my interests.*"[14] Trust is, according to this account, "grounded in an assumption that the potentially trusted person has an interest in maintaining a relationship with the truster."[15] I have argued elsewhere that this condition is too strong. I have proposed that we define the attitude negatively, as one that obtains when I have reason to believe that the potentially trusted person is not adversely disposed toward the realization of my interests.[16] A conception of trust that hinges on the potentially trusted agent's interest in maintaining a relationship in my view offends against linguistic intuitions. More crucially, however, to the extent that we think that the conferral of trust is a prolegomenon to cooperation, the restriction of trust to cases of encapsulated interests would have us forgo opportunities for cooperation through which we could significantly advance our interests and goals.[17]

So the vigilance that I introduced a moment ago can be further specified by referring to the definition of trust just mooted. My vigilance is manifested by the fact that my conferral of trust upon another individual is dependent upon my having sufficient evidence to suggest that she is not ill-disposed toward the realization of my interests.

This is still far too indeterminate, however. The account needs to be fleshed out along a number of dimensions. First, I want to introduce a distinction between trusting as an attitude and trusting as action. Now, Hardin has held that "if trust is cognitive, then we do not choose to trust."[18] At some level, this seems correct: to claim that I trust someone just means that I possess conclusive evidence of the appropriate kind, that is, evidence that speaks to her trustworthiness. It seems odd to claim that one does not trust another agent, though all available evidence points to her being entirely trustworthy. A natural interpretation of such a statement would be that the person making it is intimating that, in fact, all the evidence is not available.

On further reflection, there do however appear to be volitional dimensions to trust. First, we can decide to expend more or less effort in the search for relevant evidence. In deciding whether or not to trust a vendor on *Ebay*, I can default to the assumption that a fairly established site would have already filtered out untrustworthy vendors, or I can dig more deeply into her previous record as a vendor, as attested to by previous customers.[19] Decisions as to how much effort to expend are made often unconsciously by agents countless times in their everyday lives. But they are *decisions* nonetheless, that can be adjudged more or less rational.

Second, the locution "I trusted X with Z," where Z designates an object I have an interest in, is ambiguous as between two meanings. First, it can denote a purely cognitive attitude, to the effect that I believe that Z can be trusted to realize or at least not to undercut the interest that I have in Z. But it can also denote an action. "I trust her with my kids" would seem to denote more than just a belief. It standardly means that I have decided to act on my belief, to entrust my kids to her. And that too, results from a decision. Note, however, that the decision to act on my trust does not flow directly from the belief that a person is trustworthy. I can, in ways that are perfectly intelligible, decide not to (actively) entrust the realization of an interest to an individual that I (cognitively) trust. Especially if we admit, as I think we should, that judgments of trustworthiness admit of degrees, then we can well imagine a person deciding not to make the realization of an interest contingent upon the performance or abstention of another agent, even when she believes that that other agent seems, for the most part, to be trustworthy.

How do we decide how much effort to expend in determining whether a person is worthy of our trust or not? And what threshold of trustworthiness is it reasonable to expect a person to reach before we feel able to act on the belief we hold in her trustworthiness? A moment's reflection strongly suggests the following answer: it depends. It depends in particular on complex cost–benefit reasoning that incorporates the value of that which we are considering entrusting to another person, the costs involved in inquiring into her trustworthiness, the costs involved in *not* entrusting the realization of the interest to her, the availability of other potential cooperators, and so on. There may very well be decision contexts in which it makes sense to act on a low level of trust, and others in which it makes sense *not* to act on a comparatively higher level. It depends, to express the thought in a compact manner, on what is at stake.

A second complication that needs to be added to the account I am developing has to do with the properties that make an agent worthy of trust. Thus far, and in conformity with much of the literature on the issue, I have emphasized the attitude that the potentially trusted person has toward the truster. She is trustworthy to the extent that she is (at least) not unfavorably disposed toward the satisfaction of the truster's interests. But an agent can still find her trust to be misplaced even when the potentially trusted other possessed the requisite attitude. Though she may be favorably disposed toward me, she may not possess the capacity to carry out her role in satisfying my interest. She may not know enough, or be otherwise incapacitated. Now, there are occasions in which the possession by the potentially trusted person of a capacity to help is not required. Sometimes, all I need from the people that I trust is simply that they get out of the way, or that they not deliberately act to harm me.

But there are times when the possession of the requisite capacities matters crucially. If I entrust my child to a minder, it matters just as much to me, if not more, that she be suitably inclined to care for my child, as that she know, say, how to administer CPR were the need to arise.

This heightens the challenges that the vigilant agent faces in determining whether or not to trust another. Not only does he have to collect evidence that points toward the other agent's dispositions toward him; he also has to ascertain whether the other agent is competent or qualified to do that which he is disposed to do in the service of my interests.

So it turns out that, unless we merely fall back on our intuitive, gut-level impressions as to another agent's trustworthiness, the decision to trust another agent is a dizzyingly complex task, involving the collection of various kinds of evidence, cost–benefit calculations to do with the amount of effort that it is rational to expend in the quest for such evidence, and further calculations concerning the appropriate action to take on the basis of the evidence, given the comparative desirability of the pre-trust *status quo* and the post-trust state of affairs, suitably adjusted to account for the risk that any conferral of trust inevitably involves. Given the complexities involved, and the costs of getting these complex calculations wrong, it is little wonder that human agents often default to system 1 heuristics and simply "go with their gut."

Making sense of the gulf between avowal and action

I want in the next section to provide an account of some of the additional difficulties that attend the conferral of trust not to other individuals in "horizontal" contexts, but rather in institutionalized structures of authority. But the account thus far allows us to provide a way of answering a puzzle that Onora O'Neill has raised about trust. O'Neill observes quite rightly that there seems to be something of a gulf between, on the one hand, the attitudes that citizens profess when asked, for example in the context of opinion polls, whether they trust the members of different professions, and on the other, the decisions that their actions would seem to evince. People claim not to trust, and yet they confer trust everyday (by drinking the water that comes out of their taps, by believing, if only defeasibly, what they read in the newspapers, consulting lawyers and doctors, by voting, and so on). O'Neill's view is that in contexts in which people have a choice about whether or not to actively trust the provider of a service, we gain no real information about their level of trust from their mere avowals. She writes:

> Expressions of mistrust that are divorced from action come cheap: we can assert and rescind, flaunt or change, defend or drop attitudes and expressions of mistrust without changing the way we live. This may show something about attitudes of suspicion, but little or nothing about where we place trust.[20]

Now there is no denying that people may very well simply be venting when they tell pollsters that they do not trust politicians, journalists, lawyers, and so on. But something more subtle may be going on. We can understand human agents as having complex attitudes towards the agents that they are considering whether or not to confer trust upon. On the one hand, they may genuinely and sincerely think that the evidence suggests that they are not entirely trustworthy, or that they have insufficient evidence to determine a level of trustworthiness with anything approaching confidence. This may be what at least some citizens are telling pollsters when they are asked whether or not they trust members of this or that profession. On the other hand, their all-things-considered judgment might be that despite the fact that they do not entirely trust them, they are still better off acting on imperfect trust than withholding it, given the costs attendant upon attempting to secure further evidence, and the costs involved in not trusting, or in finding an alternative for the realization of an interest to conferring trust on agents that present themselves most readily. O'Neill is right to state that "those who *seriously* mistrust producers and suppliers of consumer goods *can* and *do* refuse to rely on them. Those who *really* mistrust the tap water drink bottled water, or boil it, or use water purification tablets."[21] This seems overstated, especially in the light of the analysis provided thus far. Clearly, people who have absolutely no trust in the agencies charged with providing them with clean water will take steps such as those suggested by O'Neill. But if our trust is partial, or based on incomplete evidence, we may judge that it is best, all things considered, to drink the water provided, given the costs of taking these steps.

I want to suggest in the next section that the complexities that accompany the decision to confer trust upon institutions may lead to citizens making erroneous judgments about the trustworthiness of institutions and of their agents. But contrary to O'Neill, I think we can make perfectly good sense of the apparent gulf between the avowals and actions of agents, without having to ascribe lack of seriousness to the former.

The requirements of vigilance with respect to institutions

Deciding whether to trust another individual is, as we have seen, a complex affair. Things get more difficult still when we have to decide whether or not to trust the institutions that in complex modern societies have such great impact upon our ability to realize our goals and interests. I want in this section to describe the difficulties that attend deciding whether or not to trust institutions. I will argue that the challenges that face us in deciding to trust institutions are fearsome. But I do so not out of a sense of despair, but rather in order to determine what mechanisms have to be put into place in order to make it the case, first, that we look in the right places for evidence that institutions are trustworthy or not, given that there are strong pressures that push us to look for that evidence in the wrong places, and second, that we be able to put institutional safeguards in place so that the obstacles to institutional trustworthiness that we have most reason to fear are if not eliminated, at least lessened, so as to decrease the dangers that accompany the conferral of trust on any agent with respect to significant interests.

A first observation follows quite naturally from the foregoing analyses. Though trust in institutions is important, it cannot be unconditional. What is true of agents in their interpersonal affairs is even truer of citizens: we need a citizen body that is vigilant. We need citizens who trust institutions that merit their trust. And so, we need citizens who to some degree evince *distrust*, who actively seek out information about the competence and the disposition of institutional agents, and for whom the conferral of trust is never a once-and-for-all affair, but who continue to monitor the institutions with which they deal for signs of untrustworthiness. Now clearly, vigilance must ideally be well calibrated. That is, we will want to avoid citizens not placing their trust in institutions that are, in fact, sufficiently trustworthy. Just as there are costs to misplaced trust, whereby citizens make themselves vulnerable to exploitation, there are also significant opportunity costs that can follow from misplaced distrust.

I will not go into any great detail concerning the precise level at which citizen vigilance should be pitched. I will however state the obvious, which is that it must if anything be pitched at a higher level than is the case in what I have here termed "horizontal" relations. This is so for at least three reasons. First, the institutions that I am interested in in this context have significant degrees of power over us. In the case of the state and of legal institutions, they can legitimately coerce us to act in certain ways rather than others, appropriate our property, and so on. Market institutions do not possess coercive authority, yet the ubiquity of the market makes it the case that citizens have to accept significant costs and sacrifices in order to immunize themselves from them. Health institutions have neither the coercive power of state institutions, nor the ubiquity of the market, yet they nonetheless exercise power over us through the quasi-monopoly they possess over the knowledge and interventions that are sometimes required in order to maintain our health. Hardin and his collaborators are thus correct in stating that "the management of power relations in a society is a key factor in determining the capacity for trust."[22]

Second, as the example of health institutions makes plain, the principal social institutions that we have to decide to trust or not are crucial for the realization of some of our most vital interests. There are few areas over which the power of the state and of its judicial institutions does not range. Whether we like it or not, most of the goods that we need in order to live comfortable lives are subject at least partially to the laws of the market. And the relations we have with health institutions are often a matter of life and death.

Third, it is far easier in most informal contexts to find substitutes to potentially trusted agents. I can always find another babysitter to look after my kids if I begin to lose trust in the one I presently employ. I can purchase my vegetables from the greengrocer down the street if the one that I presently shop at starts skimping on quality. But it is much more costly to, as it were, live "off the grid," foregoing any contact with state institutions, public utilities, mainstream health services. The non-substitutability of some kinds of agents for the delivery of goods and services necessary for the realization of their goals and interests makes citizens more vulnerable to them, and thus requires heightened vigilance on their part to ensure that they are not being exploited or neglected by the agents with which they have no choice but to interact.

Power, the importance of the interests at stake, and the relatively greater costs involved in finding substitute agents in whom to entrust the realization of these interests are salient factors that explain the need for heightened vigilance on the part of citizens.

I want now to explore some of the obstacles that get in the way of our being able reliably to collect evidence about the trustworthiness of complex institutions. The obstacles I am particularly interested in are ones that emerge, first, from the lack of fit between the particular kind of agency that institutions display, and our natural expectations about agency; second, from the particular kind of constitution of some of the most important institutional agents that we encounter; and third (paradoxically), from the setting up of institutions designed to increase the ability of citizens to collect evidence relevant to the determination of the trustworthiness of institutions.

Agency, individual and corporate

In a recent book, Philip Pettit and Christian List have demonstrated that, given a reasonable conception of what agency involves, the capacity for agency can be realized by collective agents. They defend a non-holistic but non-eliminativist view according to which group agency supervenes holistically upon the rule-governed actions of individual members of collectives.[23]

If List and Pettit are correct, then at least some institutions are agents, and thus, the kinds of entities to which it is appropriate to ascribe responsibility, and to evince attitudes such as trust. The problem I want to alert our attention to stems from the fact that institutional agents are very particular kinds of agents. The agency of institutions is a product of institutional design: it results from the ways in which the many individuals who work within the institution in question interact in order to deliver the goods or services that the institution is designed to deliver, the rules that govern their interactions within the institution, and the various oversight mechanisms that enforce these rules. Accordingly, the trustworthiness of institutions should be assessed on the basis of meso- and macro-level design features of institutions, rather than primarily upon the apparent trustworthiness of particular individual human agents within these institutions. The individual behavior of people who work within complex institutions provides us with at best very limited and fragmentary evidence of an institution's trustworthiness. Individual behavior within institutional contexts is constrained in a number of ways by the rules of the institutions. But these rules are opaque to us if we attend merely to behavior and cues delivered by the individual human agents we encounter within institutions.

The problem is that we are naturally disposed to arrive at conclusions about the trustworthiness of agents on the basis of our encounters with other human agents. The system 1 heuristics that we discussed earlier are derived from our experience of interaction with other human agents, and thus rely on features that are simply not possessed by institutional agents. We look for facial cues, tones of voice, and the like. Now, as we have already seen, these heuristics, though serviceable and efficient in a wide range of contexts, are not infallible, and they therefore make us vulnerable to exploitation, especially to agents who have learned to mimic the cues of trustworthiness so as to induce an attitude of trust. In order to avoid potentially disastrous errors in the conferral of trust, system 1 processes must be monitored and if necessary overridden by the more complex cost–benefit reasoning that I briefly described above. If what I have said about institutional agents is correct, it follows that in the case of institutional agents we must not only override the tendency to look for certain kinds of cues in individual human agents. We must also override our tendency to arrive at conclusions about the trustworthiness of all types of agents, collective and individual, on the basis of our responses to the latter type.

Focusing on individual agents rather than on the constitution of collective agents in order to ascertain the trustworthiness of institutional agents can lead us to make mistakes of misplaced trust and misplaced distrust. Institutions that are designed in order to deceive or exploit their clients, and institutions that are simply not very good at tracking their interests, can give rise to misplaced trust if the individuals with whom clients come into contact seem trustworthy. One can well imagine that unscrupulous agents often make use of the tendency of individuals to see certain kinds of physical cues as evidence of trustworthiness in order to mask the exploitative way in which the institution actually operates.

Perhaps more insidious is the risk that attending to the traits of individuals in order to determine whether or not an institution is trustworthy may in some crucial contexts induce misplaced distrust. Some institutions that have the properties that we briefly described in the previous section (power, connection with vital interests and non-substitutability) as warranting heightened vigilance on the part of citizens may actually be designed in ways that do not justify distrust, but that generate individual behavior and traits of character that may lead people to ascribe untrustworthiness to the institution as a whole. Let me explain what I mean in the next section.

Adversarial institutions

Lawyers and politicians are routinely identified as among the least trusted professionals. Now, that may be because there is something about the law and about politics that attracts morally subpar individuals. One might think for example that both domains present ample opportunity for lucrative corruption, and so those who are drawn to these professions are among the more corruptible members of society.

I want to explore an alternative explanation for the lack of trust that citizens profess towards members of these professions in opinion polls. Lawyers at least in the kind of legal system that characterizes societies such as Canada, the United States, and the United Kingdom, and politicians in the context of multiparty democracies, operate in institutional contexts that we might term "adversarial." That is, they are built on the assumption that important goods (justice, the "common good," etc.) are more efficiently delivered not by entrusting their pursuit directly to individual agents, but rather by institutionalized competition. Lawyers on both sides of a case zealously defend their clients' interests, attempt to dig up evidence that is favorable to them and to present that evidence in ways that are favorable to them. When both sides do this in the context of a rule-governed competition in which the principal motivation of the main actors in the system is partial, the hope is that justice, impartially construed, will emerge more readily than under other, non-adversarial sets of rules. Democratic politics is also premised on the assumption that agents who are motivated to a large degree by partisanship will in the context of a democratic system act in ways that conduce to the common good more efficiently than, say, in a one-party state.[24] Similar remarks might be made about markets.

The "case" for adversarial institutions of course needs to be made much more fully than this.[25] What's more, it is clearly the case that such institutions will only work if certain rules are observed by all parties within an adversarial context, and it is thus a very important task that we develop the ethics, individual and institutional, that need to be put in place and enforced if adversarial institutions are to deliver the goods that constitute their *raison d'être*.[26] My intention in the present context is much more limited, however. I want merely to point out that to the extent that key social institutions such as the law and democratic government are constituted according to an adversarial logic, it is likely that traits of character that allow individuals to thrive in adversarial contexts will be present to a greater degree among the members of such institutions than in the population at large. They will tend to attract individuals possessing these traits in greater proportion than will other professional areas, and will tend to accentuate these traits among participants in the institution.

If this is the case, then the risk for the assessment by citizens of the trustworthiness of adversarial institutions is the following: if citizens form their impressions about the trustworthiness of institutions on the basis of traits of individual agents rather than on the constitution of collective agents, and if on the whole they tend to disapprove of people who display greater aggressiveness or competitiveness than is deemed appropriate in non-adversarial contexts, it follows that they may come to distrust institutions that, *ceteris paribus*, actually warrant their trust. That is, they will form their impressions upon the traits of character of individual agents, taken in abstraction from the institutional contexts within which they are actually required, and from the institutional rules and mechanisms that best account for the agency of the particular kind of agents that collective agents organized in an adversarial manner actually are.

The role of the media

We have seen thus far that heightened vigilance on the part of citizens is warranted as a prolegomenon to their conferring trust upon certain central social and political institutions, but that certain features of these institutions, at least as we have constituted them in many modern societies, pose obstacles to their ability to collect the requisite kind of evidence about institutional trustworthiness. I want briefly to allude to a further obstacle, one that is more contingently related to the constitution of collective agents. It has to do with the role of a free press in alerting us to institutional malfeasance.

The "crisis of trust" that has elicited much of the research on trust, both empirical and conceptual, suggests that people trust key social institutions to a lesser degree than they once did, and that their level of trust threatens to become dysfunctional.[27] It could be that people have become less trusting because the institutions upon which they rely for their well-being are actually becoming less worthy of their trust. But evidence suggests that at least in some advanced liberal democracies, there is less corruption today than there ever was in the past. How do we explain the gulf between reality and perception? I want briefly (and unoriginally) to suggest that it is a perhaps unavoidable negative consequence of the increasing vigilance of media toward the malfeasance of agents in positions of institutional authority. The media may simply be more inclined to report on the wrongdoings of powerful people than they once were, thus creating a perception of increased corruption, and perhaps a growing intolerance on the part of the public to instances of corruption.

Can anything be done in order to enhance the media's contribution to the ability of citizens to confer trust appropriately?

Onora O'Neill has in recent writing been skeptical of the media's ability to contribute positively to the development by citizens of the kinds of capacities that will allow them to confer trust intelligently. Her criticisms of the media are various. Some have to do with the human-all-too-human ways in which members of the media immunize themselves from the scrutiny that they subject members of other institutions to, and with the sometimes dishonest or at the very least misleading ways in which they often conduct interviews and report.[28] But at the core of O'Neill's views about the media lies the idea that the role of the media is not just to provide readers, listeners and viewers with *information*, but rather to *communicate*. Indeed, one can as O'Neill has rightly observed, drown the population in information without actually communicating *useful* and *critically ascertainable* information to them. At the limit, information can come to be seen as a substitute for communication, when it is deliberately put forward in a manner that defies the public's ability to process and to critically assess.[29] And in her view, that imperative, tied in as it is with requirements of accessibility and assessability by citizens of information provided, justifies some regulation of press freedom, that might require of media that they declare potential conflicts of interest, that they provide readers with the *bona fides* of reporters who publish on matters requiring some degree of technical expertise, and that retractions and corrections be given the same prominence as the articles that communicated falsehoods in the first place.[30] These are entirely sensible safeguards meant to ensure that, especially when journalists report on scientific matters, their reporting be informed by expert knowledge of the matters at hand, and be exempt from conflict of interest. (In the area of biomedicine, the willingness of pharmaceutical companies to purchase favorable media coverage has been well established.)[31]

Onora O'Neill has provided us with a powerful framework with which to identify and to criticize the excesses of the media in the present regulatory environment. But her analyses must be completed by a positive account through which we can identify not just what the media should be prevented from doing, but also what their positive contribution to the capacity of a vigilant, intelligently trusting citizenry might be.

The analysis provided here can, I think, contribute to our coming to a more complete understanding of the role that media can, but do not always perform in contributing to citizens' abilities to place trust wisely. If what I have said is correct, it follows that the trustworthiness of institutions is a function not so much of the people who hold positions of authority within them, but rather of the rules that govern the institution and of the oversight mechanisms that see to it that rules are adhered to. When media focus, as they tend to do given the incentives that private media outlets vying for market shares are subject to, on the chicanery and malfeasance of individuals, they deflect our attention from the more fundamental sources of institutional trustworthiness, which have to do with the institutional context in which such malfeasance occurs. Are the actions of individuals that they report on symptoms of deeper structural problems in the very constitution of the institution in question, such as its tendency to generate conflicts of interest, or are they one-off occurrences unlikely to occur again in the institution in question given the institutional rules and safeguards that are in place? When the focus is placed squarely on individuals and their character flaws, we are led to believe that the road to the restoration of trust lies in the replacement of morally flawed officials by morally upright ones, whereas the resilience of institutional trustworthiness depends upon the institutional sources that have made corruption capable of being rooted out.

While the changes to the regulatory environment that O'Neill envisages to deal with some media failings can very well be enshrined in law and in the practice of regulatory bodies without infringing the principle of press freedom to too great a degree, the requirement that the media contribute to the emergence of an appropriately vigilant citizenry can hardly be made into a legal requirement. Rather, it should be thought of as an aspirational ideal, one that is rewarded through various mechanisms that distribute esteem and other kinds of positive incentives among members of the press.[32]

Strategies for enhancing trust

The foregoing arguments have sought to establish that there are formidable challenges lying in the way of citizens being able to confer trust in institutions appropriately. Ideally, they should avoid both the extreme of distrust whereby they forgo opportunities for the advancement of their interests because of excessive suspicion, and that of gullibility, whereby they confer trust too readily upon institutional agents about which they do not possess sufficient evidence to warrant trust. In order to achieve this optimal balance, citizens must overcome a range of obstacles that have been briefly surveyed in this essay. First, they must overcome their natural tendency to base their judgments of trustworthiness on system 1 heuristics that are doubly inappropriate in the case of institutions. As we have seen, this tendency is one that makes us vulnerable to exploitation even in interpersonal contexts. What's more, it is inappropriate in institutional contexts because it involves a confusion as to the kinds of agents that institutions are. This is especially the case for what I have termed "adversarial" institutions.

Second, they must determine how much effort they must expend in attempting to acquire the requisite kind of evidence. And third, they must determine, given the stakes involved, what level of trustworthiness is required on the part of institutional agents in order for the active conferral of trust to be rational. These cost–benefit calculations must moreover, as we have seen, be carried out in a context in which heightened vigilance is warranted, given the power that core social institutions have over them, the nature of the interests at stake, and the fact that they are largely non-substitutable.

The challenges are such that at least one group of prominent researchers on the issue of trust have concluded that it makes no sense to talk about trust in large-scale institutions such as governments. Whatever the conception of trust we adopt, they argue that "an ordinary individual cannot have the knowledge to judge a large institution or its role holders to be trustworthy for any of these reasons."[33] The best that we can do, they claim, is to devise "institutional alternatives to trust."

I want to make two comments about this pessimistic conclusion. First, I believe that it is partly an artifact of their very demanding conception of trust as "encapsulated interest." But as I have suggested above, it seems too strong a requirement that we reserve the term to contexts in which we can gain assurance that others promote our interests *because they are our interests.* Second, I do not believe that the withholding of attitudes of trust and distrust constitutes a real alternative for agents whose interests are woven in so tightly with the performance of core social institutions. As I argued above, citizens have no choice but to interact with the state, with institutions that administer health and justice and the like. If they can, it is at such a cost as to not constitute a live option for most citizens. They therefore can't help but form beliefs as to the trustworthiness of these institutions, and so we have an interest both in ensuring the trustworthiness of institutions, and the ability of citizens to acquire reliable evidence about trustworthiness. Unwarranted trust opens citizens to mistreatment and to exploitation, while excessive *distrust* can lead to dysfunctional behavior such as free-riding.

More fundamentally, however, the idea that institutional mechanisms are *alternatives* to trust, rather than the appropriate form that trustworthiness must take in institutional agents, might be a reflection of a failure to take seriously enough the nature of institutional agents. An analogy might be helpful here. What would be the best way to acquire evidence into the trustworthiness of individual agents? It would be to be able to gain insight into their character, into the "maxims" that serve as general policies on the basis of which individuals act in the full range of situations they face. Insight into these "maxims" would allow us to know whether the contribution (or lack thereof) of an agent to the satisfaction of our interests was fortuitous, and thus impossible to place trust in, or constitutive. Conversely, it would also allow us to know whether the individual *failures* of agents to act in a trustworthy way should lead us to remove trust entirely, or to maintain it.

Now, as Kant understood, the fundamental maxims that we might see as constitutive of individual character are inaccessible both to agents and those observing them, and trying to determine whether or not to confer trust in them. The best we can do to determine an individual agent's character is to infer what the agent's maxims might be on the basis of broad swaths of behavior.

I have argued above that we go wrong in trying to assess the trustworthiness of institutions on the basis of our best guesses as to the character of the individual agents we encounter within those institutions. But if this is the case, then it turns out that it might in one important respect be *easier* to determine the "character" of an institution than it is to ascertain that of an individual agent. While the fundamental maxims of individuals are hidden in the deepest recesses of their souls, those of the institutions we are concerned with in this context are public. Public institutions are governed by rules that often result from legislation, and their administrative frameworks are also most often available for public scrutiny.

What's more, they often incorporate watchdog bodies (ombudsmen, ethics committees, auditors, and the like), that have as their role to see to it that the constitutions and administrative regulations of these institutions are such that the public interests that they are meant to serve are not made more difficult to serve by institutional design flaws that can be identified and addressed. They also serve to verify that the rules that aim to ensure that the institution in question tracks the public interest in a manner sufficient to warrant trust on the part of citizens are not causally idle, in other words, that they are actually enforced within the institution, and that infractions are sanctioned, when they do not result from design flaws but rather from individual malfeasance.

So rather than seeing the fact that modern mass societies have tended to entrust the task of ensuring that institutions track public interests as proving that we can only have *ersatz* trust when it comes to institutions, why not see it as locating trustworthiness in exactly the right place, given the kind of agents that institutions are? We gain access into their "characters" by understanding their constitutions and by gauging the efficacy of the watchdog bodies that ensure that constitutions are changed when they need to be, and that infractions are duly sanctioned.

Onora O'Neill has drawn our attention to the pathologies that excessive and badly thought out institutional monitoring can give rise to. At their worst, the watchdog bodies that, according to my analysis, are key to the trustworthiness of institutions, can have just the opposite effect. Too often, the monitoring of institutions is reduced to the multiplication of demands for the satisfaction of performance indicators that create counter-productive irritants, and that in any case do not really monitor the degree to which the institution in question actually tracks the interests it is meant to serve. It tends to reduce the ethical governance of the institutions to the systematic suspicion that those working within the institutions being monitored are systematically misappropriating funds and other resources, and to the multiplication of mechanisms of "accountability" which both create a climate of distrust and suspicion within the institution, and, as Philip Pettit has shown, can actually elicit the kind of behavior they are designed to counteract.[34] O'Neill characterizes the vicious circle that the (initially well-meaning) monitoring of institutions risks setting in motion when she writes: "The pursuit of ever more perfect accountability provides citizens and consumers, patients and parents with more information, more comparisons, more complaints systems, but it also builds a culture of suspicion, low morale, and may ultimately lead to professional cynicism, and then we would have grounds for public mistrust."[35]

O'Neill goes on to argue that breaking out of this vicious cycle requires that monitoring focus on "good governance" rather than "micro-management."[36] The arguments presented here provide us with a sense of what the attempt by watchdog bodies to ensure "good governance" should focus on. In essence, they suggest that such bodies should ensure that the institutions that they monitor should be the right kinds of agents given the goods they are expected to deliver. That is, they should see to it that the regulatory environment that they operate within and the administrative rules that define roles and associated norms, what I have here called the "constitutions" of institutions, be functional to the attainment of the goods in question. When problems arise, it is crucial that their source be adequately identified. Do they result from individuals breaking rules, or on the contrary do they point to perverse incentives that are generated by flaws in institutional design? Ridding institutions of such design flaws is key to the ethical resiliency of institutions, and thus, to their trustworthiness.

An example drawn from recent Canadian history might serve as an illustration. In the late 1990s, in the wake of a referendum on secession that came to within a few thousand votes of taking Quebec out of the Canadian federation, a program was put in place and administered by prominent civil servants in order to increase the visibility of the Federal government in Quebec, in spite of very stringent rules restricting the federal spending power in Canadian provinces. The attempt at circumventing these rules was compounded by widespread misuse of the funds that were devoted to the program. The pattern of corruption was detailed in a damning report issued in 2003 by the Federal Auditor-General, and gave rise to an investigation presided over by a retired judge, John Gomery.

The report that he produced both identified culprits, but crucially it also identified structural flaws in the way in which the relations between the Government and the Public Service were governed. For various reasons, including the fact that the head of the Public Service also holds a Cabinet-level position within the government, the civil service had become "politicized." The report recommended punishing those who had been guilty of misappropriation of public funds, but it also urged constitutional changes that would immunize the civil service from the risks of politicization.[37]

The government's response, however, was to put in place exactly the kinds of micro-managing mechanisms meant to signal the government's seriousness in tackling corruption, but doing nothing to address the systemic flaws that impede the government's trustworthiness.[38] My point, however, is to show that at least in principle core institutions can be monitored by "watchdog institutions" that actually do increase the capacity of citizens to confer trust wisely. In the case at hand, the Auditor-General's report, that was widely disseminated and publicized, can be seen as having significantly increased the ability of citizens to acquire relevant information about the government's trustworthiness. And the investigation that ensued counteracted the tendency that citizens have to look to individual character and behavior of agents rather than to institutional rules and monitoring devices in order to decide whether to trust.

Conclusion

This paper has taken its cue from Onora O'Neill's quite justified complaints that the principal social institutions of modern liberal democracies have at best awkwardly responded to the challenges posed by the contemporary "crisis of trust." It can be taken as a series of friendly amendments and elaborations to many of O'Neill's insights. By providing a systematic account of the challenges posed to individuals in their decisions as to whether or not to trust others, and the additional obstacles facing citizens in their attempts at placing trust in institutions wisely, I have suggested answers to three challenges posed by O'Neill in her recent work on trust. First, by drawing a distinction between the purely cognitive and the volitional dimensions of trust, I have provided an interpretation of the puzzle aptly noted by O'Neill that emerges from the fact that the avowals of distrust proffered by citizens are not matched by their actions. Second, in response to O'Neill's observations that neither media nor the "watchdog bodies" that currently monitor core social institutions are performing their roles adequately, I have provided an analysis of the obstacles that face citizens in ascertaining the trustworthiness of institutions that has allowed me both to describe the role that media might appropriately play in order to contribute positively to the capacity of citizens to place trust wisely, and to give an account of the kinds of monitoring mechanisms that could most adequately perform their role both in augmenting the epistemic capacities of citizens, and in ensuring that the mistaken heuristics that citizens naturally bring to bear to the understanding of cases of institutional dysfunction are corrected.

I have not applied this analysis to the area that O'Neill has devoted the most attention to, that of biomedical ethics. Though I share the concern that she and Neil Manson have eloquently expressed that practices of informed consent as they are currently conceptualized and institutionalized fall short of the requirements that would warrant our placing our trust in health professionals and health systems, I believe that their positive proposals could be constructively augmented by the institutional focus urged here. The detail of that augmentation will, however, have to be given on another occasion.

Notes

1 The work of Annette Baier has been particularly important in this context. See in particular her "Trust and Antitrust," in *Ethics*, vol. 96 (1986), pp. 231–60.
2 Robert Putnam, *Making Democracy Work: Civic Tradition in Modern Italy*, Princeton: Princeton University Press, 1993; *Bowling Alone: The Collapse and Revival of American Community*, New York: Simon and Schuster, 2000.
3 Francis Fukayama, *Trust: The Social Virtues and the Creation of Prosperity*, New York: The Free Press, 1995.
4 Daniel Weinstock, "Building Trust in Divided Societies," in *The Journal of Political Philosophy*, vol. 7, no. 3 (1999), pp. 287–307.
5 Karen Jones, "Trust as an Affective Attitude," in *Ethics*, vol. 107 (1996), pp. 4–25.
6 Mark Warren, *Democracy and Association*, Princeton: Princeton University Press, 2000; Nancy Rosenblum, *Membership and Morals, The Personal Uses of Pluralism*, Princeton: Princeton University Press, 2000.

7 For some important exceptions, see the essays collected in Marc Warren (ed.), *Democracy and Trust*, Cambridge: Cambridge University Press, 1999.
8 Bo Rothstein, *Social Traps and the Problem of Trust*, Cambridge: Cambridge University Press, 2005.
9 Charles Tilly, *Trust and Rule*, Cambridge: Cambridge University Press, 2005.
10 Onora O 'Neill, *A Question of Trust*, Cambridge: Cambridge University Press, 2002, p. vii.
11 Most notably in Onora O'Neill, *Autonomy and Trust in Bioethics*, Cambridge: Cambridge University Press, 2002; and in some sections of Neil C. Manson and Onora O'Neill, *Rethinking Informed Consent in Bioethics*, Cambridge: Cambridge University Press, 2007, especially chapter 7.
12 Paul J. Zak, Robert Kurzban and William T. Matzner, "The Neurobiology of Trust," *Annals of the New York Academy of Sciences*, vol. 1032 (2004), pp. 224–27.
13 For a popular account of "dual process theory" from which the idea of two distinct modes of cognition has been developed, see Daniel Kahneman, *Thinking, Fast and Slow*, New York: Farrar, Straus and Giroux, 2011.
14 Russell Hardin, *Trust*, Malden, MA: Polity Press, 2006, p. 19. Italics in the text.
15 Ibid., p. 17.
16 Weinstock, "Building Trust in Divided Societies", pp. 287–307.
17 Hardin does not deny that cooperation can occur without trust. Indeed, he has devoted much attention in recent years in identifying ersatzes for trust in contexts in which the fairly limited definition he offers is not appropriate. If this is the case, then it is possible that the debate between a more restrictive definition such as Hardin's and the one that I propose is an uninteresting, merely terminological one. See Karen S. Cook, Russell Hardin, and Margaret Levi, *Cooperation without Trust?*, New York: Russell Sage Foundation, 2005.
18 Hardin, *Trust*, p. 17.
19 Unsurprisingly, the Internet has become an important locus for research on trust. See for example Helen Nissenbaum, "Securing Trust Online: Wisdom or Oxymoron," in *Boston University Law Review,*, vol. 81 (2001), No. 3, pp. 635–64; and Russell Hardin, "Trust on the Internet," in *Trust*, pp. 98–117.
20 O'Neill, *A Question of Trust*, p. 14. For another interpretation of the gulf between avowals and actions as regards trust, see Kieran O'Hara, *Trust from Socrates to Spin*, London: Icon Books, 2004, chapter 9.
21 Ibid.
22 Cook, Hardin and Levi, *Cooperation without Trust*, p. 41. Cf. Hardin, *Trust*, pp. 152–54.
23 Christian List and Philip Pettit, *Group Agency: The Possibility, Design, and Status of Corporate Agents*, Oxford: Oxford University Press, 2011.
24 For a defense of parties and partisanship as integral elements of democratic institutions, see Nancy Rosenblum, *On the Side of the Angels: An Appreciation of Parties and Partisanship*, Princeton: Princeton University Press, 2008.
25 For an excellent defense of adversarial institutions, see Dominic C. Martin, *Rivalité et marchés: Une éthique adversative pour les agents économiques*, PhD thesis submitted to the Département de philosophie, Université de Montréal, January 2012.
26 For some attempts at designing ethics for adversarial institutions, see Arthur Applbaum, *Ethics for Adversaries. The Morality of Roles in Public and Political Life*, Princeton: Princeton University Press, 2000. See also Joseph Heath, "An Adversarial Ethic for Business: or, When Sun-Tzu met the Stakeholder," *Journal of Business Ethics*, vol. 69 (2006), pp. 359–74.
27 For example, as Bo Rothstein has shown, belief that the government is not to be trusted correlates highly with tax evasion and other anti-social behavior. Bo

Rothstein, *The Quality of Government. Corruption, Social Trust, and Inequality in International Perspective*, Chicago: University of Chicago Press, 2011, chapter 7.
28 Onora O'Neill, *Autonomy and Trust in Bioethics*, pp. 180–81.
29 For a fascinating inquiry into the pathologies of too one-dimensional a conception of "transparency," see Archon Fung, Mary Graham and David Weil, *Full Disclosure: The Perils and Promise of Trasparency*, Cambridge: Cambridge University Press, 2007.
30 Ibid., p. 190.
31 David Healy, *Pharmageddon*, Los Angeles: University of California Press, 2012.
32 For a systematic account, see Geoffrey Brennan and Philip Pettit, *The Economy of Esteem*, Oxford: Oxford University Press, 2007.
33 Karen Cook, Russell Hardin and Margaret Levi, *Cooperation Without Trust*, p. 105.
34 Philip Pettit, "Rational Choice Regulation: Two Strategies," in *Rules, Reasons and Norms: Selected Essays*, Oxford: Oxford University Press, 2002.
35 Onora O'Neill, *A Matter of Trust*, p. 57. Cf. *Autonomy and Trust in Bioethics*, p. 132.
36 Ibid., p. 58.
37 The volume of the Report detailing recommended institutional changes is available here: http://web.archive.org/web/20070107064802/http://epe.lac-bac.gc.ca/100/206/301/pco-bcp/commissions/sponsorship-ef/06-03-06/www.gomery.ca/fr/default.htm. For a broader discussion of the constitutional issues raised by the scandal, see Donald Savoie, *Breaking the Bargain: Public Servants, Ministers, and Parliament*, Toronto: University of Toronto Press, 2003.
38 See my "Du bon usage des commissions d'enquête et des rapports qui en émanent", in *Éthique publique*, vol. 13, no. 1 (2011), pp. 225–32.

13

RESPONSES

Onora O'Neill

Context: A philosophical elephant?

These penetrating essays on my philosophical work are descendants of papers given at a 2009 conference held at the British Academy. Reading the finished versions has confirmed my suspicion that I have cast my net rather wide; probably dangerously wide.

I have been writing philosophy for a large number of years, and know that there are unclarities, hiatuses and gaps, not to mention straightforward errors, in my published work. I also know that I have changed my views, both when others pointed out difficulties I had overlooked (or perhaps devised!), and when I have noticed them for myself. So it seems little short of a miracle to find that astute and sympathetic commentators have unearthed so much coherence in writings that I have often seen as successive and incomplete attempts to capture a range of disparate matters that seemed important for specific reasons, occasions, projects or audiences. Instead of comments that resemble the reports of the blind men of Indian legend, whose several descriptions of the elephant they were touching did not fit together, these essays reveal something of the shape of the philosophical elephant that I have been tracking, and even suggest that it may be a svelter and less baggy beast than I have sometimes feared.

In responding to these generous discussions I shall start by saying something about two themes that have been recurrent and basic in my work: acting and reasoning. I will then turn to questions about my reading of Kant's ethics, to discussions of agency and autonomy, to practical ethics, and will end with some comments on trust and trustworthiness. I shall not be able to respond to all the questions raised and arguments developed, but will try to address at least some of them. But first a sketch of the anatomy of my philosophical elephant.

Kant on action and reason

I began working on action and reason in the late 1960s, when I embarked on a PhD under John Rawls at Harvard. After a time, and rather to my surprise, the work took a Kantian turn.[1] My central question both in the thesis and in the book that it later became[2] was how reasoning could bear on action. This seemed, and still seems, to me the elephant in the room that is all too often ignored or pushed to the margins in philosophical work in ethics and political philosophy.

As I came to see matters, reasoning bears on matters that have propositional form and content. Principles of action have propositional form, and the act and agent descriptions they incorporate have propositional content. So they provide an apt focus for reasoning. If they articulate standards or norms that can be used to shape action, they may also be apt for practical purposes. However, any given act satisfies many descriptions and many principles, and there has been perennial disagreement about *which* principles of action are relevant for ethical and other practical reasoning. Seemingly Kant resolved this problem by asserting that practical reason bears on *maxims*, by which he means the principles that agents may adopt and enact at or through some time. But his answer has been widely disputed.

With some misgivings I initially took the (rather traditional) view that the maxim of an act is an agent's intention in acting. Later (as Marcia Baron, Thomas Hill and Neil Manson all note) I came to think that this way of construing maxims puts too much weight on the possibility of knowing agents' intentions, and is incompatible with Kant's strikingly severe views of the limits of self and other knowledge. I then revised my views, and suggested that maxims were better thought of as the governing or underlying principles of acts, which can be ascribed to agents on the basis of what they do, rather than being identified with intentions that agents consciously adopt. Still later I came to think that maxims are best construed simply as practical principles that agents can make their own, adopt for action and seek to satisfy.

In short, I gradually – and confusingly – moved from viewing maxims *introspectively*, by way of seeing them *ascriptively* to seeing them *prescriptively*.[3] A prescriptive or practical understanding of maxims sees them as articulating standards or principles that agents can seek to adopt, and if circumstances permit, to enact or instantiate. It sets aside the (necessarily retrospective, rather than practical) task of establishing which of the many principles that a particular act actually instantiates should count as its maxim. A practical understanding of maxims has advantages. It focuses on the practical task of *making* a principle one's maxim, rather than the cognitive task of *discovering* which maxim one has adopted, or others have adopted. It sees maxims as standards or norms to be enacted, rather than as intentions to be inspected or detected (at least in a few morally superior acts). And it readily allows for the thought that a given act can satisfy numerous maxims.

Maxims and moral worth: Marcia Baron

These points are, I think, relevant to Marcia Baron's probing discussion of Kant's account of moral worth. She reconsiders the importance that Kant attaches to a distinction between acts that merely conform to – i.e., satisfy – principles of duty and those that are done 'out of' duty: a preoccupation of the earlier part of Kant's *Groundwork*. If we assume that maxims are introspectively knowable states of agents, then it seems we should try to discover 'out of' which maxims acts are done. But we cannot. As Kant unhelpfully insists, the human heart is opaque, and we cannot tell whether even a single act has ever been done purely 'out of' duty. Acting 'out of' duty is not a knowable property of morally superior achievements; rather it articulates a standard that can serve as a paradigm of moral worth. The notion of acting 'out of' duty is *normative* for dutiful action – but insurmountable epistemic difficulties prevent us from knowing whether or not particular acts live up to this ideal. All of this caused me, as it has caused others, many of the problems that Marcia Baron raises, and she rightly notes my discomfort as I tried first to hang on to a view of maxims as intentions, and then to construe them as underlying intentions. Since concluding that the best understanding of maxims is prescriptive, I have come to agree with her closing comment that 'the moral worth of actions seems to me of minor significance' (see p. 15).

Reasoning and constructivism: Melissa Barry, Thomas Hill

Reasoning can bear on action only if it provides ways of discriminating among principles of action, offering grounds for seeking to make some one's maxim and to reject others. In earlier work I had noted Kant's view that instrumental reasoning is indispensable but insufficient for ethical reasoning, his insistence that ethical claims cannot be derived from examples and his inference that practical reason must therefore be at least in part non-instrumental. But I had said nothing about his conclusion that the basic principle for non-instrumental reasoning, the Categorical Imperative, is the 'the supreme principle of practical reason' or about his claim that it can be formulated in a number of seemingly quite distinct ways.

From the mid 1980s I began to think more systematically about Kant's repeated claim to offer a critique and vindication of reason, and since then have found this topic deep and intriguing. So I am particularly pleased that Melissa Barry and Tom Hill both focus on this aspect of my work, and specifically on my arguments for thinking that Kant offers an account not only of the way ethical claims can be 'constructed' using the meagre tools that reason provides, but of the way in which we can also think of reason itself as 'constructed'.

In a highly perceptive paper, Melissa Barry argues that this move takes the idea of construction a step too far: a very plausible fear! As she sees it, it is one thing to use an account of reason as the basis for constructing ethical principles, but 'the ambition of providing a constructivist vindication of practical reasoning itself' (see p. 33) must fail. I agree with her that construction *ex nihilo* is not possible, but do not share her conclusion that attempts at complete constructivism are more accurately characterized as forms of limited constructivism (see p. 33), or that reason must be viewed as foundational, so beyond justification (so casting doubt on any justifications it supposedly confers).

The alternative route that I explored draws on many passages in Kant's later writings, and argues not from any putative *foundations of reasoning*, but from what one might call (by analogy with Hume's account of the *circumstances of justice*) the *circumstances of reasoning*. Kant sees those circumstances as arising among any plurality of agents whose communication and interaction is not antecedently coordinated by a pre-established harmony (instinct, divine plan or other). Free agents can offer one another reasons for believing those claims only if they put forward considerations that (they take it) those others *could follow in thought*, i.e., understand; they can offer one another reasons for action only if they put forward proposals that (they take it) those others *could adopt for action*. In the event – indeed very frequently – those to whom reasons are offered cannot or do not understand them, or adopt them. So the thought is simply that we do not even *offer* others reasons for belief unless we aim to be intelligible to them, and do not even *offer* others reasons for action unless we make proposals that we think adoptable by them.

This minimal conception of reasoning may seem to offer at best a necessary condition for reasoned thinking or acting, in that it requires only that what we offer to others as reasons must seek to be intelligible to or adoptable by those others. It covers reasoning of all sorts, including the many sorts of theoretical and practical reasoning that are conditional on contingently shared assumptions. In a wide range of writings, Kant discussed conditional reasoning, covering not only technical and prudential reasoning, where specific aims are assumed, but also a great deal of ethical reasoning that is conditional on one or another assumption that is not itself reasoned, which he speaks of as heteronomous reasoning, that will reach only those who accept the assumptions on which it is conducted. He contrasts such reasoning with reasoning that is *not* conditional on contingently shared assumptions, so is fit to reach 'the world at large', so can count as public reasoning.

In speaking of reasoning that is fully public, Kant set out a very different view of public reason from those found in contemporary work. Contemporary accounts, including those given by Habermas and Rawls, see public reason as citizens' reasoning that is to serve purposes ranging from deliberative democracy, through political legitimation to the justification of principles of justice. Kant did not offer an account of reasoning in which the entire public *actually* participate or *is (merely) free to participate*; nor did he try to show how principles of justice could be grounded in reasoning that relies on the meagre political commitments common to fellow citizens in bounded liberal democracies, whatever their individual beliefs and outlooks share. His more elementary approach to public reasoning sees it as reasoning that is *fit* to be public, in that it seeks to be intelligible to or adoptable by each and all. That is why the fundamental principle of practical reason – the Categorical Imperative – is no more than the *modal* injunction to 'act only on maxims that can be willed at the same time as universal laws' (G421). Kant's focus is on the necessary conditions for *possible* communication or interaction with others, without restriction.

Why, one might ask, does ethical reasoning have to offer reasons *to all*? Many have thought otherwise, and have claimed that ethical reasoning may, even must, draw on the established beliefs, conventions or ideologies of particular communities and traditions, so will be fit to reach some but not others. Kant saw this as a mistake. Reasoning that is premised on local or contingent beliefs, conventions or traditions is incomplete reasoning because it offers reasons only to some and not to all, and assumes various contingent beliefs as premises. Such reasoning, as Kant sees it, is inevitably less than fully public. It is *heteronomous reasoning*, in that it assumes some *other* source or authority, and while many admirable acts reflect heteronomous reasoning, the touchstone of reason is *not* to rely on extraneous or arbitrary assumptions. Fully reasoned belief and action seek to rely on reasons that could be offered to *all* others, so aim to be fully public in the Kantian sense.

Many of these issues are illuminated by Thomas Hill's perceptive and careful contrasts between the forms of constructivism that our teacher John Rawls developed and those that I subsequently explored. He offers an instructive assessment of my claims that the Rawlsian versions are 'more remote from Kant's texts, narrower in scope, and subject to several serious objections' (see p. 42). I have only minor points of disagreement with his account of differences between Rawls' position and the one that I have tried to work towards. Perhaps the only significant – if long-standing – disagreement between us is that he thinks that I claim that 'reason can vindicate ... only the universal law formula of the Categorical Imperative and ... the general principles of means-ends coordination' (see p. 45). My view is rather that any coherent interpretation of the formulations of the Categorical Imperative must take seriously Kant's claim that they are equivalent, and seek to construe the differences between them as providing different perspectives on the same requirement on principles of thinking and acting. If no interpretation of the formulations of the Categorical Imperative can preserve a claim of equivalence, much of the structure of Kant's ethics will fall apart.[4]

Thomas Hill is also right that I am more optimistic than Rawls in thinking that reasoning may allow us to justify not only certain principles of justice, but aspects of morality, and he is right in thinking that I try to base my arguments on more meagre assumptions. However, I do not claim to have assumed less but justified more. The Kantian construction of reason seeks to justify more than principles of justice, but does not (directly) justify principles with the specificity of Rawls' principles of justice. Kant's fundamental principles of duty are less determinate than Rawls' principles of justice, and his subsequent discussion of principles of justice relies on a realist view of the necessities of enforcement and enforcing institutions to reach more specific conclusions. His extensive discussions of the derivation of duties, the justification of institutions and the demands of judgement trace many further steps that are needed to move from an account of reasoning about action to practical, including political, conclusions.

Perhaps one useful way of articulating some of the differences between Rawls' constructivism and my own is that Rawls stresses the *pluralism of beliefs*, but I have stressed the *plurality of agents*. Rawls asks how those who share citizenship in well-ordered societies, but have diverging beliefs and outlooks, can reach agreement. He argues that as citizens they share enough to reach consensus or agreement, at least on fundamental principles of justice.[5] However, he accepts that potential reasoners who are *not* citizens of liberal democratic societies may be ignored by or excluded from this conception of public reason.

In exploring the weaker Kantian approach to public reason as setting standards that any plurality of agents must meet if they are to offer others reasons, I had to do without the advantage of an appeal to common citizenship. Doing so had advantages and disadvantages. It allowed me to work towards a wider view of the scope of reasoning, but yielded only a weaker conception of public reason. Rawls deploys a specifically political, indeed civic, conception of public reason, and consequently aims (especially in his later work) to reach conclusions only about justice. I tried to work with a less specific, modal account of public reason and to reach a wider range of normative conclusions.

Reason and hope: Katrin Flikschuh

Kant's vindication of reason bears not only on his account of ethics and justice, but on his account of religion 'within the limits of reason'. Katrin Flikschuh's deep and interesting paper takes up some of my claims about Kant's approach to religion. The common ground between us is that Kant does not think it possible to provide theoretical arguments – let alone proofs – for the existence of God or for atheism. However, Kant went far beyond these negative claims. In many of his later writings he insists that we are committed both to the possibility of discovering empirical truths about the natural order, and to a conception of ourselves as free agents. The two standpoints of nature and of freedom are both indispensable, yet neither is reducible to the other. We cannot grasp or know how nature and freedom are connected, yet cannot avoid seeing ourselves as agents and our action as requiring justification as well as explanation.

If I have a puzzle about Katrin Flikschuh's reading of my rather meagre work on Kant's writings on religion and on politics, it is that she concludes that I subscribe to some form of radical secularism. That was not my intention. As I read him, Kant denies that we can establish truths about a supernatural order, denies that we can show that the natural order is all that there is, and concludes that our orientation to the insurmountable limits of human knowledge should be articulated as reasoned *faith* or *hope* rather than knowledge. This thought is adumbrated in Kant's famous remark that he had found it necessary to 'deny knowledge in order to make room for faith (Glaube)' (*Critique of Pure Reason* B xxx), and developed in many discussions of faith and hope (which he sees as closely linked, if not identical) in his later writings.

As I understood his position, Kant rejected rationalist articulations of hope that see it is as tracking belief, but with reduced certainty. Kantian hope is not a form of optimism about the way things are or are going to be. Hope within reason, unlike belief within reason, is constrained only by the impossible and not by the merely improbable, let alone by the balance of probabilities. For that reason, Katrin Flikschuh's example of everyday hopes, such as hoping her son will learn his multiplication tables if she practices with him, is an example of reasonable expectation rather than of Kantian hope.

The parallels that I drew between hopes articulated in other-worldly and in this-worldly terms had a specific purpose. My aim was to display the parallels between Kant's comments on the interpretation of sacred texts, including those of traditions whose vision of religion is not other-worldly, and his accounts of certain indispensable this-worldly hopes. All religions have their everyday practices and traditions of exegesis (cf. 'ecclesiastical faith', *Kirchenglaube*), but they can also be read as articulating hopes that transcend the here and now (cf. 'philosophical theology', *Religionsglaube*, 'moral religion'). Hopes that transcend the here and now, whether articulated in other-worldly or this-worldly terms, are not a matter of reasoned expectation, and are not defeated by probabilistic arguments. Kant articulates them variously as hopes that virtue and happiness will be coordinated, that freedom and nature are compossible despite our lack of theoretical insight into their connection, and that we can reasonably seek to shape the world (in some small part) and the human future in line with principles of reason and morality.

Insofar as such hopes are intelligible but may be realised at some time, they lie, as Kant phrases it, 'within the limits of reason'. This is why I did not see Kant's discussion of hopes for the far future of this world in his writings on human history, progress and destiny as signs of a commitment to secularism, let alone to radical secularism (which seemingly assumes that empirical reasoning has a completeness that Kant denies). He puts the point as follows:

> History may give rise to endless doubts about my hopes, and if these doubts could be proved, they might persuade me to desist from an apparently futile task. But so long as they do not have the force of certainty ... this uncertainty cannot detract from the maxim I have adopted, or from the necessity of assuming for practical purposes that human progress is possible.[6]

A political inflection of Kantian hope would therefore not be something like hoping to win the next election, or hoping that a specific policy can be implemented, but a hope that the human condition can improve, a hope that Kant thinks reasonable as long as there is no decisive counter-evidence.

So much, at least for present purposes, on the philosophical elephant. Once I had reached some clarity about the nature and scope of practical reasoning, I began to write more on practical issues. Most of what I have written, including what I have written on Kantian themes, says nothing about these larger issues or about the way in which reasoning can bear on action, but focuses on ways in which normative reasoning can bear on various ethical and political questions, and in the first instance on the possibility of saying something about requirements or obligations, and their implications for action in various situations.

It is a refreshing aspect of this collection of papers that my interlocutors have not taken me to task for claiming that in practical reasoning duties or obligations are more basic than rights, and indeed provide the most plausible basis for justifying rights. I see it as a considerable advantage to approach ethics from the perspective of agents and their obligations, rather than that of recipients and their rights. However, since I am constantly taken to task for this unfashionable view, I am happy to bracket the problems that are sometimes alleged to arise from taking it here, noting simply that I have always thought it important in writing on ethics and political philosophy to allow both for 'perfect' duties, including obligations of justice, where duties have corresponding rights and for 'imperfect' duties that lack corresponding rights, of which many are generally seen as virtues. Taking this broad approach, that prioritises the requirements on agents over the entitlements of recipients, has provided room for forays both into political philosophy, and into the ethics of personal, family and social life, as well as for inquiries into matters that straddle personal and public life, such as discussions of trust and trustworthiness and of the ethics of communication.

Agency, consent and autonomy

If agency and action are the point of departure for practical reasoning, then it is important to take some view of agents' capacities for action. I have addressed questions about those capacities in many contexts, particularly in discussing questions of justice, conceptions of (individual) autonomy, and action and policies that are taken to reflect these conceptions. These essays take up my approach in a great variety of ways, but a common theme in several of them is a focus on consent and individual autonomy.

Consent and opacity: Neil Manson

In 'Informed Consent and Referential Opacity' Neil Manson dissects some of the difficulties of my writing in this area, as only a close collaborator can.[7] He rightly points out that I have stretched the notion of referential opacity beyond its standard use to cover sentences in which two terms denoting one and the same item cannot be substituted for one another *salva veritate*. I do not think that I am alone in stretching the term, but agree that it is a stretch. I extended the use of the term from sentences to propositions, then from propositions that express beliefs (that may be true or false) to propositions that express consent. My focus was on the implications of a divergent understanding of terms that are taken to refer to a single matter, that is often a feature of informed consent transactions. It may be true that A and B both consented to the terms of a given consent transaction, yet false that A consented to what B consented to.

Reading Neil Manson's comments I am now less sure that even a generous view of opacity provides enough for an adequate focus on features that distinguish genuine from bogus, justifying from ethically pointless consent. I suspect that it highlights one, but only one, of the things that can make consent inadequate. Consent indeed fails to legitimate where the terms proposed and the terms consented to are understood in differing ways – even, perhaps especially, where a shared vocabulary masks the discrepancy. If so, it is unclear whether or what the consent given legitimates. Opacities, mismatches and other infelicities may all vitiate consent, which can fail in many ways.

As Neil and I argued in *Rethinking Informed Consent in Bioethics*, the prospects for a complete remedy for these failures are slender. If 'fully informed' consent is fundamental to justification, consent transactions will not justify much, since we can unavoidably consent explicitly to little, and give 'fully' informed consent to even less. However, the gap between the understanding assumed by proposers and that assumed by those who ostensibly consent to their proposals can widen for *many* reasons, *any* of which may undermine the justification that consent supposedly provides. Hence the need to consider both the wider ethical framework within which consent can be used to waive obligations that would otherwise be binding, and the range of epistemic and ethical norms that adequate processes of consenting must respect. Hence also the irrelevance of the idea that defective consent can be made good simply by providing more information (cf. Neil Manson's discussions of 'the deficit model', p. 87).

Towards the end of his paper Neil Manson asks whether consent is particularly problematic for Kantian ethics, because of the difficulty of identifying the maxim 'out of' which any act was done. This is an intriguing question: what (if anything) links Kant's views on the opacity of the self, and consequently of the maxims agents adopt (see p. 220), to the opacity that I saw as making consent problematic? Had I stayed with my initial reading of maxims as inner states of agents (see p. 220), there would I think have been rather close links. For on that reading, as Manson puts it, 'the way that a maxim is described matters to whether or not it is universalisable' (see p. 91) leading inexorably to the question 'Which description of a maxim is the relevant one for moral evaluation?' (see p. 91). That was indeed a difficulty with which I struggled for many years, but it faded when I concluded that, given Kant's comments on the opacity of the self, a prescriptive or practical view of maxims was textually as well as philosophically preferable. Once we take a practical view of maxims, the impossible task of deciding which description of a maxim is relevant for moral evaluation is replaced by the practical task of adopting principles that *can* be willed as universal laws and rejecting principles that *cannot* be willed as universal laws. In acting, we do not *find* ourselves possessed by a specific maxim, but *decide* whether or not to *make* a specific principle our maxim.

Nevertheless, some of the problems of a subjective view of maxims can resurface in the context of consent transactions. Given that consent will be problematic if what is consented to by one party differs from what the other proposes, a practical approach to consent is not a simple matter. The remedy, I think, for this and for related problems, including those of aligning trust with trustworthiness (see below), is to give more explicit and thorough attention to the complex normative requirements on adequate communication or interaction. As I came to appreciate the pervasive importance of adequate communication in this and other contexts, I also began to work more systematically on the ethics of communication.

Consent and autonomy: Suzanne Uniacke

In engaging with practical questions about agents and agency, I found myself writing in a period, beginning in the 1970s and still continuing, in which conceptions of autonomy became ever more prominent in discussions of philosophical, political and topical issues. On the surface this might seem congenial to anyone who takes Kant seriously. However, it became increasingly clear to me that contemporary conceptions of individual autonomy are not versions of Kant's conception of autonomy (although various discussions misleadingly claim Kantian ancestry).[8] Articulating the differences between *Kantian autonomy* and conceptions of *individual autonomy*, and the degree to which some of the latter can be operationalised in informed consent requirements, then became a preoccupation. It is a theme on which both Suzanne Uniacke and Marilyn Friedman comment.

Suzanne Uniacke's discussion of informed consent in medical contexts examines my claim in *Autonomy and Trust in Bioethics* that a 'limited focus on informed consent, rather than on any more extensive conception of autonomy, serves reasonably well in medical ethics because it suits the real context of illness and injury'.[9] In that work I tried not only to point out how many conceptions of individual autonomy are now in play, but to show that some of the more exacting ones are unsuitable for clinical contexts, where individual independence (variously understood) is often eroded by pain, disability and frailty. My worry was that placing too much emphasis on patient autonomy, as variously understood, can demand too much of patients and burden them. That is why I suggested that informed consent requirements, even if they do not successfully operationalise any of the more ambitious conceptions of individual autonomy, have a point – if only a limited point.

However, as Neil Manson and I later argued in *Rethinking Informed Consent in Bioethics*, the temptation to 'improve' informed consent requirements, that has been so prevalent in clinical and research ethics, and is supposed to secure more respect for more exacting conceptions of individual autonomy, can overtax the capacities of those invited to consent. The result will then not be more or better respect for patients or for their autonomy, however conceived, but only pretence of such respect. We may end up with 'consent transactions' that achieve consent that is not genuinely informed, or patients and research subjects who do not feel that they have genuinely chosen that to which they have supposedly consented. We need, I think, to be cautious *both* about laying too much weight on autonomy *and* about trying to make consent requirements do too much work.

In her paper on these themes Suzanne Uniacke uses some well chosen examples to suggest that consent requirements can and should do more work in some contexts than is often proposed, or than I had discussed. She argues that there are reasons to think that current informed consent requirements in medical practice are not strong enough, because while they respect choices that patients make from a 'menu of options' offered by medical practitioners, they do not respect choices that are 'off the menu'. She points out that some 'off the menu' choices are made with a high degree of reflection and thought, and argues that they should count as expressions of autonomy and deserve to be protected.

The case she mainly discusses is that of a patient who foresees future inability to communicate, so executes an advance directive asking for continuation of nutrition and hydration, whatever his future situation, up to death. However, the relevant GMC guidance leaves the decision on withdrawing nutrition and hydration after loss of abilities to communicate to the medical team or doctor, who must take account of but need not comply with the patient's previously expressed *views* and *best interests*, and need not even take account of the patient's previously expressed *wishes*. This is an interesting case, and Suzanne Uniacke concludes that it reveals a defect in the GMC guidance on ceasing to provide nutrition and hydration to patients who have executed advance directives. She points out that the High Court's decision (reversed on appeal) that in such cases a patient's wishes should count 'was widely regarded as a strong defence of the view that the medical law and the human rights principles ... are grounded in the moral value of patient autonomy' (see p. 95). It may well be true that the decision was widely so regarded, but I suspect this tells us only that there are lots of conceptions of individual autonomy around. Some people will think that individual autonomy is extended by respecting others' (past) wishes; others will not think respect for (past) wishes central to individual autonomy.

The practical question is whether patients' wishes for or choices of treatment that is 'off the menu', either in the present or for the future, should be respected. Clearly there cannot be a blanket requirement on doctors to respect such choices. A patient who expresses a wish to receive organ transplants or indefinite artificial respiration, either now or for the future, may be making a demand too far on those who provide and fund health care. Equally, doctors cannot be required to provide treatment that they believe will harm patients. The difficult case is that of treatment that is not unaffordable or unfair, will not harm the patient, and is chosen by a particular patient either for the present or for the future. Continuing provision of artificial nutrition and hydration may be such a case. Nevertheless, I doubt whether it is desirable to amend the GMC guidelines by adding a requirement to consider, let alone respect, patients' wishes on this matter (expressions of wishes need not, it is worth noting, even be consistent). Guidelines have to take account of the fact somebody has to judge at what stage of a person's dying continuing nutrition and hydration not merely does not benefit, but actually harms the dying patient. Rather than trying to establish a right to have the wishes or choices a patient has expressed unconditionally respected, it seems to me that a more appropriate standard for the care of dying patients is the use of a well-articulated standard of care, such as the Liverpool Care Pathway (endorsed by the Department of Health) which sets out safeguards for decisions to discontinue nutrition or hydration at the very end of life.[10]

An appeal to any generic conception of individual autonomy is a blunt tool for addressing such cases, for several reasons. First, there is a wide range of interpretations of individual autonomy, many of which do not interpret respect for autonomy as a matter of unconditional respect for wishes or choices, since they see choices that are not reasoned, stable, reflectively endorsed or the like, let alone wishes, as less-than-autonomous choices. Second, even if a choice to receive nutrition and hydration, whatever future circumstances, is ethically important, so are other considerations. Advance directives are inevitably not adjusted to the details of future circumstances. While there are hard cases, I suspect that removing all discretion from doctors – acting in consultation with relatives, with other physicians and with the terms of advance directives, as the GMC advice suggests – would simply generate new problem cases.

The other examples Uniacke discusses are of patients who remain competent, but reject recommended treatment in favour of another treatment that is not recommended. These cases seem to me to raise rather different issues, since there is no question of the degree to which an advance directive should be treated as establishing requirements, let alone rights. The issue is more straightforwardly whether physicians should provide treatment that is 'off the menu' because they judge it suboptimal (I take it that the unavailable and unaffordable remain off the menu). In such cases a standard move is for a patient to seek a second opinion, or to refuse treatment, and once again I cannot see that doctors can be required to provide treatment they judge suboptimal. As a practical matter, patients in this situation can, and often do, refuse the recommended treatment and may (then or later) be offered a treatment that medical practitioners think (or earlier thought) suboptimal.

Consent and disability: Marilyn Friedman

Marilyn Friedman also discusses aspects of individual autonomy, and in particular of the 'feminist critique of independence'. She focuses on a charge made by Eva Kittay and others, that liberal conceptions of the ideal citizen and the ideal conditions under which she chooses political principles fail to incorporate consideration for the severely cognitively disabled. In Friedman's view, Kittay is mistaken: 'We can appreciate the valuable consequences of dependence without having to jettison all notions or ideals of independence' (see p. 111). Friedman extends my suggestion that independence is *relational* (it is independence *from* something) and *incomplete*, by adding that it is *differentiated* (e.g., economic and psychological independence may diverge), and concludes that "independence" has a relatively clear and ascertainable meaning and is not a myth or fiction at all. She therefore rejects Kittay's startling claims that in the 'reigning liberal understanding of justice', those with 'severe or profound cognitive disabilities' can 'never be citizens' and 'have no rights associated with their needs.'[11]

However, Friedman concludes that because I focused on oppression rather than on severe cognitive disability in discussing dependence and independence, I have not reconceptualized citizenry for the severely cognitively disabled. I think that this is true, but that the reality (as

Friedman also thinks) is that while exclusion from citizenship due to oppression is in principle fully remediable, exclusion arising from severe cognitive disability is not. That does not mean that the severely cognitively disabled 'have no rights associated with their needs'. An older political vocabulary would have made the point by saying that those with severe cognitive disability (as also children, the senile, the comatose) can enjoy and should be guaranteed passive citizenship and a range of rights and protections, but cannot exercise active citizenship.

Friedman sensibly distinguishes the task of justifying foundational political principles, such as principles of justice from the practical problem of how to treat different or nonstandard groups of persons within actual, functioning liberal societies. But if the tasks are distinct, then ways of approaching the foundational task that invoke an autonomously rational citizen who chooses political principles under idealized conditions indeed say nothing about the situation of the cognitively disabled. I would add that they also say nothing about the situations of averagely independent persons, or of excessively and obnoxiously independent persons. Appeals to idealised conceptions of independence or versions of individual autonomy may or may not offer the best prospect for justifying fundamental matters of justice (in my view there are more plausible ways of approaching fundamental tasks), but they neither make nor assume empirical claims about the various levels of individual autonomy or independence actually found.

Any discussion of the rights of the disabled, including the cognitively impaired, belongs outside discussions of foundational issues. Friedman suggests otherwise. This does not seem to me correct. Foundational arguments generally aim to establish only the most general principles of justice, and assume that their elaboration and institutionalisation will need further argument and debate, as well as constitutional and legislative action. Direct democracy without intermediate institutions – for example, Bills of Rights, the rule of law, the institutionalisation of executive powers – may notoriously give short shrift to various minorities, among them the severely cognitively impaired. But we do not have to fantasise that this is the only option.

As Friedman points out, Kittay might see it as one of the *advantages* of Rawls' earlier approach to the foundations of justice that it invokes an idealised conception of choice in an Original Position, in which social and individual features are masked, as the hypothetical choosers know that capacities may fail for some, so will have hypothetical reason to take account of the interests of those who lack various capacities, including those with severe cognitive impairments. So it seems to me misleading to import the idea of *consent*, and unnecessary to worry about the consent of the cognitively competent crowding out that of the cognitively impaired.

The Rawlsian Original Position is by definition blind to variations in competence and incompetence *of all sorts*, so does not need to be corrected by introducing special measures. The Original Position, whatever problems it has, is not a tea party and neither the severely cognitively impaired, nor any other group, are 'excluded from the table'.[12]

Rawls' later justificatory strategy for principles of justice (which Friedman does not discuss) invokes the idea of agreement among fellow citizens, and here questions of inclusion and exclusion make sense and are significant for the configuration of justice across borders. This later strategy takes a closer-to-empirical view of agents in foundational arguments about justice, seeing them as fellow citizens in a liberal democratic, bounded society who can reach or fail to reach agreement. However, if the justification of principles of justice is to rest on the possibility of agreement among fellow citizens, there will be no way of including those who cannot engage in discussion or join in processes of discussion and agreement.

Practical ethics

Conceptions of agency, individual autonomy and consent underlie and permeate many current discussions in ethics and political philosophy. Questions frequently surface about who counts as agent and subject, who bears which obligations, and what they ought to do or provide for which others. These practical questions have surfaced at many points in my work both in political philosophy and in ethics.

Agents of justice: Simon Caney

Political philosophers have classically seen individual human beings as agents, but have additionally treated states as agents, that can hold (at least) obligations of justice. This exception in favour of states has often been justified by reference to their supposedly special status as creations of and legitimated by the action of their individual citizens. However, political philosophers have often been reluctant to see other bodies corporate as agents, let alone as bound by obligations of justice. Such a limited account of the relevant agents is problematic for an account of justice that seeks to be adequate for a world in which there are many powerful non-state actors that are not individuals, and in which action at a distance and across state borders is ubiquitous.

Nor is it even tempting to take such a restricted view, once we think of principles of action as prescriptive rather than as reflecting inner states. There is no deep reason why bodies corporate of many sorts should not count as agents, or carry obligation. There are, however, difficulties enough in working out which non-state actors can or should shoulder which obligations, how existing non-state actors might be improved, or new and more effective ones constructed, and how institutional failure to live up to obligations should be handled. What has seemed clear to me for a long time is that powerful agencies that shape the world and others' lives cannot plausibly be relieved of obligations by denying that they are competent to carry them.

Simon Caney discusses the diversity of non-individual agents who can carry obligations of justice by focusing on some limited comments I have made on some types of corporate agents, and suggests how they could be widened and extended. I had argued[13] that if we distinguish primary from secondary agents of justice – agents that establish just or unjust structures and agents that work within such structures – we will have reason to think that there are various sorts of *agents of justice* in addition to states and individuals. I concluded in particular that transnational corporations and NGOs are often secondary agents of justice. Caney argues that the distinction I had drawn between primary and secondary agents of justice would be better drawn as a distinction between two *roles* that agents may have, rather than as a difference between two *types* of agent, since some may contribute to both tasks. And he argues that a wider range of institutional agents, including international agencies, may act as agents of justice, and also that those individuals who are victims of injustice may have special competence and obligations in the construction of justice. I agree on all counts.

Autonomy and reproduction: David Archard

Issues about agency also permeate discussions of human reproduction. Such decisions are after all decisions to bring into the world a human being who (even if all goes well) will depend on other effective agents for many years. I have discussed aspects of the ethics of reproduction intermittently for many years. When I first wrote on them, as David Archard notes, public and philosophical concerns were often centred on some of the risks of *unwanted fertility*, and in particular on their implications for child poverty and suffering, especially in poor countries, and on the forms of reproductive control exercised in some states, whereas recent debates have increasingly focused on *unwanted infertility* and the possible remedies offered by new reproductive technologies.

In the main, David Archard shares my conclusion that there are no unconditional rights to procreate, but we approach this conclusion by differing routes. In arguing that rights to procreate are constrained by obligations to form feasible plans to rear any child that is born, I did not begin from a claim that individuals (or couples) have a liberty right to what later came to be called 'reproductive autonomy'. Nor did I use J. S. Mill's harm principle to identify the permissible limitations on this supposed liberty right. There were simple reasons why I did not take this route. Most obviously, I was not working within a Millian (or other Utilitarian) framework, within which the standard arguments for the harm principle were developed and are deployed. Later I also came to suspect that the harm principle offers less robust guidance than its advocates hope, because judgement of the likely harms of a prospective act, or of the likely harm of types of act, are often considerably less secure than would be helpful for practical purposes.

My point of departure was rather that successful human reproduction leads to the birth of a child, who will unavoidably depend on others for long years, and my claim was that those who decide to reproduce have a duty to form and pursue some feasible plan for the child to be brought up, whether by themselves or willing others. Archard puts forward a slightly different claim, and suggests that progenitors' 'right to procreate [is] constrained by a duty to ensure that those they bring into existence can be expected to enjoy at least a minimally adequate standard of upbringing' (p. 158). I may have thought this – but I said very little indeed about the *standard* of upbringing to be achieved or about *expectations* about that standard, and should probably have said more.

Concerns with questions about the harms that progenitors might do have become more prominent since Derek Parfit's later and well-known discussion of the case of a young girl who has a baby whom she cannot expect to give a good start in life, although she could have expected to give a (different) child born to her when older a good start. Parfit suggested that in this case the proper comparison is not with the better life of the potential subsequent child, but with the harm of non-existence, which not being born ensures. If one assumes that non-existence is very nasty indeed, then it is easy to conclude that a child's progenitors are quite unlikely to harm it by bringing it into the world, because even a thoroughly miserable life will (supposedly) be better than non-existence. Procreation is then judged permissible 'so long as any child created enjoys a life that is at least (but not necessarily any much) better than non-existence' (p. 158). This line of thought absolves progenitors of demanding responsibilities: almost any life a child leads will be better *for that child* than no life at all.

Parfit's example and its subsequent widespread discussion are evident in the background of David Archard's discussion of the question whether reproductive rights are constrained by a duty to provide a tolerable life or merely (on analogy with Millian liberty rights) by a duty not to harm any child that is born. I had assumed without discussion, that neither progenitors nor others have rights to harm children, nor in particular rights to harm a child they have brought into the world. However, in discussions of human reproduction the harm principle is now often invoked for more arcane and limited purposes, which focus very largely on the harm of being born with poor prospects. Once it is assumed that not being born will be worse than being born with miserable prospects, the harms that are most often *actually* inflicted on children receive little attention. The entire discussion brackets issues of child abuse and neglect, and the serious ways in which children's rights are often violated.[14] This seems and seemed to me a tendentious way of looking either at progenitors' rights or at the harms that children are likely to suffer.

Archard rightly points out that I also said little about alternative approaches, in which progenitors are not absolved merely by providing a life that is better than no life at all, but may be thought to have a duty to provide a *tolerable* life, or an *adequate* life, or a *decent* life, or a *minimally decent* life, or a life that meets some other standard. One reason that I did not was because I was looking at matters prospectively. Any human project that lasts over many years is highly uncertain, and what can be demanded is closer to having a *feasible* plan than a *reasonable* expectation or *definite* standard. Once again, this way of thinking depended on taking an agent rather than a spectator perspective on ethical questions.

When I resumed occasional writing on the ethics of reproduction many years later, the entire context of discussion had changed. Preoccupation with the fate of abandoned children remained a concern, especially among those who write or work on development and poverty. But in the rich world, the advent of new reproductive technologies had led to a huge increase in interest in the predicament of *unwanted infertility*, and relative neglect of the consequences of *unwanted* or *irresponsible fertility*. In more philosophical writing, this new focus was expressed in increasingly confident claims that reproductive rights were broader than the long acknowledged prohibitions on forced reproduction and the canonical 'right to marry and form a family'.[15] A number of prominent philosophers claimed that their rights to 'reproductive autonomy' included rights to receive assisted reproduction if infertile.

I doubt whether invoking various conceptions of 'reproductive autonomy' has provided better arguments for the configuration of obligations and rights that bear on human reproduction. As in other areas of life, a wide range of conceptions of individual autonomy have been in play. Some of the more conspicuous advocates of 'reproductive autonomy' equated it with mere, sheer choice, bounded only by the rights of others; others drew analogies with rights of self-expression.[16] Others left it unclear how individual autonomy was to be interpreted, and how the claims of (a specific conception of) individual autonomy was to be judged against other claims. With a lot of premises one can arrive at lots of conclusions, and with a lot of attention to individual autonomy it is easy to overlook how the less than autonomous will fare. An individualistic outlook that emphasises the autonomy of progenitors, variously conceived, does not provide an optimal framework for thinking about the needs or rights of children, or about the duties of those who bring them into the world.

Trustworthiness and trust

In every domain of life we aim and hope to achieve not simply more trust, but specifically more trust in the trustworthy, and (if we can) less trust in the untrustworthy. What we care about is *well-placed* trust; what we fear is *misplaced* trust. So there is little prospect of saying much about the practical problems of trusting if one is unwilling to say anything about trustworthiness. Yet it is quite common for current discussions of trust to say remarkably little either about trustworthiness, or about the demanding task of distinguishing trustworthiness from untrustworthiness.

Trust before trustworthiness? Annette Baier

Annette Baier disputes many of the claims that I have made about trust, so it should be useful to try to sort out the issues that divide us. She defines trust as 'willingness to be vulnerable to the trusted, to rely on their competence and goodwill' (p. 175), and claims that it is more fundamental than trustworthiness. This seems to me to be a correct characterisation of trusting attitudes that will cover everything from blind trust to intelligently placed trust, but one that is not useful for practical purposes because it brackets the very considerations that matter for placing trust well. For practical purposes we are interested not simply in trusting attitudes, but in placing trust well – and any account of well-placed trust depends on an account of trustworthiness.

Baier's account of trust is congruent with many in the sociological and psychological literatures (to which she refers), and also with those taken in the gigantic public relations industry, including those parts that carry out public opinion polls and market research. Each of these bodies of work takes an essentially empirical approach to trust. They aim to answer questions such as 'Does A trust B?', 'Does C trust people of type D?', 'How much does E trust F?', 'Does G trust people (professionals, institutions) of type H?' or 'How much do people of type X trust people (professionals, institutions) of type J?'. In many contexts, particularly in commercial and political life, where reputation is critical to success, information about others' levels of trust can be both useful and economically valuable. Some excerpts from such information are widely reported in the media in developed societies; others remain closely guarded in commercial or political confidence.

However, empirical work on attitudes of trust does not offer an adequate framework for addressing normative, including ethical, questions about the intelligent placing and refusing of trust. In working out whom to trust for what purposes it is of little help to know whom others trust, or how much they trust them. We are not lemmings, and knowing how others are placing or refusing trust would be useful to us only if we also knew whether or not their trust was well placed.

Placing trust well, even in simple matters, is hard. Annette Baier claims that 'O'Neill confuses placing trust with deciding to rely on someone or something'. Would that matters were so simple! In placing trust in another for some particular purpose we typically need to make a judgement of the other person's competence and honesty, as well as their reliability, in the relevant matter. Such judgements do not, of course, need to achieve certainty, but they are epistemically challenging even in quite familiar contexts. This is why I think it useful to spend time thinking about the task of placing and refusing trust intelligently not only in face-to-face contexts, but in the more demanding contexts in institutional life, or in dealing with experts whose claims we cannot check for ourselves. My discussions and criticisms of the uses and misuses of specific forms of accountability in institutional and professional life have been offered not as an alternative to trust – an aim that I continue to argue is incoherent – but as a way of understanding more about the task of placing and refusing trust intelligently in settings where doing so is demanding.

In the end, the claims about priority on which Annette Baier and I differ reflect the very different purposes with which we discuss trust. She, I think, is interested in the phenomenon of trust, whether or not it is well placed, so can bracket consideration of trustworthiness or actually claim that it is secondary. Attitudes of trust can indeed diverge from, or disregard questions about trustworthiness, often at great cost to those who place their trust poorly. I am concerned with the practical demands of trust, so think that it matters that it be placed in the trustworthy and denied to the untrustworthy, and that we need therefore to grasp the importance of placing trust in the trustworthy.

Misplaced distrust: Karen Jones

Karen Jones shares my concern with the practical task of placing and refusing trust well, and has interesting things to say about misplaced mistrust (or distrust). I agree with her that misplaced mistrust, even if not as harmful as misplaced trust, can still produce great damage. She notes that misplaced mistrust is not always due to the poor judgement or suspicious attitudes of those who distrust, and suggests that it might sometimes reflect 'something missing from the trustworthy person or institution that is unable or unwilling reliably to signal to would-be trusters that they can be counted on' (p. 187). I agree that this is an interesting and underexplored problem, and would add that misplaced mistrust may not reflect failings in either party, since it may reflect dearth of evidence or lack of contact.

Karen Jones then defends 'affective attitude accounts of trust', arguing that we can 'acknowledge that trust contains an affective component without thereby seeing it as impervious to reasons or unable to be discriminating' (pp. 186–87). She distinguishes between *basic trustworthiness*, in which B is trustworthy to A in respect Z, from *rich trustworthiness*, in which B is trustworthy to A in respect Z, *and* B 'signals' to A that he is trustworthy in this respect. Clearly there is much to be said in favour of 'rich trustworthiness', since it helps A to judge better whom to trust in which respects (provided that B's signalling is trustworthy).

However, it is unclear to me why Jones describes 'rich trustworthiness' as requiring 'signalling', rather than communication. She writes that:

> Signaling is communicative and takes place against a vast social background including norms and shared understandings of what can be expected of whom. Some of the background norms are moral, others professional; some are localized, others broadly based. [...] Because we live in a world in which how we present ourselves and who we are taken to be carries with it social meanings, we are inevitably signaling, rightly or wrongly, who can rely on us for what. [...] Signaling can be accomplished in many ways, including but not limited to: appearance, comportment, words, glances, deeds, certificates, titles, institutional roles. (p. 190)

But all of this is surely true of all communication. Communication is not solely linguistic, often includes gestures or other social signals, relies on a multiplicity of norms and may or may not receive adequate uptake by intended and other audiences. The use of the term 'signalling' suggests that Jones may have some distinctive type of communication in mind, but if so I have failed to grasp what is distinctive.

She poses the key question for an understanding of 'rich trustworthiness' by asking 'When and why does signaling fail? Who is responsible for its failures?' (p. 191), and notes that 'Signaling is ... consummated only when it receives the right kind of uptake by the intended audience' (p. 192), but that a wide range of emotional factors and many sorts of stereotyping may influence that uptake:

> Our trusting can, and often does, part company from our believing: trust operates at a different level from mere belief. It is the largely unreflective result of our social experiences and reflects our prejudices and cognitive habits at least as much, if not more than, our judgments about trustworthiness. To think of trust as simply a matter of judgment and choice is to locate trust and distrust too shallowly within the agent's psyche and so not to see the kinds of pathologies to which it is vulnerable. (p. 195)

I think that the contrast drawn here between belief and trust is misplaced, not because I assume that trust is immune from affect and pathologies, but because belief too is subject to affect and pathologies. And just as the communication of trustworthiness is subject to distortions and pathologies, so too is the communication of beliefs. Trust is indeed not 'simply a matter of judgement and choice', and nor is belief.[17] In communicating to others that I am trustworthy in some respect, both my communication and the audience's uptake may be influenced by prejudices and stereotypes, by inhibitions and preconceptions. Communication is like that. Any adequate account of the epistemic and ethical norms that are relevant to judging or communicating trustworthiness takes it that norms matter *not* because communication always lives up to them, but on the contrary, because it does not. Normative considerations are relevant where things can go wrong.

The possibilities of misplaced trust, misplaced mistrust, and miscommunication about trust are the reasons behind my insistence that normative standards matter if we are to say anything about the intelligent placing of trust. Because trust and mistrust can be misdirected, and because there are many ways in which they can be misdirected, it matters to work out what steps we can take to direct it well.

Trust is indeed not 'simply a matter of judgment and choice' (p. 195), but this is no reason for setting aside judgement and choice if our aim is to place trust well – and to 'signal' trustworthiness well. Judgement and choice are the ways in which we take steps to correct or allow for our own or others' prejudices or stereotypes, blindness or error, to place trust intelligently rather than blindly, and to communicate to others where they have reason to place and refuse trust. The pathologies of trust, like the pathologies of testimony are real; the remedies are incomplete, but they are not negligible.

It may be that Karen Jones is wary about the normative remedies for misplaced trust and misplaced mistrust that judgement can provide, because she thinks of judgement and choice solely individually, so as unresponsive to social context. That is not a view I share, and as I put the matter in the preface to my 2002 Reith Lectures 'we need social and political institutions that allow us to judge where to place our trust'.[18] Since then I have spent a lot of time writing on the social practices and institutional structures that are used to support the placing and refusal of trust, and seeking to understand why some of them work and others fail, at worst even exacerbating the problems they seek to remedy.

Judging trustworthiness: Daniel Weinstock

Daniel Weinstock joins me in seeing the placing and refusal of trust as a practical matter, and notes with regret that whereas 'empirical work [on trust], both survey-based and historical has begun to emerge … properly normative work lags sorely behind' (p. 200). That is also my view, and Weinstock's paper addresses a broad range of contexts in which normative work could be, and some in which it has been taken forward.

He notes that some of the literatures on trust separate discussion of 'horizontal' trust that 'obtains among agents in (largely) face-to-face contexts, outside of formal structures of authority' (p. 199), but that the more difficult problems arise in situations that require 'vertical' trust where 'agents must decide whether or not to trust agents who hold positions of institutional authority over them, or to trust "faceless" institutions with which they have relations that are largely unmediated by sustained human contact' (p. 200). He then offers astute comments on some of the remedies sought, and their success or lack of success where trust has to be of 'faceless' others.

I believe that there is much to be discovered here by closer empirical study (with a normative purpose!) of those institutions and professions that are widely trusted. Like him, I suspect that much depends on good governance rather than zealous micro-management. I also think that once again communication is crucial, and agree with many of his comments on the adequacy and inadequacies of institutional and media communication. However, diagnosing inadequacies is easier than identifying effective remedies, and to identify those remedies I think that we need to think more capaciously about the ethics of communication.

Defective communication is probably one of the sources of persistent difficulty in the placing and refusing of trust intelligently, but unfortunately some fashionable remedies for these defects can themselves fuel mistrust. For example, it is often said that *transparency* is a useful antidote to untrustworthy behaviour. The hope is that it will have two beneficial effects. On the one hand, knowledge that their conduct will be exposed to public gaze will lead institutions and those who staff them to behave better; on the other hand, the public will be better able to judge where they should and should not place their trust. The supply side will have incentives; the demand side will have information.

Needless to say, matters are seldom so straightforward in institutional life. Those who are subjected to transparency requirements will also realise that there are incentives for representing what they do in a better light, rather than for changing it: they may invest in public relations, spin, communication strategies and soft words. Those who are supposed to benefit from transparency may still find it hard to grasp what is going on, despite the torrents of communication lavished on them. Weinstock's focus on these issues mainly discusses the role of the media, which I too think of central importance if communication is to support the intelligent placing and refusal of trust. However, the media operate within a far wider world of corporate and political communication, of spin and press releases, of public relations and advertising, and often enough of communication whose sources and funding is hidden, and whose purposes may not be evident. If the media are to become part of the remedy rather than the problem of defective communication, we need to find ways of securing better standards of communication without jeopardising press freedom. If we are to offer a fuller account of the intelligent placing and refusal of trust, it will be important to engage with this wide world of communicative activity.

Notes

1 I was surprised because I'd assumed that rational choice approaches to reason and action would offer more, but concluded that they do not – despite and because of lavish reliance on implausible assumptions.
2 *Acting on Principle: An Essay on Kantian Ethics* (New York: Columbia University Press, 1975). The book was originally published under my then married name (Onora Nell) and will shortly be reissued by Cambridge University Press.
3 For explicit discussion of this shift see Onora O'Neill, 'Kant's Virtues,' in *How Should One Live? Essays on the Virtues*, ed. Roger Crisp (Oxford: Oxford University Press, 1996), pp. 77–97.
4 See 'Universal Laws and Ends-in-Themselves,' *The Monist*, 1989, 341–61, reprinted in *Constructions of Reason: Explorations of Kant's Practical Philosophy* (Cambridge: Cambridge University Press, 1989) and 'Self-Legislation, Autonomy and the Form of Law,' in *Recht, Geschichte, Religion: Die Bedeutung Kants für die Gegenwart*, ed. Herta Nagl-Docekal und Rudolf Langthaler, *Sonderband der Deutschen Zeitschrift für Philosophie* (Berlin: Akademie Verlag, 2004), pp. 13–26.
5 John Rawls, *Political Liberalism* (New York: Columbia University Press, 1993) and *Law of Peoples* (Cambridge, MA: Harvard University Press, 1999), esp. pp. 62ff.
6 Immanuel Kant, 'On the Common Saying: That May be Correct in Theory but it is of no Use in Practice,' in *Kant's Political Philosophy*, 2nd edn (trans. H.B. Nisbet) (Cambridge: Cambridge University Press, 1991), pp. 61–92. For more extended discussion see my 'Historical Trends and Human Futures,' *Studies in History and Philosophy of Science* A 39, 2008, 529–34.
7 See Neil C. Manson and Onora O'Neill, *Rethinking Informed Consent in Bioethics* (Cambridge: Cambridge University Press, 2007).
8 I was first alerted to the differences by Thomas Hill. See Thomas E. Hill Jnr, 'The Kantian Conception of Autonomy,' in his *Dignity and Practical Reason* (Ithaca NY: Cornell University Press, 1992), pp. 76–96. My most extensive discussion of the theme is in *Autonomy and Trust in Bioethics* (Cambridge: Cambridge University Press, 2002) and my most recent in *Autonomy and Public Reason in Kant* in Mark Timmons and Robert Johnson, eds, *Reason, Value, and Respect: Kantian Themes from the Philosophy of Thomas E. Hill, Jr*, Oxford University Press, forthcoming.
9 *Autonomy and Trust in Bioethics*, p. 49.
10 For a summary of the Liverpool Care Pathway see http://www.liv.ac.uk/media/livacuk/mcpcil/migrated-files/pdfs/lcpv12newdocuments/LCP%20Relative%20Carer%20Information%20Leaflet%20-%20Nov%2009.pdf. This particular instrument has become controversial, and, it is said, is misused. I doubt whether any replacement can give weight to all wishes, or reported wishes.
11 Eva Feder Kittay, 'When Caring Is Just and Justice Is Caring: Justice and Mental Retardation,' in *The Subject of Care: Feminist Perspectives on Dependency* (Lanham: Rowman & Littlefield, 2002), p. 270. See p. 271.
12 So Kittay's worry that they 'do not have a place at the table where their fates are decided' is misplaced. Eva Feder Kittay, 'The Personal Is Philosophical Is

Political: A Philosopher and Mother of a Cognitively Disabled Person Sends Notes from the Battlefield,' *Metaphilosophy*, 40, 2009, p. 620.
13 Mainly in 'Agents of Justice,' *Metaphilosophy*, 32 (2001), 180–95, and 'Global Justice: Whose Obligations?' in *The Ethics of Assistance: Morality and the Distant Needy* (Cambridge: Cambridge University Press, 2004), edited by Deen K. Chatterjee, pp. 242–59.
14 Archard suggests that some commentators claim that I deny that children have rights. I have in fact written a fair amount on children's rights, most obviously 'Children's Rights and Children's Lives,' *Ethics*, 98, 1988, 445–63; and 'The "Good Enough" Parent in the Age of the New Reproductive Technologies,' in *The Ethics of Genetics in Human Procreation*, ed. Hille Haker and Deryck Beyleveld (Vermont: Ashgate, 2000), pp. 33–48.
15 *Universal Declaration of Human Rights*, Article 16. The Declaration did not make the egregious assumption that the childless have no family.
16 See my discussion in *Autonomy and Trust in Bioethics* of the various accounts of reproductive autonomy offered by Ronald Dworkin, John Robertson and John Harris.
17 Relevant bodies of work include studies of cognitive distortion, biases and heuristics; parts of behavioural economics; work in social epistemology. On the specific issue of pathologies of testimony, see Tony Coady, *Testimony: A Philosophical Study* (New York: Oxford University Press, 1992); Axel Gelfert, 'Kant on Testimony,' *British Journal for the History of Philosophy*, 14, 2006, 627–52.
18 *A Question of Trust* (Cambridge: Cambridge University Press, 2002), p. vii.

INDEX

accountability 176, 187, 188, 196, 214, 238
action 4–5, 9–76, 204, 219–26
advance directives 229–30, 231
adversarial institutions 208–9, 212
affective attitudes 7, 186–87, 194–96, 238–39
agency: consent 5, 77–129; hope 63, 65–66; medical ethics 2; rationality 23, 26–27, 32, 33, 45; reason 3, 4, 21–22, 61–62, 77–129, 226–33; trust 207–8
agents of global justice 6, 133–56, 233–34
Alder Hey inquiry 82, 83–84, 88
ambiguous Right 68–69
Ameriks, Karl 56–57, 64, 74
ANH *see* artificial nutrition and hydration
Anscombe, Elizabeth 1
appraisal respect 98
arbitrary principles 22, 24, 38, 39, 43–44, 44–46, 50
Archard, David 6–7, 157–71, 234–36
artificial nutrition and hydration (ANH) 94, 95–96, 103, 107–8, 229–30, 231
attitudes: affective 7, 186–87, 194–96, 238–39; trust 202, 203, 204, 237
audits 175, 182, 184
authority 4, 23–24, 43, 44–46, 61, 204–5, 223; *see also* control, power
autonomy: moral 58; patient 5–6; procreation 161, 162, 167–68, 170, 234–36; rational 26; reason 3, 77–129, 226–33; respect 27; will 28, 30, 31
avowals 204–5, 216

Baier, Annette 7, 175–85, 190–91, 237–38
Baron, Marcia 4, 11–16, 220–21
Barry, Melissa 4, 221–24
basic trustworthiness 7, 187–90, 191, 238–39
belief 82, 195, 202, 222, 223, 224, 227, 239–40
Bhandary, Asha 124
bioethics 3, 79–81, 86, 87, 88, 92, 94–110, 157–58, 164, 229; *see also* medical contexts
Boswell, John: *The Kindness of Strangers* 159–60
Bretton Woods institutions 140
Bricker, Philip 70–71
Burke v. The General Medical Council 5, 94–97, 99, 102–3, 107–8

Caney, Simon 6, 133–56, 233–34
capacity 27, 203, 206, 216, 226–27, 229, 232
Castelfranchi, Cristiano 177–78, 180
Categorical Imperative (CI): consent 89–90, 91; constructivism 28, 29, 31, 221, 223; independence 112–19; maxims 39–41, 41–42; moral worth 11–12, 14, 15; practical reasoning 20
children: care of 7, 157–70, 202, 203, 236; right to procreate 234, 235–36; trust 177, 179
Christian religion 55, 58–63
CI *see* Categorical Imperative
citizens, liberal 119–27
citizenship 199–216, 231–32, 233
civil rights 49
co-referring terms 81–82, 83

INDEX

coercion: agents of justice 147–48, 148–49, 150; consent 90, 122, 125; cooperation 22; power 48, 50, 122; procreation 166; prohibitions of 39, 45; rights 69; trust 206
cognitive aspects: ability 119–27, 231–33; agents 178; trust 195, 202, 216
collective agents 207, 208, 209
commitment 13, 21–27, 30, 188
common authority 19, 23–24
communication: consent 88, 89; ethics of 3–4; patient autonomy 94–95, 96; trust 190–91, 192, 193–94, 210, 239, 240, 241–42
competence: decision to trust 177, 178, 183, 184, 238; drawing on resources 189; institutions 205; rich 192; social 191
complete constructivism 18, 19, 33, 222
compliance: agents of justice 135, 136, 137, 140–41; respect 6, 98, 99–100, 102, 103, 104, 106
conditional reasoning 46, 222
consciousness 72–73, 81
consensual sex 80
consensus 50, 224
consent 5, 77–129, 226–33
consideration respect 6, 98–99, 100, 101–2, 104, 106–7
constitutive principles 29
constructivism 2–3, 4–5, 17–36, 37–54, 221–24
contingently shared assumptions 222
control: hope 65, 66, 70; independence 115; trust 177, 182, 183; *see also* power, authority
convergence of reasons 5150
cooperation 22
coordination 19–20, 21–23, 24–25, 27, 31, 223
Copenhagen criteria 140
corporate agency 207–8, 233, 234
corruption 59, 138, 171, 182, 208, 210, 215
cosmopolitanism 151, 152
cost–benefit reasoning 203, 208, 212
crisis of trust 200, 210, 215
culture 48, 115–16, 119, 191–92

Dancy, Jonathan 184
decisions: informed consent 79–93; patient autonomy 94–95, 97, 105–6; procreation 167; prudence 68, 70; trust 177, 202, 216
deductive reasoning 45
default trust 180, 182
defective communication 241–42
defective consent 228
deliberate trust 180
democratic politics 209
dependence on others 6, 111–29, 165, 189, 231
derivative principles 39, 45, 116
design, institutional 207, 215
desires 28, 29, 30, 31, 46–48
developing countries 149
difference principle (Rawls) 120
direct democracy 232
disability 119–27, 231–33
discipline of reason 61–62
disclosure of information 86–87
discrimination 189
disease 180–81
disposition to evil 58–59, 60
distrust: avowals 216; institutions 8, 205, 208, 209, 212–16; misplaced 205, 208, 238–40; monitoring 214; trustworthy 7, 186–98; *see also* mistrust, trust
divine assistance 55, 59, 68
divinity 63
doctors 177, 188, 195, 196
doctrinal belief 67, 73
Dunkel, Arthur 142–43
duty: childcare 235; fundamental principles 224; justice 134, 141, 142, 145, 146; moral actions 4, 12–13, 14, 221; practical reasoning 226; procreative 157–71
Dworkin, Ronald 161, 164

emotions 194, 195, 239
empirical reasoning 224, 226
encapsulated interest of trust 201, 212
environmental degradation 135–36
equality 26, 121, 123, 151, 183
equity rights 68–69
ethics: communication 3–4; constructivism 37–54; faith 56; informed consent 227–28; practical 131–71, 233–36; procreation 7; reasoning 221, 222, 223; society 61, 63; standing of agents 20–21

245

INDEX

EU *see* European Union
European Union (EU) 139, 140
euthanasia 150
evidence: lawyers 209; tampering 194–95; trust 202, 203, 204, 205, 210, 212, 213
evil 56, 58–61, 116
executive roles 135
existence 163–64, 165, 166, 167, 169
existential hope 66, 67, 69
existential prudence 72, 73
expectations 65–66, 187, 190, 225, 235
experience 181, 207–8
expert knowledge 211
explicit consent 80–81
external monitoring *see* monitoring

faith 55–76, 225
Falcone, Rino 177–78, 180
false consciousness 81
fear 178, 179–80, 183–84, 195, 198
Feder, Ellen 112
Feinberg, Joel 169
feminism 111, 231
fertility 105, 167–68, 234, 236
Fineman, Martha Albertson 112, 113
finitude 67, 85, 86, 88, 89, 91, 92
first-order desires 30, 31
first-order duty-bearers 145
Flikschuh, Katrin 5, 55–76, 224–26
formal principles of reasoning 18, 26, 28, 31, 32
foundling homes 158, 159–60
Frankfurt, H. 30
free-choosing adults 123
freedom 62, 63–64, 66, 161, 162, 242
Fricker, Miranda 85
Friedman, Marilyn 6, 111–29, 231–33
Fukayama, Francis 199
fundamental principles: Categorical Imperative 11, 223; consent 89–90, 91; constructivism 39, 45; duty 20, 224; maxims 40; practical reason 223

Galston, William 114–15
Gauthier, D. 21–22
General Medical Council (GMC), UK 94, 95–96, 229–30, 231
global justice 6, 133–56, 233–34
GMC *see* General Medical Council
God 55–68, 73, 224
the good 123

good governance 214, 241
goodwill 175, 177, 187

Hardin, Russell 201, 202
Hare, John 55, 56, 58–61, 67, 72, 73
harm: patient autonomy 230; principle 162–63, 164, 234–35; right to procreate 165, 166, 235–36; trust 175, 178, 180
Harris, John 161, 164, 165, 168
health institutions 176, 180, 206
hermeneutical injustice 85–86
heteronomous reasoning 222, 223
heuristics 201, 203, 207, 212, 216
hierarchical normative systems 26
Hill, Thomas E. Jr. 4–5, 37–54, 221–24
Holton, Richard 188
honesty 238
hope 5, 55–76, 224–26
horizontal trust 199–200, 206, 241
Hruschka, Joachim 74
human agents 207, 208
human tissue 82, 83–84, 88
humanitarian intervention 150
Hume, David 30, 31, 63, 179, 222

IBRD *see* International Bank for Reconstruction and Development
idealism 64
idealizations 46–48, 112–13, 120, 232
identity-based prejudice 195, 196
ideological consent 81
ILO *see* International Labour Organization
IMF *see* International Monetary Fund
impartiality 151
imperfect duties 226
income-earning 114, 115, 117, 118
incompetence 196
independence 6, 97, 111–29, 229, 231, 232
indicative trust 192
individuals: agency 207–8; autonomy 94–110, 112, 229–31, 231–33, 236; character 213, 215; trust 175, 176, 178, 209, 211, 213
infertility 161, 234, 236
information 80, 85–87, 89, 192–93, 205, 210, 237
informed consent 5, 79–93, 227–28, 229
innate evil 58, 59, 60–61

246

INDEX

institutions: agents of justice 136–37, 139–43, 233–34; trust 7–8, 182, 194, 199–218, 241
instrumental reasoning 46–48, 221
intelligent accounts of trust 186, 238, 240
inter-personal relationships 111–27
International Bank for Reconstruction and Development (IBRD) 148
international institutions 139–43, 148, 151, 152
International Labour Organization (ILO) 139
international law 150–52
International Monetary Fund (IMF) 140
intuition 201, 203

Jackson, Robert 138
Jones, Karen 7, 177, 186–98, 238–40
judgement: patient autonomy 229–30, 231; trust 195, 196, 201, 202, 238, 240–42
justice: agents of 6, 133–56, 233–34; consent 124; constructivist reasoning 18, 20; instrumental reasoning 46–47; liberal legitimacy 124; marginalization of women 121; morality 43; the person 123; procreation 166; reasoning 223–24

Kant, Immanuel: autonomy 116–17; consent 87–92; constructivism 2–3, 19, 32; *Critique of Pure Reason* 41, 57, 61, 62; *Doctrine of Right* 68; *Groundwork for the Metaphysics of Morals* 13, 14, 15, 68, 72, 73, 221; reason 1, 4, 5, 9–76, 219–26; *Religion Within the Limits of Reason Alone* 55, 58, 60, 61, 62, 63, 67; *Perpetual Peace: A Philosophical Sketch* 68, 71; trust 213
Kavka, Gregory 160
Kittay, Eva 112, 120–21, 123, 231, 232
knowledge 65, 70, 225
Korsgaard, Christine 17, 28–31, 32, 33, 37

large-scale institutions 212
law 150–52
lawyers 208–9
legal contexts 135, 150–52; *see also* regulations

legislation, self–29
legitimacy: liberal 6, 49, 50, 51, 124–27; political 146, 147–48, 149
liberal theory: conceptions of the ideal citizen 231; democratic societies 224, 233; independence 119–27; legitimacy 6, 49, 50, 51
life-governing fundamental maxims 40
limited constructivism 18, 31, 33, 222
List, Christian 207
Locke, John 144, 179
Luhmann, Niklas 175–76, 182, 183

Machiavellian prince 68, 71
McMahan, Jeff 151
malfeasance 210, 211, 214
Manson, Neil 5, 79–93, 216, 227–28, 229
marginalization 44, 48, 49, 119, 121
market institutions 206
maxims: Categorical Imperative 39–41, 42; consent 91, 228; evil 58, 59; Kant's three great 39; moral worth 4, 11–16, 220–21; prudence 70; public reason 223; trust 213
means-ends coordination 223
media 184, 197–98, 200, 209–11, 241
medical contexts: informed consent 79–81, 229; patient autonomy 5–6, 94–110; procreation 169; trust 182–83, 188; *see also* bioethics
meta-ethics 37
Mill, J.S. 15, 234
minimal conception of reasoning 222
minimal goodwill 175, 178, 184
minimalist sense of autonomy 5, 6
minimally decent life 161–63, 164, 165, 166–67, 170, 236
misplaced distrust 186–98, 238–40
misplaced trust 205, 208, 237, 238, 240
mistrust 175, 176, 178, 179–80, 182, 204–5; *see also* distrust, trust
monitoring: trust 7, 175, 176, 177, 181, 182, 183; watchdog bodies 213–14, 216
morality: constructivism 39; hope 55–76; justice 43; limits 144; philosophy 17–36; reasoning 223–24; worth 4, 11–16, 220–21
multiple act-descriptions 39–40
mundane hope 65, 66
mundane prudence 69, 72, 73

nature 62, 63, 66, 224–25
neighbour trust 179–80
NGOs *see* non-governmental organizations
Nietzsche 26
non-arbitrary principles 22–23, 24, 45
non-consensual actions 90
non-constructed principles 31, 32
non-doctrinal belief 67, 68
non-existence 6, 7, 158, 160, 163–64, 165, 166, 169, 170, 235
non-governmental organizations (NGOs) 137, 139, 147, 149, 234
non-identity 163, 168–69
non-instrumental reasoning 221
noncompliance 143–44
nonconstructivist, coherentist methods 18
norms: agents of justice 145–52; compliance with 140–41; consent 5; ethics 38; medical treatment 103; misplaced trust 240; reasoning 226; referential opacity 86; trust 190
Nozick, Robert 1
Nussbaum, Martha 123

objectivity 17–36
obligations: agents of justice 133, 136, 137–38, 141, 142, 146–52, 233, 234; patient choice 102–8; permissive consent 88; practical reasoning 226; rich trustworthiness 193
O'Neill, Onora 219–43; *Acting on Principle* 2, 39, 91; *Autonomy and Trust in Bioethics* 3, 83, 97, 157, 161, 229; 'Begetting, Bearing and Rearing' 157; 'Between Consenting Adults' 80; *Bounds of Justice* 3, 42, 133; *Constructions of Reason: Explorations of Kant's Practical Philosophy* 2, 37, 40, 89; *Faces of Hunger: An Essay on Poverty, Development and Justice* 2; *Having Children: Philosophical and Legal Reflections on Parenthood* 157; *A Question of Trust* 3; *Rethinking Informed Consent in Bioethics* 3, 87, 88, 89, 90, 227, 229; *Towards Justice and Virtue: A Constructive Account of Practical Reasoning* 2–3, 4, 20, 134
opacity, referential 5, 79–93, 227–28
opinion polls 204, 237
oppression 231–32

the Original Position (Rawls) 18, 46, 232–33
overlapping consensus 50–51

Parfit, Derek 163, 168–69, 235
Patel, Jayant 196
patient: autonomy 5–6, 94–110, 229–31; trust 181
perfect duties 226
performance indicators 214
permissive consent 5, 88
Pettit, Philip 207, 214
plurality of agents 20, 21, 23, 222
political constructivism 37
political contexts: constructivism 5, 38; independence and dependence 6, 119–27; legitimacy 146, 147–48; practical faith 55–76; Rawls 48, 49–51; trust 199–200, 208–9
population policies 166
poverty 165–66
power: agents of justice 138, 139, 140, 142–43, 145–46; coercive 48, 50, 122; institutions and trust 206; referential opacity 85–86; trust 182, 183, 200; *see also* control, authority
practical contexts: ethics 131–71, 233–36; faith 55–76; independence 120; maxims 228; objectivity 17–36; philosophy 1; reason 41, 55–76, 57, 220
prejudice 195, 196
prescriptive approaches 220, 228, 233
press freedom 242
presuppositions 26–27, 51
primacy of practical reason 57, 61, 62, 64
primary agents of justice 133–37, 141, 142, 143, 152, 234
primary motives 12, 13, 14
principles of Right 72–73
probabilistic arguments 225
procedural approaches 87–88, 89, 103–4, 106, 176, 178
procreation 6–7, 157–71, 234–36
professionals: judgement 229–30, 231; provision of treatment 94–95, 100–101, 102, 103–4; trust 175–76, 179, 181, 182–83, 241
profit obligations 141, 142
property rights 166
propositional issues 82, 83, 85, 220, 227
prostitution 80

proxy consent 126
proxy measures 192
prudence 55–76, 118, 119, 222
public reason 48, 222–23, 224
Putnam, Robert 199–200

quality control 182
quality of life *see* minimally decent life
quasi-states 138
Quebec, Canada 215

racism 195, 196, 198
radical secularism 56, 66, 67, 68, 73, 74, 225–26
radiotherapy 105
rationality: agency 23, 26–27, 32, 33, 45; authority 4; autonomy 26; finitude 85, 86, 88, 89, 91, 92; fundamental maxims 40; reflection 105–6; sharing principles 89–90; value 41
Rawls, John: agents of justice 138; constructivism 18, 37–38, 42–44, 44–51, 222, 224; independence 120; *The Law of Peoples* 42, 138; the Original Position 18, 46, 232–33; political legitimacy 147; *Political Liberalism* 42, 44, 49, 50; rationality 1, 2; *A Theory of Justice* 18, 42, 44, 46–47
reactive attitudes 188
real-world ethical debates 1
realism 17–19, 31–33, 43
reason 1–5, 9–76, 201, 203, 219–26
recalcitrance 195, 196–97
recognition respect 98
referential opacity 5, 79–93, 227–28
reflection 29, 31, 33, 100, 105–6, 126–27
regulations 166, 167–68, 210–11, 213–14; *see also* legal contexts
relevance 88, 89, 192
religion 5, 55–76, 149, 164, 224–26
remedial responsibilities 142
reproductive autonomy 161, 167–68, 234, 234–36
respect: agents of justice 136; autonomy 5–6, 27, 94–110, 229, 230; diverse values 43; rational agency 23, 26, 32; trust 188–89
responsibilities: agents of justice 136, 137, 141, 142, 143, 145, 146–52;

procreation 7, 157, 158, 161, 164–65, 166–67, 168
revolution, right to 69
rich trustworthiness 7, 187–90, 191, 192–94, 239
Right 56, 57, 68–69, 72–73, 74
rightness 4, 11–16
rights: patient autonomy 94–108, 230, 231, 232; permissive consent 88; practical reasoning 226; procreative 157–71, 234–36
risk 80, 84, 105, 106, 181, 182–83
Robertson, John 161, 163, 164–65
Rousseau, Jean-Jacques 158–59, 160, 161, 164
Ruddick, William 157
Ruggiero, Renato 142–43
rule-governed competition 209

sacred texts 225
Salgo v. Leland Stanford Jr. University Board of Trustees 84
Scalon, T. 32–33
schools 192–93
second-order desires 30
second-order duty-bearers 145
secondary agents of justice 135, 136–37, 234
secondary motives 12, 14
secularism 56, 58–64, 66, 67, 68, 73, 74, 225–26
self-consciousness 28–29
self-determination 100
self-discipline 61
self-expression 164
self-legislation 29
self-monitoring 7, 181
self-perceptions 194
self-preservation 143–44
self-sufficiency 114, 116, 117, 121
self-trust 177
sharing principles of rationality 89–90
single mothers 113–14
slavery 80, 160–61
social context: authority 43; consent 81; dependency 112, 113; independence 117, 118; trust 179, 190, 191, 193, 196, 199
sovereignty 69
the state: agents of justice 6, 138, 147, 150, 151, 152, 233; international

organization membership 139; trust 206; welfare provision 113–14
stereotypes 195, 239, 240
substantive principles 21–27, 28, 29, 31, 32
supervision 175, 176, 177
supreme moral principle 13
suspicion 191–92, 212, 214
Sutherland, Peter 142–43
system 1 heuristics 201, 203, 207–8, 212

tacit consent 80
technical reasoning 222
teleology 67, 73
temporal hope 63
temporal prudence 70–71
three-place trustworthiness 188–90, 194
thresholds: adequacy 165, 166; cognitive capacity 127; trustworthiness 202–3
tissue donation 82, 83–84
TNCs *see* transnational companies
tracking belief 225
trade power 142–43
traditions and beliefs 112, 113, 223
transcendence 56, 57, 63–66, 67, 68, 73–74
transnational companies (TNCs) 138–39, 141–43, 234
transparency 146, 190, 193, 241
trust/trustworthiness 3, 7–8, 66, 70, 173–218, 237–42; *see also* distrust, mistrust
truth 5, 82, 88, 89
tyranny 125, 126

uncertainty 70, 71, 72, 226
unconditional rights to procreate 234
unconditioned norms of reason 31
Uniacke, Suzanne 5–6, 94–110, 228–31
unified will 28, 30, 31
unintelligent accounts of trust 186
United States of America 120
universal law formula 41, 45
universalizability 2, 11, 12, 14, 20, 41

vertical trust 200, 241
victims of injustice 143–44
vigilance 205–7, 208, 209–10, 211, 212
vindication of reason 43–44, 44–45, 46, 221–22, 224
virtue 56, 118, 225
volitional trust 202, 216
vulnerability: dependence 112, 118, 119, 122; rational agents 27; responding with care 124; trust 7, 175, 179, 180–81, 187, 212

watchdog bodies 213–14, 215, 216
Weinstock, Daniel 7–8, 199–218, 240–42
welfare recipients 114, 115
Western culture 48
will 58, 178
willing 28–31, 178–79, 192
wishes of the patient 94–108, 229–30
women 6, 111–12, 117, 118, 119, 121, 122
World Bank 139, 140, 148
World Trade Organization (WTO) 139, 140, 142–43
WTO *see* World Trade Organization

Young, Iris 114–15

www.routledge.com/philosophy

Also available...

The Routledge Companion to Ethics

Edited by **John Skorupski**

'This fine collection merits a place in every university, college, and high school library for its invaluable articles covering a very broad range of topics in ethics. ...With its remarkable clarity of writing and its very highly qualified contributors, this volume is a must read for anyone interested in the latest developments in these important areas of thought and practice. Summing Up: Highly recommended.' – *CHOICE*

The Routledge Companion to Ethics is an outstanding survey of the whole field of ethics by a distinguished international team of contributors. Over 60 chapters are divided into six clear sections:

1. History 2. Meta-ethics 3. Ideas and Methods from Outside Ethics 4. Perspectives in Ethics 5. Morality 6. Debates in Ethics

The *Companion* opens with a comprehensive historical overview of ethics, including chapters on Plato, Aristotle, Hume, and Kant, and ethical thinking in China, India and the Arabic tradition. The second part covers the domain of meta-ethics. The third part covers important challenges to ethics from the fields of anthropology, psychology, sociobiology and economics. The fourth and fifth sections cover competing theories of ethics and the nature of morality respectively, with entries on consequentialism, Kantian morality, virtue ethics, relativism, evil, and responsibility amongst many others. A comprehensive final section includes the most important topics and controversies in applied ethics, such as rights, justice and distribution, the end of life, the environment, poverty, war and terrorism.

The Routledge Companion to Ethics is a superb resource for anyone interested in the subject, whether in philosophy or related disciplines such as politics, education, or law. Fully indexed and cross-referenced, with helpful further reading sections at the end of each chapter, it is ideal for those coming to the field of ethics for the first time as well as readers already familiar with the subject.

2010| 880 pages | PB: 978-0-415-41516-3 | HB: 978-0-415-41362-6
Learn more at: www.routledge.com/9780415415163

Available from all good bookshops

Taylor & Francis

eBooks
FOR LIBRARIES

ORDER YOUR FREE 30 DAY INSTITUTIONAL TRIAL TODAY!

Over 22,000 eBook titles in the Humanities, Social Sciences, STM and Law from some of the world's leading imprints.

Choose from a range of subject packages or create your own!

Benefits for you
- Free MARC records
- COUNTER-compliant usage statistics
- Flexible purchase and pricing options

Benefits for your user
- Off-site, anytime access via Athens or referring URL
- Print or copy pages or chapters
- Full content search
- Bookmark, highlight and annotate text
- Access to thousands of pages of quality research at the click of a button

For more information, pricing enquiries or to order a free trial, contact your local online sales team.

UK and Rest of World: **online.sales@tandf.co.uk**
US, Canada and Latin America: **e-reference@taylorandfrancis.com**

www.ebooksubscriptions.com

ALPSP Award for BEST eBOOK PUBLISHER 2009 Finalist

Taylor & Francis eBooks
Taylor & Francis Group

A flexible and dynamic resource for teaching, learning and research.